The Soul of Politics

The Soul of Politics

Beyond "Religious Right"
and "Secular Left"

———

JIM WALLIS

With a foreword by Garry Wills
and
a preface by Cornel West

A HARVEST BOOK

HARCOURT BRACE & COMPANY

San Diego   New York   London

Requests for permission to make copies of any part
of this book should be mailed to: The New Press,
450 West 41st Street, New York, New York 10036.

Library of Congress Cataloging-in-Publication Data
Wallis, Jim.
The soul of politics: beyond "religious right" and "secular left"/Jim Wallis;
with a foreword by Garry Wills; and a preface by Cornel West.
p.   cm.—(A Harvest book)
Originally published: New York: New Press; Maryknoll, NY:
Orbis Books, 1994.
Includes bibliographical references and index.
ISBN 0-15-600328-7
1. Christianity and politics. 2. Political science—Philosophy.
3. United States—Politics and government—1993– I. Title.
[BR115.P7W26   1995]
261.7—dc20   95-18526

The introduction was revised for the Harvest edition.

Text set in Sabon

Printed in the United States of America
First Harvest edition 1995   B C D E

TO THE PEOPLE OF SOUTH AFRICA,

WHO HAVE TAUGHT THE WORLD

THE POWER OF HOPE

Contents

Part Three
Toward an Alternative Vision

CHAPTER EIGHT

Foreword
by Garry Wills

In the 1960s, when campuses were violent for peace, one enclave seemed safe. Trinity Evangelical Divinity School in Deerfield, Illinois, is a seminary adjacent to Trinity College. If Richard Nixon could have chosen a school to send his children to, Trinity would have looked like the ideal choice—rural, old-fashioned, patriotic, respectful of authority.

But in 1970 a young man drove up to campus and set off tremors that can still make its professors quiver. Jim Wallis had been a campus activist on peace and racial matters at Michigan State University. He was no more radical, then, than most students upset by the Vietnam War; in fact, the most radical thing he had done up to this point was precisely this going to Trinity. Why would a leftist of even the mildest sort choose a churchy backwater for his seminary training? The faculty and alumni were sincerely puzzled by that question and feared that he had chosen this tranquil pond for the outsize splash he could make in it.

But, from another angle, Trinity was the obvious and entirely right place. Born into a devout family of Plymouth Brethren, who have a tradition of lay ministry, Wallis had grown up with prayer and the Bible as natural a part of his life as sports and schooling. Despite the inevitable adolescent questioning, he did not need to give up his faith just because he felt there were injustices in society. Quite the opposite: it was the Bible that made him sensitive to injustice. He suspected, before he knew, that evangelicals had not always been submissive to patriotic authority. He saw that there is something radical in their approach to the Bible, and that the really unnatural aspect of modern evangelicalism is its marriage to the materialistic gospel of middle America.

Alumni tried to expel Wallis when he organized protests, prayer vigils for peace, and appeals to forgotten texts of the Bible. But he gathered a group of idealists around him and launched a magazine that the students kept publishing after graduation—first in nearby Chicago, and then in Washington, D.C. I first became aware of the magazine—called *Sojourners* by then—when one of its editors, Wes Michaelson, came to seminars at the Institute for Policy Studies, on whose board I was serving. Michaelson was an aide to the evangelical senator Mark Hatfield of Oregon and had written for him the resolution for a day of fast and penitence over Vietnam. That was denounced as unpatriotic—until Hatfield revealed that the text was Abraham Lincoln's from a resolution to do penance during the Civil War.

That was typical of the Sojourners way of reclaiming a lapsed but authentic heritage. Some patriots wanted to take the flag away from protesters during the troubled sixties, though the demonstrations often spoke for the most patriotic values. In the same way, the religious right wanted to take the Bible away from religious dissidents, though it is the Bible that inspires dissent from worldly values.

It is a popular mistake to think all evangelicals are cast in the Pat Robertson mold. Most African Americans are evangelical Christians, as were many abolitionists. Wallis has been able to make his case to many people, including Billy Graham, who chose *Sojourners* as a forum for his first denunciation, on American soil, of nuclear weapons and the arms race.

As a praying community in the nation's capital, one that stands with the poor in their neighborhoods, the Sojourners remind me of Dorothy Day's early Catholic Workers, another radical group that flourished in what was perceived as a conservative and superpatriotic church. Day, too, appealed to deeper traditions than the traditionalists like to acknowledge. Those who read this book will see how far Wallis has, by now, traveled from his Trinity days. He meets with gang leaders, with religious figures from non-Christian lands and peoples, with politicians and bishops and—always—with the poor. It is a sight that would have cheered Dorothy Day. In fact, I'm sure it does.

Preface
by Cornel West

Jim Wallis is the major prophetic evangelical Christian voice in the country. He refuses to allow the religious right to have a monopoly on morality and spirituality; he also calls for the secular left to speak to the crucial issues of personal meaning and individual values. In short, he is part of a new wave of public intellectuals—such as Michael Lerner, Eugene Rivers, Katie Cannon, and Rosemary Ruether—who understand that the rich prophetic elements of religious traditions are indispensable for fundamental social change in America. Jim Wallis is an extraordinary example of a Christian visionary thinker who grounds his reflection in concrete action.

This book is a kind of manifesto that lays bare the spiritual impoverishment of America in light of a social analysis of power, wealth, and privilege. His concern about the soul of politics is rooted in a deep understanding of the emptiness of public life and the mean-spiritedness of social life in America. His powerful vision flows from his intimate experiences of fighting poverty and hopelessness on the streets of Washington, D.C., Detroit, Chicago, Los Angeles, and other cities in this country. His basic focus on race rests on the conviction that racism is America's most scarring form of idolatry. Yet he also realizes that moral consistency requires him to keep track of other forms of dehumanization—male supremacy, vast economic inequality, homophobia, and pending ecological catastrophe. His major message is faith, hope, and love—yet it is put forward with a sense of urgency and insight rarely seen in our cynical time. I hope and pray his voice resounds across this land—and that we pay heed to it!

Introduction
The World Isn't Working

The world isn't working. Things are unraveling, and most of us know it.

Tonight, the urban children of the world's only remaining superpower will go to bed to the sound of gunfire. Bonds of family and community are fraying. Our most basic virtues of civility, responsibility, justice, and integrity seem to be collapsing. We appear to be losing the ethics derived from personal commitment, social purpose, and spiritual meaning. The triumph of materialism is hardly questioned now, in any part of our society. Both domestically and globally, we are divided along the lines of race, ethnicity, class, gender, religion, culture, and tribe, and environmental degradation and resource scarcity threaten to explode our divisions into a world of perpetual conflict.

Our intuition tells us that the depth of the crisis we face demands more than politics as usual. An illness of the spirit has spread across the land, and our greatest need is for what our religious traditions call "the healing of the nations." The fundamental character of the social, economic, and cultural renewal we urgently need will require a change of both our hearts and our minds. But that change will demand a new kind of politics — a politics with spiritual values.

Several decades ago, Mohandas K. Gandhi warned against what he called the seven social sins: politics without principle, wealth without work, commerce without morality, pleasure without conscience, education without character, science without humanity, and worship without sacrifice.[1] These social sins today provide an apt description of our leading institutions and cultural patterns; they are the accepted practices of the life of the nation.

Gandhi's social sins point to the crucial relationship between our ethics and our public life. That relationship is the subject of this book. *The Soul of Politics* seeks to address the spiritual center and the moral heart of our political discourse. It is not a book about political policy; rather, it is a book about political vision. My contention is that we will not get very far in developing new policy directions until we deal with ethical issues. I am writing not just to liberals or conservatives; I am writing to anyone—left, right, or in between—who believes that we need a new political conversation. Neither am I writing only to religious people; this book is for anyone who longs for a new political vision with real moral values.

Several thousand years ago, the writer of the Proverbs warned, "Where there is no vision, the people perish."[2] That ancient warning also applies to our contemporary situation. Without a vision, we are indeed perishing.

The old political categories we have known are almost completely dysfunctional now. Ideologies and policies of liberal and conservative, left and right, have run their course and come to a dead end. During the American election year of 1992, public television's Bill Moyers commented that none of the candidates had adequately spoken a "language that evokes the common bond of a diverse people."[3] Moyers believes the American people have a desire to transcend the old paradigms of politics, "a deep yearning to go beyond left and right, to go beyond the nostrums of both the conservative and the liberal movements as they have been manifest in our time."[4]

Liberalism is unable to articulate or demonstrate the kind of moral values that must undergird any serious movement of social transformation; the critical link between personal responsibility and societal change is missing on the left. Conservatism, on the other hand, still denies the reality of structural injustice and social oppression; to call for individual self-improvement and a return to family values while ignoring the pernicious effects of poverty, racism, and sexism is to continue blaming the victim.

Both ideological options fail to deal with the enormity and complexity of the social crisis we now confront. For example, the urban chaos of drugs, guns, and violence cannot be touched by liberal sociology or conservative piety. Real solutions require a much deeper understanding of the relationship between structural destruction and self-destruction. The destruction of structures is caused by systematic social, racial, and economic injustice, the destruction of self by the lack of character, family, and community. Very few politicians are making the connections between the two. This book seeks to do that.

We will explore a deeper analysis of the globalization of the economy and the degradation of the popular culture. We will examine a kind of violence born not only of poverty but also of perverse values, a disintegration caused not only by the lack of good jobs but also by the lack of spiritual formation, a crime rate rooted not only in economic disparity but also in the nihilism of a society whose materialism is its only real god.

What we seem to have lost is something as simple as respect—for each other, for the earth, and for the kind of values that could hold us together. Most of the social, economic, and political issues we now face have a spiritual core. The profit-driven structures of the global economy will inevitably produce an ever-widening gulf and conflict between us unless we submit our economic policies and institutions to the ethic of community. Rapidly changing demographics and our ingrained habits of racism and sexism will create increasing cultural polarization unless we act to assert our common humanity and equality as the children of God. The insatiable momentum of our consumerism will ultimately poison both our environment and our hearts unless we learn our right relationship to the earth and its abundance. These are some of the themes we will pursue.

Not only will we probe the deeper moral roots of our social crisis, but we will also try to suggest ways to find common ground on the issues that divide us. *We can find common ground only by moving to higher ground.* Constituency-based politics, with its factional interests, will not lead us to this higher ground. Politics has been reduced to the selfish struggle for power among competing interests and groups, instead of a process of searching for the common good.

A vision of politics must be articulated that clarifies the essential moral issues at stake in any political discussion. Spiritual values must enter the public square. We are not calling here for the invasion of sectarian religion or theocratic grabs for power but rather for the contribution of neglected values to the political process. Most of us believe that institutional religion and the state must remain separate. But without moral values, our political life quickly degenerates into public corruption, cultural confusion, and social injustice.

This book suggests that only a prophetic political morality has the capacity to transcend old ideological categories and forge new relationships and connections between people and issues. Out of these new configurations of moral concern will come the creative political initiatives we so desperately need.

Deep in the American soul exists the conviction that politics and morality are integrally related. We need a politics that offers us something we haven't had in a long time: a vision of transformation. A new sense of direction will require a moral compass that we can trust. We must seek a "politics of conversion," [5] as Cornel West, an African-American Christian intellectual, has said. Jewish editor Michael Lerner hopes for a new "politics of meaning."

The politics of power will never yield to the politics of community without real transformation. But the moral issues at the heart of the public debate are often unrecognized and ignored or, worse yet, manipulated and twisted for politically self-serving and ideological purposes.

We witness the spectacle again each election year. Genuine moral discourse and discernment seem so out of place in the media's political coverage and the endless polling of voters. When moral issues do come up they tend to be narrowly defined and often become the basis for excluding others rather than opening doors to compassion and justice.

Political discussions around local or national elections reduce many citizens to a choice of the lesser of two evils or the temptation to withdraw altogether in support of hopeless nontraditional candidates. More often, the result is noninvolvement. Only half of us bother to vote anymore, and the level of real citizen participation, especially between elections, is alarmingly low for the health of political democracy. Instead of letting our best moral values remove us from politics, perhaps it is time for us to trust those values and allow them to become a bridge, both to the majority of disaffected citizens and to the still-unmarked path to a morally sound political vision.

We must broaden and deepen our definition of politics beyond "Republicans and Democrats." Americans today often find themselves with an unrepresented point of view on many issues, a political ethic not being articulated by the extreme views of the opposing camps.[6] Hence they frequently cast negative votes— votes *against* candidates rather than *for* their opponents. Bill Clinton assumed a mandate he didn't have when the voters rejected George Bush in 1992. Two years later, the voter rejection of Clinton and the Democratic leadership in Congress was too quickly interpreted by the Republicans as an endorsement of a comprehensive conservative revolution. Today it seems clear that both major parties are failing us.

Especially repugnant to many Americans is the bitter partisan warfare that impoverishes and paralyzes our public discourse. We long for political leaders who would be community builders and not polarizers, public servants who practice the art of bringing diverse peoples together for projects of common good, instead of power brokers who represent only those who have the most clout. Building consensus, creating common ground, and finding workable solutions to intractable problems are far more difficult tasks than endless ideological posturing and partisan attacking.

Politics is the discourse of our public life. There are real limits to what politics can provide to better the human condition. But politics can make a great difference, for good and for evil, in the ways that we live together. Political leaders can appeal to people's best instincts (as when Martin Luther King Jr. proclaimed, "I have a dream") or manipulate their worst impulses (as when George Bush exploited the case of Willie Horton).[7] Which values or fears are awakened or appealed to is, perhaps, the best moral test of politics and politicians.

It is possible to evoke in people a genuine desire to transcend our more selfish interests and respond to a larger vision that gives us a sense of purpose, direction, meaning, and even community. Real political leadership provides that very thing; it offers to lead people to where, in their best selves, they really want to go.

A new framework, new language, and new visions could emerge from resurrecting our most basic personal and social values. Many of those values derive from the cores of our best religious traditions and are common to people who have long been politically and culturally separated from one another. This book suggests that central to any new politics will be a new spirituality—indeed, a renewal of some of our oldest spirituality—creating a moral sensitivity that refuses to separate political ideas from their consequences for human beings and for the rest of the creation.

For example, the U.S. Census Bureau tells us that more people are now in poverty than at any time in the last three decades and that 40 percent of the poor are children.[8] Close to half of black and Hispanic children live in poverty[9] while in the wider society 10 percent of U.S. households own almost 70 percent of the nation's wealth.[10] These are profound realities if we are to take our religious traditions seriously.

Similarly, the fires of Los Angeles and other cities still smolder, yet racism does not appear near the top of the nation's political agenda. And how often do we hear the epidemic rates of rape and violence against women in this country discussed as a fundamental social crisis? The breakdown of families, the abuse of sexuality, and the undermining of personal moral responsibility have also led to a multitude of problems. The disintegrating economy is a top political issue, but what about the rampant consumption that is poisoning our souls and our environment while prompting our children to kill each other in their schools? Meanwhile, pictures of mass starvation and bloody ethnic conflict dominate the international scene, and a morally consistent foreign policy beyond old doctrines of national interest has yet to be articulated. It is the moral character of these and other "political" issues that we shall hope to reveal.

We are at a critical juncture of history. The Cold War is over. Profound economic, ethnic, and environmental challenges lie before us in a time that cries out for alternative vision. But where will such vision be found? And who will the visionaries be? They may be found in unlikely places.

We must expand our definition of political leaders to include others besides elected officials. We should include people like Daniel "Nane" Alejandrez, a barrio veteran, who directs the Coalition to End Barrio Warfare, an organization active in over fifty cities across this country. Nane and his *compañeros* at Barrios Unidos are beginning a series of community-based economic development projects to provide alternatives to the drug traffic and help strengthen local neighborhoods.

We should include Fred Williams, an African-American community activist who, after a new wave of drive-by shootings against Latino families in Los Angeles, brought black young people along with him to stay overnight in the homes of Hispanic families. A clear message was sent and the violence subsided.

We should include Dr. Janelle Goetcheus, who with her family left a comfortable white middle-class existence to establish medical facilities in Washington, D.C., for homeless street people, undocumented immigrants from Latin America, and children at risk in the nation's capital. Her persistent advocacy for those with no health care has made her a thorn in the medical establishment's side and has won her the distinction of Family Physician of the Year from the American Academy of Family Doctors.

We should include Don Mosely and other members of Jubilee Partners in southeast Georgia, who have provided hospitality and assistance to almost two thousand refugees from Vietnam, Central America, Bosnia, and other troubled areas. An offshoot of Koinonia Farm's early experiment in racial reconciliation, Jubilee seeks to practice the ancient spiritual discipline of welcoming the stranger.

We should include Eugene and Jackie Rivers, who, along with a core of young black men and women from Harvard University, Massachusetts Institute of Technology, and other prestigious schools in Boston, have moved into drug-infested, violence-torn Dorchester to establish the Azusa Community, an African-American congregation dedicated to reclaiming the street youths who have been abandoned by virtually everybody else.

We should include Lucy Poulin and an intrepid group of Mainers, who have created a whole network of economic cooperatives, housing construction projects, and cottage industries in one of their state's poorest counties. In the tradition of Dorothy Day's Catholic Worker Movement, Home Co-op has created a land trust, homeless shelters, organic gardens, a service center, and a welcoming community for the rural poor.

We should include Nathan Jernigan, a Howard Divinity School graduate from the projects of Chicago, and Barbara Tamialis, from the suburbs of Detroit, who co-direct the program at our own Sojourners Neighborhood Center, twenty blocks from the White House. Sixty African-American young people are doing more than improving their reading, math, and other educational skills here. They are becoming "freedom fighters" who are learning to remember their past, claim their present, and choose their future.

All of these men and women have learned that political morality must grow from experience, from the concrete human situations that need attention, rather than from mere theoretical and ideological concerns. They demonstrate that social change will be based upon reclaiming the moral values of personal responsibility, social compassion, and economic justice. New visions of community spirit, democratic participation, and political empowerment can transcend both liberal and conservative categories. Transforming individual character, social policy, and our physical environment is the key to change.

We should not place our trust exclusively in government programs or in appeals to personal self-improvement; neither can we rely merely on private voluntarism or on public spending. Rather, we must generate a new moral and political will to change our lives and our communities. Both private and public support will be needed for the kind of community-based initiatives that empower individuals and families to change their own circumstances and their neighbors' well-being.

We need to articulate clearly the essential moral character of the many crises we confront, the connections between them, and the choices we must make. By being faithful to a moral vision of politics in our own lives and communities, we will make our best contribution and offer our most profound participation. The little islands of hope we create are harbingers of a different political future for this country.

We begin this future not by searching for new systems to replace the ideological dinosaurs that have failed us. Instead, we start by subjecting all projects, initiatives, decisions, and policies to new criteria: whether they make justice more possible for all of us and especially for those on the bottom, whether they allow us to live in more harmony with the earth, and whether they increase the participation of all people in decision making. In other words, we must learn to judge our social and economic choices by whether they empower the powerless, protect the earth, and foster true democracy.

All these criteria are directly derived from our best moral, religious, and political traditions and serve as examples of how our spirituality could help shape a new social direction. Gandhi said that when you begin a new project, "Recall the face of the poorest and most helpless [people] whom you may have seen and ask yourself if the step you contemplate will be of any use to [them]. Will [they] be able to gain anything by it? Will it restore [them] to control over [their] own life and destiny?" [11]

The relationship between politics and morality is absolutely vital to the future. The profound public longing for a more fair and responsive political process is a signal that a new politics may be possible. Politics must begin to address moral values and do so from all points on the political spectrum.

Regardless of our political backgrounds, we could agree that the political status quo is simply not morally acceptable. Too many people are not making it and are being left behind. Neither the injustices built into our social system nor the irresponsibility they generate is tolerable any longer. Controlling the poor is not the only alternative to abandoning them. In most of our religious traditions, justice is best understood as the establishment of a right relationship between peoples, among communities, and with the earth itself. It's time to reclaim those traditions.

We will build a different future not with a negative message, but with demonstrations of what a morally based politics looks like. We need concrete examples, and many will be presented in this book. I do not prescribe a detailed political program; instead I invoke and invite the values of a new political vision that will make practical solutions possible.

A prophetic politics rooted in moral principles could again spark people's imagination and involvement. We need a personal ethic of moral responsibility, a commitment to justice with the capacity also for reconciliation, an economic approach governed by the ethics of community and sustainability, a restored sense of our covenant with the abandoned poor and the damaged earth, a reminder of shared values that calls forth the very best in us, and a renewal of citizen politics to fashion a new political future. But to shape a new future we must first find the moral foundations and resources for a new political vision.

During the civil rights movement it was said that our perspective comes from what we see when we get out of bed in the morning. The things we see, hear, taste, smell, and touch each day determine our view of the world. More than the things we've read or the ideas we've heard, it is our *vantage point* that most affects our social and political perspective.

For me, that perspective comes from waking up in one of the poorest and most violent neighborhoods of Washington, D.C. A popular slogan today is that you can't understand America and the world from "inside the beltway." That's only partly true. Indeed, the reality of this country cannot be comprehended from inside the offices of the Washington lobbyists, media pundits, and politicians who inhabit the corridors of power. What they wake up to in the morning are the busy schedules, sheltered lives, and the privileged positions of those who fill the upper echelons of American decision making.

But just a few blocks away are neighborhoods like mine, where poverty and despair provide a stark and revealing counterpoint to the wealth and power of official Washington. Here people wake up to a profoundly different reality. The contrast between their view and the view from government halls provides the most revealing insights into the truth about this country and indeed the rest of the global economy. It is from the vantage point of this contrast, and from living and working for twenty years on the margins, that I now write.

Part One

The Conversion
of Politics

Chapter One

Signs of a Crisis
The Politics of Violence

Los Angeles. The whole nation watches transfixed as the City of Angels explodes into an orgy of violence and raging infernos of fire. People of all cultures loot in the streets, and commentators argue, back and forth, about social injustice and cultural breakdown. But few seem to comprehend fully the meaning of the obvious rage and despair.

Boston. A young man fleeing two pursuers with automatic weapons ducks into a church during a worship service, believing he will be safe there. His assailants don't even pause at the church door as they rush in and open fire. The choir stops singing, the preacher dives under the pulpit, and the congregation crouches beneath the pews as the sanctuary is sprayed with bullets. Later, at a press conference, indignant church leaders decry the blasphemous violation of holy thresholds and sacred space. But an African-American street pastor offers a different and prophetic word: "If the church won't come into the streets, the streets will come into the church."

Washington, D.C. All the Sunday morning talk shows focus on the nation's violence and crime, which seem out of control. Nobody is safe, says a worried-looking David Brinkley. Desperate-sounding politicians and police chiefs speak of crime bills and gun registrations, and a concerned president speaks of the breakdown of work, family, and community. What's most clear is that the political and media elites haven't got a clue about what to do.

Palestine. Eighth century B.C.E. The prophet Isaiah delivers oracles to the children of Israel and to the neighboring Egyptians about the plight of their societies:

> Their land is filled with silver and gold, and there is no end to their treasures; their land is filled with horses, and there is no end to their chariots. Their land is filled with idols; they bow down to the work of their hands, to what their own fingers have made. And so people are humbled, and everyone is brought low.[1]

The consequence, says the prophet, of a society's greed, social injustice, and idol worship is a judgment that comes in the form of spiritual degradation, violence, and the breakup of community. The people turn on one another—"and they will fight, one against the other, neighbor against neighbor, city against city, kingdom against kingdom."[2] The people's "spirit" will be "emptied out."[3]

A WAKE-UP CALL

Could the escalation of violence on our nation's streets become the crisis that wakes us all up to our cultural and political bankruptcy and the urgent need for redirection? The violence that has overtaken us as a society might, indeed, be the clarion call that rouses us from our long political slumber. The very violence that has so gripped the nation with fear could become the impetus for going deeper than we have before in trying to diagnose and solve our many social calamities.

The violence is not the problem; it is a consequence of the problem. And, in some redemptive way, the violence could be a catalyst for political renewal. How? Because, at root, the character and brutality of the violence show that it is a profoundly moral and spiritual crisis that we face. This is a crisis of the spirit. A cruel and endemic economic injustice, a soul-killing materialism, a life-destroying drug traffic, a persistent and pervasive racism, a massive breakdown of family life and structure, and an almost total collapse of moral values have all combined to create a climate of violence throughout this country and a coldness of heart on our streets that make even veteran urban activists shiver.

It is, in fact, the cold disregard for others' lives and property (and even their own lives) among many young people that creates the greatest danger and causes the gravest concern. Kids walking into convenience stores and just "blowing people away" is, indeed, very scary. Yet, their frightening disregard for human life is a bitter reflection of the way these same young people have been utterly disregarded by their society. Their coldheartedness is now a judgment upon our coldness toward them. Indeed, we are reaping what we have sown.

Crisis is the word that best describes our domestic and global situation, and we hear it used over and over again. Many have noted that the Chinese symbol for the word *crisis* is a combination of the symbols for the two words *danger* and *opportunity*. It is no longer news to say that our society is in a state of crisis. Most people sense the danger and are searching to find the opportunity.

The cry and hope for change lie just beneath the surface of most contemporary public discourse and come raging to the forefront in our electoral campaigns. When we make a political shift, our hope that change is possible begins to rise. But that hope is fragile, and simply a change in leadership at the top is unlikely to resolve the deeper issues, which are both structural and spiritual.

The crisis is more serious than being offtrack. The truth is that we are in a time of transition, an in-between period when the old is dying and the new has yet to be born. The values, assumptions, and structures that have governed us for so long have come to their logical end, and we now find ourselves at a dead end. But new values, patterns, and institutions have not yet emerged. We are caught in the middle, stranded between paradigms. And our society is suffering a crisis of leadership, just when the established institutions charged with that task are at their lowest ebb of credibility, confidence, and respect.

America today lacks any coherent or compelling social vision. Things just seem to happen to us and all we seem to be able to do is hope for the best while fearing the worst. The media is daily filled with images of mounting problems and growing crises that we sense must be somehow connected, but we are not sure how.

Contradictions is the word that describes our state of mind and heart. We are increasingly buffeted by contradictory realities. A rampant individualism separates us from one another, and yet we feel a deep longing for community and a sense of belonging. Consumerism has reached unprecedented proportions and excesses, far eclipsing citizenship as the dominant means of social participation in affluent societies. But at the same time, we experience a profound hunger for seeing life as more than an acquisitive venture. Never have more people been socially abandoned to poverty and misery, yet at the same time the human intuition and need for compassion seem to be on the rise, especially within youthful hearts. A series of related ecological crises threatens the very fabric of our lives, but a substantial change in consciousness about our relationship to the earth is now occurring and has the potential to reshape social habits and economic policies.

Perspective is the word that best speaks, in the midst of our many crises and contradictions, to what is most needed and longed for today—a sense of how things fit together. How do we make sense of issues and events that threaten to overwhelm us? Even more important, how do we connect the fundamental questions that confront us with values and beliefs that are worthy of our allegiance? Perspective provides a way of seeing and understanding, a stance from which to respond, and a foundation for acting in the world.

Perspective fundamentally has to do with values—moral values and ethical commitments. As we have already observed, virtually all of the critical challenges we face today have a central spiritual reality. At the heart of the social, economic, and political issues that rage around us are fundamental questions that challenge our most basic sensibilities. Our values do shape our politics, and the growing realization of that is a sign of hope.

Poverty, by itself, does not necessarily generate violence; it's the loss of hope that creates violence. When the children of my neighborhood are planning their funerals instead of their futures, it is a sure sign that we, as a society, have lost our sense of hope.

READING THE SIGNS OF THE TIMES

Many signs help us interpret the causes of our present crisis. A sign is an event, a condition, an observation, a characteristic, or a phenomenon that helps to reveal the sources of our problems. Signs point us to the root causes, values, and structures that have led to our predicament.

If we pay attention to the signs of the times, we can come to understand both the nature of our many problems and their potential solutions. The fact that one political side speaks only of moral behavior while the opposing side speaks exclusively of social oppression is very revealing. The signs of the crisis one singles out often betray one's own political perspective.

The predictable and exhausting arguments between conservatives and liberals have left us antagonized, demoralized, and confused, with no consensus even about what positive steps we can take together to move forward. By taking a more honest look at the signs of the crisis than either ideological camp has been willing to do, we may find some direction for more creative and effective responses. All the signs of our crisis must be squarely faced. What are these signs of crisis?

Signs of Crisis

The vast urban territories where so many young people live today have become virtual war zones; home has become a place to survive. Some see our urban unraveling as a problem to be solved; others see it as a sign to be heeded. The urban chaos provides a case study of what happens when the values of social justice and personal responsibility are both abandoned.

Kids killing kids is not just a crime problem; it is a parable of pain that points to illness in our cultural soul. This is not only an urban problem; it is a crisis that extends to the places where we all live. Violence is not confined to the eruptions that flash across our media screens; it is far deeper and much more pervasive. The very structures, habits, and values of our society are being prophetically interrogated by the "culture of violence" that is becoming normal to us; that is a sign of the crisis.

Seventy thousand manufacturing jobs lost in South Central Los Angeles before the Rodney King verdict is a sign of the crisis. So are the wages, conditions, and environmental degradation endured by the third-world workers who now have those jobs.

The white racism that survived integration by selectively assimilating some blacks while inflicting upon poor black communities the worst conditions since slavery is a sign of the crisis. Similarly, a global economy that wondrously connects one-fifth of the world's population while abandoning the other four-fifths of the world's people is a most telling sign of the crisis.

The particular jeopardy of women is also a sign of the crisis. Economic inequality, the social marginalization of mothers and children, and epidemic rates of rape and domestic violence combine to make life dangerous for half the population.

The scenario of countless television murders and exploitative sexual messages casually witnessed each day by our children is a sign of the crisis; so is the aggressive marketing of tens of thousands of useless and harmful products to our daughters and sons in our own homes as they sit transfixed before the electronic spiritual formation that occupies fifty to one hundred hours of their every week.

The unprecedented disintegration of family life is, indeed, an alarming sign of the crisis and is a primary cause of the chilling lack of respect for human life that is now prevalent on our streets and in our national psyche. Similarly, the reducing of sexuality to a commodity and the disconnecting of sex from committed, covenantal relationships is a sign of the crisis that has damaged our spirits, spread dreaded disease, and undermined the fabric of our lives and society. The vital connections between good work, good parenting, and good sexual values must be reestablished if the quality of our family life is to be restored.

The poverty of middle-class life is a sign of the crisis. Our shopping mall culture keeps consumers busy in an age of hitherto-unknown materialism fraught with emptiness, loneliness, anxiety, and a fundamental loss of meaning. A most revealing sign of the crisis is the blank, sad, or angry looks in the eyes of the young who congregate both on the wasting corners of urban streets and in the wasteful corridors of suburban shopping centers. But a moral focus on consumerism makes both liberals and conservatives uncomfortable, perhaps because both sides are so deeply caught up in it.

The most painful and dangerous sign of the crisis is what is happening to our children. When our children become our poorest citizens; our most at-risk population; the recipients of our worst values, drugs, sicknesses, and environmental practices; our most armed and dangerous criminals; the chief victims and perpetrators of escalating violence; an object of our fears more than of our hopes, then their plight has become the sign of our crisis. When children talk about their favorite kinds of caskets instead of bikes or cars, it is a sign we can no longer ignore.

An overarching sign of our crisis is our poisoned environment. From our toxic wastes to our toxic values, from the pollution of our air and water to the pollution of our hearts and minds, from the destruction of our forests and agricultural land to the destruction of local economies and cultures, from a world full of carcinogens to a world full of weapons, from our alienation from the earth to our alienation from one another, we are a society in crisis.

Social oppression and cultural breakdown are the twin signs of our age. One has to do with structural injustice and the other with the collapse of values. Some will speak only of oppression and some only breakdown. It is the heart of the tragic split between liberals and conservatives. But to miss the reality of either is to misunderstand the dimensions and depth of our present crisis. Both oppression and breakdown are real, and the two are integrally related. Understanding the realities of both social oppression and cultural breakdown, and the dynamic connection between the two, is the beginning of political and spiritual wisdom.

Signs of Hope

But other signs call us to hope. Even the widespread recognition of crisis is a hopeful sign. The realization that political ideology cannot save us along with the deep longing in many places for a new spirituality is a very positive sign. A new kind of politics could also emerge—one that transcends old political categories and gets to the roots of our problems.

Despite the predatory character of market forces, compassion for the economic system's many victims is also on the rise. While hate crimes against racial, ethnic, and sexual minorities have increased, the desire for an authentically multicultural and pluralistic national community is also growing in many places, especially among the young. And despite the media-sponsored ethics of selfishness and sexual promiscuity, many people are deciding to take control of their own lives and are choosing to value relationships and family over material goals and short-term gratification. In many hearts and minds, our relationship with the earth and all its creatures is being restored. And, in the face of this deepening crisis, the religious community may be waking up.

THE FAILURE OF POLITICS

But the politics we witness each day on the national media stage is clearly not working, nor is it satisfying the deeper questions of justice or community. The underlying moral issues, dilemmas, and choices that confront us have yet to be clarified or adequately addressed in the domestic political discussion.

We have begun to see the rhetoric of change in response to the profound disenchantment of the electorate, but the substance of new vision and direction has yet to manifest itself. Voters will cast their lot for almost anyone who claims to be an outsider and speaks the language of change, but most still believe that little can be done to turn things around.

The ritual of public polling has now almost completely replaced genuine citizen participation in political life. Candidates compete against each other with quick media sound bites, negative attack ads, and carefully calculated images on the stage of television, which has become the primary—and virtually only—arena of public political discourse. After the exchange of symbols, code words, and dishonest slander, a poll is taken and the winners declared. An election is merely the final poll.

The media celebrities who modestly claim only to report the news are clearly its arbiters now. Corporate conglomerates have taken over the news business. Television has taken over the role that party bosses once played in selecting political candidates and issues. Producers and their telegenic news superstars define the issues for the public and decide who does and does not get to speak to them. The commentators tell us what reasonable people should think about the issues, and then they take another poll to see what we think about what they have told us. Right on cue, the eager politicians, along with their own pollsters and "spin doctors," take the results and announce their positions on the major questions of our public life.

This closed system of media-oriented political entertainment continually preempts genuine public dialogue and debate about the issues that most affect people's lives and the character of the nation. It also gives enormous advantage to those in society whose money and power already control the political landscape. The triumph of technique over substance now governs American politics.

Our public discussion proceeds so continually from the top down that the idea of local, national, and global issues being debated at the grassroots level and then filtering *up* the political process is now foreign to us. We have almost completely forgotten how such a democratic town meeting tradition influenced our earlier history.

Yet who has time to be a citizen? Studies in recent years show that more Americans are working longer hours, have multiple jobs, and are taking fewer vacations or days off than in times past. Adding the demands of family and household responsibilities, who has energy for public debate? What does it mean when the grindstone of our economy effectively leaves politics and political participation to the elites?

Presidential Politics

The public reaction to elite politics dramatically erupted during the U.S. presidential campaign of 1992. Billionaire H. Ross Perot became the highly ironic symbol and lightning rod of widespread discontent. However, as is characteristic of America's media politics, the substance never followed the symbols. Neither Perot's highly orchestrated TV events nor Bill Clinton's appearances on MTV and the Arsenio Hall show have generated the awakening of grassroots citizen politics that our political crisis requires.

President Clinton has indeed sought to move beyond old political stereotypes by portraying himself as a "New Democrat." Anxious to present himself as more than a tax-and-spend liberal, he has used the White House as a bully pulpit to speak to the wider moral issues of personal responsibility that Democrats have often avoided. But the president's hopeful rhetoric about values, caring, and change has yet to translate into a coherent and compelling social vision. And public doubts about aspects of the president's (or the first family's) personal behavior have chipped away at the moral authority of the Clinton administration.

It is refreshing to have someone in the White House who is genuinely moved and anguished by the poverty and violence experienced by inner-city children, instead of a president who always seems to talk about such things as if he's speaking only to white suburban dwellers. Yet what has emerged in this presidency is Clinton the compromiser rather than Clinton the visionary. On issue after issue, the myriad of vested interests that control Washington has successfully intervened to make promises into pittances. A pattern emerges: A lofty goal is stated; a proposal is offered to achieve about one-twentieth of the original idea; and after wrangling in the Congress and the media, one-fiftieth of the vision is approved—subject to further modifications.

Some would say that these compromises are inevitable in politics, which is, after all, "the art of the possible." But something deeper may be at work here—a president who seems more comfortable trying to please everyone and be successful than a political leader who knows the strength of his convictions and principles and is willing to stick by them. E. J. Dionne Jr., writing in the *Washington Post,* said at the end of the administration's first year that "Clinton no longer looks like he's really going to change things."[4]

Most significant, what is least changed is the cynicism and distrust that most Americans still feel toward their government. Restoring citizens' trust in their political leaders would require that those leaders consistently articulate and demonstrate a new vision and agenda and be willing to lose some political battles in the process.

At this point in history public trust would demand, too, that the new visions go beyond the now hopelessly outmoded categories and solutions that still govern and paralyze our public discourse. Clinton has not yet done this. He is still controlled by traditional Democratic approaches, while his Republican opponents seem to care only to discredit him so they can regain the White House. Neither side has shown the intellectual rigor and moral courage needed to work together to find new and creative solutions to our most pressing problems. This is what a disgruntled electorate is still waiting to see.

In the absence of a clear vision, the Clinton administration is still vulnerable to the attacks of conservatives, like popular radio talk show host Rush Limbaugh, who love to point out the obvious contradictions of liberalism. But this vitriolic pundit and his clones refuse to take moral responsibility themselves for fueling the engines of racial and gender division, scapegoating the poor, and mocking environmental responsibility. These conservatives of the hard right regularly echo the mean-spirited diatribe of Pat Buchanan's us-and-them rhetoric at the Republican Convention of 1992. Hate talk is not harmless; it leads to hateful and sometimes violent behavior.

Future Republican presidential hopeful William Bennett speaks eloquently of the need for public virtues, while nearly ignoring the moral demand for social and economic justice that lies at the heart of all of our best philosophical and religious traditions. His political competitor, Jack Kemp, is virtually the only one in the Republican party to speak of racism and poverty as real and moral issues, though his preference for old trickle-down solutions offers no new economic alternatives.

There have been glimpses of hope in the Clinton administration: when the president remembers his campaign calls for a New Covenant; when Hillary Clinton demonstrates the courage and competence that confirm a new status for women apart from her husband's position; when Al Gore stands with religious leaders to launch new environmental initiatives; and when our children can see a government that for the first time really looks like America in its great diversity. Whether these symbols lead to substance in racial, economic, gender, and environmental justice will be the real test of this presidency.

Underlying Issues

The politicians of the major parties have yet to articulate and demonstrate a new vision of politics, based on a renewed sense of both personal and social morality. Neither the Democrats nor the Republicans have confronted the underlying cultural forces of our society that are key to political transformation.

For example, when have we heard a national politician speak of the materialism of American society as a moral issue, even though its powerful influence virtually shapes the whole social order and establishes the limits of political change? How many public officials are willing to talk about the ethics of selfishness, individualism, and the relentless pursuit of power that so dominate contemporary political life and social policy? What candidate will be honest enough to talk about the power of money over the political process and both political parties and be willing to offer a personal example of real financial integrity by simply refusing the contributions of special interests and the notorious political action committees?

Where are the political leaders who demonstrate the integral relationship between personal responsibility and social justice, who replace the politics of constituency with the politics of community, who patiently teach the disciplines of economic sustainability and environmental stewardship instead of mouthing the empty promises of endless growth, and who help us all rediscover the almost forgotten ethic of public service? We may have to look beyond what we now call politics to find leaders who will address these underlying issues.

With American demographics changing so quickly and a multicultural future emerging so clearly, a fundamental renewal of the "arts of democracy," as Frances Moore Lappé and Paul Martin DuBois have described it, is crucial now.[5] A significant increase in the participation of ordinary citizens in the political process would bring more deep-seated change than would hoped-for changes in the behavior of the leaders at the top. Indeed, more citizen participation is likely the key to changing leadership. A revitalization of citizen politics could begin to bring the deeper and wider moral perspective that our political crisis and confusion now demand. We require nothing less.

The struggle to reshape the meaning of politics is one we must all engage in. By its very nature, it is a community activity, a populist search. Politics must no longer be left to the elites who have taken over the processes of public decision making in this country.

Indeed, our personal habits of political acquiescence have been central to our problems. When politics is almost exclusively defined at the top of the society, it invariably will be defined more by power than by moral values. The search for a more ethically rooted politics is too important a task to be left to the powerful alone. It is a journey we must make together.

Chapter Two

Can Politics Be Moral?
Beyond Liberal and Conservative

"Politics isn't moral!" shouted the cab driver. "Wish it could be," he added wistfully. The hustling Yellow Cab entrepreneur had asked why I was in New York. When I told him it was to see a publisher, he curiously asked me what my book was about. Like almost everyone else I talk with, he was very interested in the subject of politics and morality.

Our public life reflects our moral values, one way or the other. We've all seen how politics can reflect our worst values of selfishness, greed, divisiveness, fear, and power. Yet we long to see how politics could reflect our best values of compassion, community, diversity, hope, and service. Reconnecting politics to our best values is now the most important task of political life. The old political morality has left us paralyzed. Our times cry out for a new political morality, one that will provide the ground for new possibilities.

But reawakening to a politics of renewed moral conscience will shake us to our very foundations. The alternative to the passive politics of the status quo is a prophetic politics of personal and social transformation. However, the movement from one to the other will change our very understanding of politics.

SHAKING THE FOUNDATIONS

At 5:00 A.M. my bed began to shake. Suddenly, the whole room started shifting and moving, like a ship in a big storm.

Sleepily, I rubbed my eyes and remembered I was in Los Angeles. It didn't take long to figure out that I was experiencing my first earthquake. This tremor was small compared to the major quake that would hit the beleaguered city in January of 1994, but it seemed symbolic of the thunder that rumbles over our cities from threatening storm clouds.

This startling awakening seemed quite appropriate in the City of Angels, where events just weeks before had shaken the whole nation. The devastation rocked not only L.A. but several other cities too. A small delegation of national and international church leaders had come to Los Angeles in the wake of the uprising following the verdicts in the first trial on the beating of Rodney King. We were there to listen and, we hoped, to act on what we would hear.

The day after the earthquake, another ground-shaking metaphor was given to us by a former gang member and now a street organizer, who described his city as a volcano that finally erupted. "Trying to cool it off," he said, "is like blowing on hot flowing lava; it can only singe your lips." We wanted to meet the young gang members who had become so central to the life of Los Angeles and its urban crisis. He set up a meeting.

We met in a dilapidated junior high school, surrounded by Jordan Downs, Nickerson Gardens, and Imperial Courts, the huge housing projects in Watts where the famous Crips and Bloods street gangs were born. More than a dozen young men, ranging in age from about 13 to 18, sat with us in a large circle. Wearing their characteristic gang colors, the young people eyed us with a mixture of suspicion and cautious hope. As I looked into their faces, I was struck by the realization that these kids were the young men of whom America is so afraid. Certainly, youths like these and their counterparts in neighborhoods like my own in inner-city Washington, D.C., have shown themselves capable of terrible violence. Yet sitting here this day, they also looked very young and strangely vulnerable.

Members of both the rival Crips and Bloods testified that the rebellion (what they all called the civil disturbance in Los Angeles) was not the most important event. Rather, they said, the more notable event occurred earlier, when the gangs stopped fighting. Their truce had begun even before the violence following the jury's verdict. "It's more than a truce," said one young gang member. "It really is a coming together." One after another, the young men described their cease-fire as one of the most important historical events ever for African-American men. It was a moment, as one said, "when young black males finally began putting our heads and hearts together."

The profound alienation of being young, black, and male in abandoned inner-city territories rang throughout our conversation. "Can't trust nobody who keeps degrading you," said one teenager, as the rest nodded their assent. Stories of constant police harassment, even since the truce, peppered the discussion. The connection to slavery was very strong in the consciousness of these young men. "We won't be slaves anymore," they had determined. Though slavery officially ended in the United States 130 years ago, it is still a deeply felt metaphor for the contemporary experience of these young people.

Many said the gangs were the only thing happening in their communities. "All your friends are in gangs and you are too. . . . There's nothing else to do down here. . . . We don't have any positive role models. . . . We don't have plumbers, teachers, even shoe shine men in our families. . . . Gangs are like families."

Feelings of betrayal ran deep. "The system told us that if we stayed in school, were nonviolent, grew up, got a job, we would get a piece. Didn't happen." Claiming that "everybody wants to make it legitimately; no one wants to be a drug dealer," they pointed out, "It's white men who sell us the drugs. We ain't got no ships and planes to bring it from overseas." In painful detail, these young men described life in their communities, saying, "We gotta give people something to do—something positive; we need some jobs."

Waking Up

For years, these youth and thousands like them have been "stealin' and killin', 'cause that's all we knew." But now, they said, "we woke up." When I asked what woke them up, they said it just didn't make any sense to keep killing each other anymore. One young man said, "We don't want our community to be on the bottom all the time."

Why now? "I don't know, man, we just woke up," said a thoughtful-looking 18-year-old in a backwards-turned baseball cap. "We just woke up." After hearing the same response from gang members making truces in other cities, the meaning of the young man's words began to dawn on me. I recalled that waking up is a spiritual metaphor for conversion.

Here were young people identifying the sources of their community's problems and deciding to do something about it. Here were teenage black males talking about the world they wanted to create for their children and grandchildren. I've heard such talk among the young in Central America and South Africa, but not for many years among the angry and marginalized youth of American inner cities. I began to wonder, with fragile hope, if this might be the beginning of a new social and political consciousness among our urban youth who are most at risk. The numbers and influence of gang members could make them a potentially significant factor in cities such as Los Angeles and across the country.

Most importantly, these gang youths' understanding of the problem went deeper than their reaction to unjust social conditions. They began to speak of the personal and spiritual roots of their situation as well. Though they all felt abandoned by the religious community, the young gang members spoke of their need for that community to reach out to them now. "We need spiritual power," they kept saying. "We can't do this by ourselves." They spoke of the need to "find themselves." In a dramatic moment, one young teenager exclaimed, "We've got some habits that only God can cure!" Everyone who heard his confession realized he wasn't just speaking for himself. He had identified our situation too — the crisis the whole society now finds itself in. They virtually pleaded with us, saying, "We've been trying to find God for so long." When one of the pastors in our group asked what the churches could do to help them, a young gang member replied, "Help us find a relationship to God. We need our churches to lead us to the Lord."

Talk like that can be shocking, even for religious leaders trying to find solutions to social problems. The call for connecting social justice with spiritual renewal today is coming *from the streets.* A new politics requires an old spirituality — a remarkable connection these young people are making between personal and political transformation. I found myself wishing I knew more politicians and religious leaders with such insight.

"Don't rebuild L.A. the way it was," they told us. "Revitalize and restore the hope of the people, and the people will rebuild L.A." That's the key word — *hope.* Somehow, hope had arisen here in a place where most would have considered it impossible. That hope was coming from no outside institution (including religious institutions and political parties), but from somewhere within the gang members and their own reality. It was enough to make even the most cynical believe in the unpredictability of history. Near the end of our conversation, the former gang member who had organized the meeting said, "Hope is the evidence of things not seen."[1] I suspected he had a grandmother who had once taken him to church.

Later in the week, I had conversations with more young gang members and was given a document offering their proposals for rebuilding Los Angeles, entitled "Bloods/Crips Proposal for L.A.'s Facelift."[2] Its recommendations were thorough and far-reaching, covering areas such as education, economic development, health care, law enforcement, housing, welfare reform, recreation, and much more. Along with calling for public action, their proposals also spoke to what the gangs intended to do for themselves. They were the best proposals I had seen coming out of Los Angeles and were greatly superior to the ideas emanating from the official city rebuilding commission, the White House, or Congress.

Taking Responsibility

In the months that followed, these gang leaders began networking with their counterparts in cities around the country to organize a national Gang Summit. The plan was to attempt a national gang truce and to redirect the energies of hundreds of thousands of young men and women toward personal transformation, economic development, and the rebuilding of their communities. A few of us were asked to serve in an advisory capacity as observers and as a support group for this ambitious project.

Among other things, the National Urban Peace and Justice Summit held in Kansas City in the spring of 1993 broke down old political notions and ideological polarities. Intense conversations focused on economic development and moral responsibility, political empowerment and spiritual renewal, strengthening local communities and rebuilding families, seeking changes in public policy and stressing the importance of individual behavior, and calling on government to take its rightful role as well as engaging churches, other voluntary organizations, and the business community.

I couldn't figure out whether the Gang Summit initiative was "liberal" or "conservative"; it didn't really matter. The truth is that the creative enterprises that could most make a difference now, like the Gang Summit, go beyond the old categories of liberal and conservative.

I hear the young men and women (the role of women in

the gangs is significant despite the media focus on young men) asking if politics can be moral. They don't believe it is right now. But they also know that the changes necessary to make it so will have to include changes in themselves.

OLD INSTITUTIONS AND OPTIONS

The nation's trust in its political institutions, politicians, and parties is at an all-time low. Public resentment toward the media is even higher. And just when the spiritual nature of this crisis is becoming more evident, the major religious institutions of our society generate little confidence or devotion either.

Left and Right

The dominant political ideologies of liberal and conservative, left and right, seem equally incapable of discerning our present crisis or leading us into the future. Politics has become almost completely dysfunctional. We long for something more truthful, more insightful, more compassionate, more wise, more humble, and more human.

Conservatives have tended to dwell on only some aspects of our social crisis, while liberals continually focus on the other dimensions. Neither side is fully candid in its diagnosis, and both sides have vested interests in which solutions are chosen. Conservatives talk endlessly about personal morality and responsibility (remember the Moral Majority), while liberals seem to only know the language of human rights and social compassion (witness the ACLU). What has so divided and polarized these virtues, which are all at the center of our great moral and religious traditions?

As social critic Cornel West points out, the "liberal structuralists" and "conservative behaviorists" are both right and both wrong.[3] To speak only of moral behavior, apart from oppressive social realities, just blames the victim; and to talk only about social conditions, apart from moral choices, is to keep treating people only as victims. Only a social analysis and practice that transcends the two approaches and forges new options has any chance of succeeding in an increasingly volatile and dangerous cultural context. The culture war that is raging between the advocates of social justice and the preachers of moral rejuvenation must come to an end, not simply to make a truce between embattled intellectuals but also for the sake of our endangered children, who have become the chief pawns and victims of our absurd bifurcations.

Here's an example. In any good community center that deals with the problems of youth, the youth workers will spend most of their time talking about how the young people can get their lives together, find the spiritual and moral resources to make responsible choices, and take control of their own futures. Self-respect and mutual respect, cultural identity, community spirit, and social responsibility are all central to the youth workers. But when describing the wider society, those same youth workers often will speak about the economic, racial, and social oppression that lies at the root of the problems their kids face.

Why must we constantly choose whether to stress responsibility or oppression? Must it be either/or? Why do those from conservative groups speak only of the personal and family values needed for change, and those from more liberal organizations stress the social causes, when anyone who really lives and works on the streets knows that both are fundamentally involved? It's time to start talking to one another instead of just at one another; or, more accurately, it's time to stop our ideological battles in political process, which are often motivated by the competition for power and scarce resources. What is called for now is that particular combination of which the prophets most often spoke—justice *and* righteousness. Why don't we call our own ideological cease-fire for the sake of the children?

Captive Forces

The inability of either liberalism or conservatism to lead us forward is increasingly clear. Both have become captive to economic and political forces and have forgotten their best impulses.

Liberalism's best impulse is to care about the disenfranchised and insist that a society is responsible for its people. But liberalism became captive to large distant institutions and impersonal bureaucracies that are more concerned with control than caring, and the result became more dependency than empowerment.

Conservatism's best impulse is to stress the need for individual initiative and moral responsibility. But because of its attachment to institutions of wealth and power, preference for the status quo, and the lack of a strong ethic of social responsibility, conservatism has virtually abandoned the poor and dispossessed.

Neither the liberal solution of control nor the conservative solution of abandonment offers much hope for those left behind. Liberals have most often spoken of justice and conservatives of liberty. But the genuine resurgence of either justice or liberty among the dispossessed of our society threatens both liberal and conservative politicians, whose power and livelihoods are beholden to established structures.

The personal and social transformation we now require will be a threat to the ideologies of both dominant political forces. Genuine self-determination of previously disempowered peoples is always frightening to those who rule. It's one thing to sing the praises of democracy, especially for other countries; it's quite another to encourage its authentic emergence on one's home turf. Both liberal and conservative ideologies are captive to the past and are now obstacles to urgently needed new solutions.

SHATTERING OLD FRAMEWORKS

Today, the political world does feel as if it has been hit by an earthquake, both domestically and internationally. The end of the Cold War has thrown many former assumptions into the air. Old political frameworks are suddenly inadequate, and new ones have yet to emerge. Many people are unsure where to look for new political directions; it is a time of both uncertainty and possibility.

There are periods in history when social crisis threatens to unravel society. But such times are often also eras of transition, invitation, and opportunity. The New Testament word for such a time is *kairos*. It means a time pregnant with possibilities. We may be at such a moment.

At these historical junctures, ideological analysis and solutions are inadequate. Old political categories prove increasingly useless. Kairos instead calls for a deeper discernment and a bolder action. We see a crisis, we feel a hope, we discern a word, and we hear a call.

It is a renewal of the heart to which we are now summoned. The crisis of our times calls out for our conversion. Our structures, values, habits, and assumptions are in need of basic transformation. Neither politics nor piety as we know them will effect such a change. Rather, a new spirituality is required, a spirituality rooted in old traditions but radically applied to our present circumstances.

Breathtaking Changes

The historical changes we've recently witnessed are breathtaking. It's as though a great logjam in the river of history has suddenly been released. Momentous events have broken the grip of the East-West conflict that held the world captive since the end of World War II. The Cold War not only forced us to live on the edge of the nuclear sword, it also served as a cover for the oppressive dynamics between the rich nations of the Northern Hemisphere and the poor nations of the South. For almost half a century, two superpowers controlled the world's playing field, while other nations either sat on the sidelines or were ground underfoot. It seemed as though the Americans and the Soviets controlled history itself and even had the power to end it in a nuclear collision of giants that would destroy the earth.

The intensity of the ideological conflict obscured many other questions. Since the old East-West warfare ended, underlying questions have now come into view. Economic polarization, environmental disintegration, the vulnerability of children, and the violence generated by racial, gender, and ancient ethnic conflicts are all now painfully visible. New democratic hopes are exploding at the same time that cynicism about political institutions and leadership is at a high point.

New Options

I remember standing at the Berlin Wall in the summer of 1983. After a speaking tour in then West Germany, I was being taken into East Berlin on a short visit carefully arranged by church groups from each side who were stretching the limits of what was then possible. Since I was an American who grew up at the peak of the Cold War, actually seeing the infamous wall firsthand proved to be an emotional experience.

A feeling of great evil dominated the place. I stood there gazing at the twisted barbed wire and armed guards and pondered how this wall of division and oppression extended around the world, running through all of our hearts and minds. It was a wall against the possibility of human reconciliation and political change. It also symbolized the false choices the world was being forced to make. On one side lived a philosophy we described as godless materialism; on the other side, the god of consumerism reigned supreme. Any middle-class American in the postwar era knew this only too well.

But on that trip to Germany, I found signs of change on both sides of the wall. In West Berlin, I met an old couple who had been married by Dietrich Bonhoeffer, the courageous young pastor who was executed for resisting Hitler. The couple's eyes still sparkled as they told me stories of the Confessing Church, a movement that sought to defend authentic faith against the state religion of the Third Reich.

I visited the little church in Barmen where the leaders of the Confessing Church gathered to make their theological declaration (the Barmen Declaration) against the encroachments of Nazism. Most encouraging were the young West German theologians who were beginning to speak of a "new confessing movement" in response to the idolatries of a global economy that crushes the poor in a new holocaust of hunger and death.

In East Berlin, I also met young theologians and pastors who were raising a spiritual and political challenge to their repressive regime and whose churches would soon become centers for dissent and dialogue among East Germans wanting a different future for their country. After a complicated process of changing subways and directions many times to elude any possible followers, we were able to meet with small communities of Christians who operated at great risk outside official structures and who were prepared to pay any price for freedom.

Like some of the Soviet dissidents I would meet in Moscow several years later, these German visionaries from both East and West seemed determined to help shape a future different from what existed on either side of the wall. Rather than simply being swallowed up into the West, those from the East said they were hoping for some new options.

For decades the old options locked us into international polarities of left and right and domestic politics of liberal and conservative. Ideology produced the great macrosystems of capitalism and communism. The latter rose in response to the abuses and injustices of the former, and communism finally collapsed under the weight of its own hypocrisy, repression, and failure. The August Revolution of 1991 in the Soviet Union irrevocably overturned the October Revolution of 1917 and immediately opened up space for better alternatives in a world stuck in the ideological ice of the Cold War, a world enduring the moral poverty of having only two options.

Beyond East and West

The fall of communism does, indeed, provide a new opening for social transformation. It is an opportunity unparalleled in our lifetimes. But it depends on our ability to grasp a new notion of politics based upon ethical values and moral vision. It is possible for us to shed the ideological straitjackets that have constrained political discourse for so long; we could jettison the old polarities of left/right, liberal/conservative that have ruled our minds and numbed our hearts.

Communism collapsed because of its own failures rather than because of the much-proclaimed victory of the West (though the expensive competition of an endless arms race did help bankrupt the Soviets—a deliberate tactic on the part of the U.S.). The failure of Marxist communism was principally ethical, even theological. Communism terribly overestimated how much humanity could be changed from the top down through enforced social engineering, while it fatally underestimated the corruptibility of the self-appointed elites who would carry out the utopian task. Communism was fatally undermined by not taking seriously the reality that evil resides not only in structures, but also in the human heart. Ideology supplanted ethics in a horrible willingness to sacrifice countless human lives on the altar of ideological necessity. The inefficiency of the system merely compounded its moral failure.

The revolutionary promises of 1917 were never fulfilled. A controlled society that would lead to a workers' paradise never moved beyond control, and control became the only real political goal in static systems that outlawed human creativity. The ideological dream was quietly replaced with a stifling and murderous bureaucracy and a passively resentful populace. It was the stagnation, backwardness, and, ultimately, the loss of energy and hope that made perestroika and glasnost necessary. The party line couldn't hold. Nobody believed it anymore, and history finally caught up. When the house fell from internal decay it did so even more quickly than anyone had predicted. Interestingly, no one in the West predicted the collapse, including the ever-vigilant CIA and our fiercest anticommunists.

Meanwhile, world capitalism had produced an increasingly stratified global economy, controlled by fewer and fewer transnational corporations wielding more power than most governments. Today, small entrepreneurs and family farmers have been replaced in large numbers by the employees of huge corporate conglomerates. The results of that dramatic development for economic and political freedom have yet to be honestly faced by either liberals or free-enterprise conservatives. Yet the consequences on the quality of our lives—our food, our books, our culture, our environment—have been enormous.[4]

For years, U.S. Cold Warriors justified their own brutal military adventures and moral double standards by pointing to the oppressiveness of communism. Today, the level of public cynicism toward government bureaucracies, corporate institutions, and media elites in the West is a critical warning sign. The moral victory declared over communism by monopoly capitalism and aggressive consumerism now rings hollow from a moral perspective.

Much idealism was lost on Marxist ideology; generations of capitalism's moral dissenters put their frail hopes in one revolutionary incarnation after another, only to be eventually betrayed. The most systematic challenge to the West finally collapsed—its best impulses having died long before—and the world was left with still no alternative to the many sins of a global corporate economy.

Instead of heaping simplistic and self-serving congratulations upon the West in the face of the East's collapse, as many politicians have done, we could respond more deeply to this historical moment by seriously committing ourselves to self-examination. The so-called free market still presides over an obscenely unjust distribution of the world's resources, the continuing degradation of the environment, and the relegation of huge segments of humanity to misery and silent extinction.

The lack of any systematic alternative does not remove capitalism's own evident failures to resolve the problems of injustice and inequality. Can these ever be resolved in a system based solely on profit? We are learning that just as communism violated ethics out of ideological necessity, so free-market capitalism violates ethics when its devotion to profits overrides every other human or ecological consideration.

The state religion of communism has been replaced so far only with the Western religion of materialism, an idol that holds great attraction for those recently set free from the idolatries of state totalitarianism. But the shimmering promises of the good life of Western consumerism are now withering in many former communist countries as the harsh realities of the market economy are experienced for the first time. Former so-called economic rights under repressive regimes are now belatedly appreciated by many, and dangerous new nationalistic and racist movements are flourishing.

The most exciting development following the collapse of communism has been the growing convergence between dissenters on both sides of the old East-West divide. New political leaders in Europe, like Czechoslovakia's Vaclav Havel, are offering a new definition of politics and the civil society.[5] These new leaders opposed communism but are not eager to simply embrace the materialism of the West. Their counterparts in the West are also eager to begin a new political and economic dialogue. I remember several conversations with Czech economists and other Eastern European leaders who hope to chart a new direction. This alternative perspective has unfortunately been mostly overrun with the pace of the West's so-called victory.

The West Wind

Ultimately, our great macrosystems have both failed, especially morally and spiritually. They have failed the poor, the earth, and the human heart. The two superpowers have also succeeded in militarizing most of the world, leaving a legacy of weapons, conflict, and social neglect that we will be living with for some time. Both ideologies have come to the end of their usefulness, despite the fact that, thus far, only one has been forced to admit its failure.

Despite the rhetoric of Western triumph over the collapse of communism in 1989, polls in the early 1990s suggest that the American people sense something very basic is wrong at home. Underneath the specific fears of many Americans is the reported belief among a majority of the population that the country is "offtrack" and headed in the "wrong direction."[6]

Political columnists report that people are deeply worried about their own lives and their children's future. The social crises they worry about are many: violent crime, an unstable economy, competition with the Japanese and the Europeans, loss of jobs, spiraling health care costs, family instability, drugs, AIDS, failing education, the lack of affordable housing, disintegrating cities, hunger and homelessness, and so forth.

The post–Cold War American economy reveals financial scandals at the top, deep insecurity in the middle, and utter poverty at the bottom. And the frightening problems of our environment, whose threatened collapse hangs like a cloud over all of our heads, have become increasingly urgent, especially to the young who worry about the world they will inherit.

For societies in decline, control becomes a priority. Dreaming becomes illegal. Vision is a threat to political leadership bereft of it. In the Eastern bloc, that was all brutally apparent, but in the West it has come about more gradually and subtly. Our loss of vision is represented by media conglomerates that control the flow of information and shape the images appearing on our television screens and by the increasing commercialization of the popular culture, resulting in a kind of uniform banality. Because the money-controlled media has become the gatekeeper, deciding which social ideas or political options are made visible, most alternative visions are filtered out of public view.

Most Western political leaders drew all the wrong lessons from the tumultuous happenings in the Eastern bloc. They saw the fall of communism as vindication. But that perspective is as shortsighted as it is self-serving. Rather, the fall of communism was prophecy. History will overtake the West as well; it's only a matter of time. Here, too, the system is failing while we struggle to keep up the illusions. Our disintegrating inner cities are but the domestic sign of a global economy that is unraveling.

Yesterday an "east wind" of freedom and democracy blew out the old. Tomorrow a "south wind" of justice and liberation will free the oppressed majority. We cannot cheer political democracy for Polish workers, Lithuanian farmers, and Chinese students and stand by while the structures of our global economy block freedom and justice for West African laborers, Central American campesinos, and Filipino slum dwellers. When the wind from the south flies in, bearing the hopes of the world's poor on its wings, a chilly gale will be felt by the northern global power centers that today run the world's system of economic apartheid. The unpredicted 1994 uprising of the Zapatista Indian campesinos in Mexico's Chiapas province, in rebellion against their government's neglect of them and embrace of NAFTA, is but a first sign.

Yesterday an ugly wall of ideological repression came crashing down in the East. Tomorrow the invisible walls of international trade and finance, which support a global system of economic, and therefore political, injustice, could also come tumbling down in a "west wind"—just as quickly and unexpectedly.

It's hard to stop the wind when it begins to blow.

MOVING FORWARD

As with communism, a failure of ethics is at the root of our many related crises and has the potential to undo the West, too; conversely, the reassertion of fundamental ethical values could bring the moral and political renewal we so desperately need. With the fear of communism now set aside, we could finally choose to face up to the moral contradictions inherent in our own systems, contradictions we have conveniently accepted for so long. Is it not time to stop arguing ideology and begin to speak in terms of what is right and wrong? Would not finding real and practical solutions to our undeniable problems be a better definition of politics than the endless pursuit of power?

Breaking free of ideological restraints offers new opportunities for cooperation among diverse people across the ideological spectrum. Conservatives who have genuinely worried about the totalitarian dangers of command economies and the effectiveness of huge welfare states could now be free to engage in a new involvement for the sake of the poor. They could take even more seriously their deep concern for human freedom and individual liberty by demonstrating a real commitment to justice for the masses of people who have been shut out and left behind. It's time for principled conservatives to prove they are not just providing intellectual and political cover for wealth, power, and right-wing self-interest, but that they genuinely care about their own best and most basic convictions.

Liberals could now be free from the constant accusation of being sympathetic to communism; they no longer have to carry the baggage of failed leftist regimes. They could take more seriously their expressed concern for the disenfranchised by making a real commitment to the kind of personal and community values that make social change possible. It's time for liberals to show they are less committed to particular models and ideologies than to the poor themselves, and more committed to finding solutions that really work.

We might all move out of our various camps and enter into a fresh dialogue with one another about the path ahead. Again, the best way to common ground is the path to higher ground. Only a heightened level of moral discourse in the public debate will bring us together.

Will godless communism simply be replaced by the god of Western consumerism, or will the true moral values of justice and liberty find rejuvenation? Will ideology be replaced with ethics in the construction of social and political alternatives? We have seen enough of the messianic promises of both the right and the left. Indeed, because of the demonstrated human capacity for both great good and terrible evil, ethics must become the touchstone of our political life. Virtue must be the fuel for our visions, integrity the measure of our programs. Grand schemes must give way to practical solutions that give new life and hope.

Chapter Three

Politics and Religion
Toward a Prophetic Spirituality

Not in polite company. That's where you were not supposed to talk about either politics or religion. Perhaps it was because these two subjects were too important and would interrupt the small talk. Or maybe it was because they were potentially so divisive that they might spoil the party.

Well, that has changed over the years. Both politics and religion are hot topics these days. But now the discomfort seems to be discussing them *together*.

I recall, painfully, as an evangelical teenager being told by my church that Christian faith had nothing to do with either racism or war. (In truth, most of the good church people quietly supported both, succeeding in keeping their politics and religion separate.) But my heart was rising to the moral challenge of the civil rights movement and the Vietnam War.

The intuition that my faith did indeed have something to do with politics was the principal cause of my separation from the little church that had nurtured and raised me. Now in exile, I found a new home in the civil rights movement and the black community. There I learned what the relationship really was between the two forbidden topics in polite white society.

The civil rights movement was built on the foundation of the black churches. The illuminating oratory of Martin Luther King Jr. and the other preacher-activists of the movement made the integral connection between faith and politics clear.

I suppose it was inevitable that I would become a preacher-activist too. The nature of the intersection between religion and politics became a continual personal and vocational reflection.

The topic has now become more complicated. The evangelical folks I grew up with finally became involved in politics and now insist that faith indeed has real political implications. The issues that drew them in were abortion and the cultural breakdown of American society.

Their political involvement became quite alarming to many liberal Christians who had long insisted on the rightful relationship between religion and questions of public policy. It was one thing to support the religious call of black ministers to the barricades of civil rights. It was quite another to accept the religious right mobilizing on behalf of the unborn.

In his provocative book, *The Culture of Disbelief,* Yale law professor Stephen Carter reflects on the thorny problem. Carter contends that a prejudice against the influence of religious commitment upon political issues now characterizes many sectors of American society, including the media, academia, the law, and the corridors of political power.[1]

Religious conviction is trivialized and becomes quickly suspect when it seems to be affecting matters political. While disagreeing with many of the tenets of the religious right, Carter defends their seeking to affect politics from their own faith perspective.

An African American and a constitutional lawyer, Carter claims that the American doctrine of the separation of church and state forbids the establishment of any religion by the state but not the influence of religious values in the public square. Along with others, such as historian Garry Wills,[2] Carter suggests that religious faith has always helped shape American politics and that such influence can serve very positive as well as terribly negative ends.

Spiritual and religious values, indeed, can contribute in a

time of social crisis to a renewed vision of politics. Yet, one need not be a member of a church, synagogue, or mosque to appreciate that contribution. In fact, one need not be a religious person at all. Anyone who believes that moral issues are at stake in our political choices can understand the need for renewal. Most people would probably agree that beneath the social, economic, cultural, and political problems we confront lie critical questions concerning our deepest values. Our crisis is also one of the spirit—deeper than just the turns and twists of secular politics.

A new politics will require the spiritual resources of our best moral and religious traditions. More and more people, religious or not, are searching for a new spirituality as well as for a new politics. The two must be joined and proceed together. The new spirituality that could guide our search for a new politics will most likely be found in the renewal of the moral and spiritual traditions we already know. In America, that will come from rediscovering our Jewish and Christian biblical traditions as well as learning from Native American spiritualities, appreciating the insights of other faith experiences, and remembering the moral imperatives of the political philosophies that shaped the founding of our nation. All have direct contributions to make in recovering our political ethics.

History and experience tell us that religious vision can turn into sectarian divisiveness, justifying some of our worst human behavior. On the other hand, our best religious impulses can remind us of what kind of people we really want to be; authentic faith can lift us to the heights of our humanity. Religious vision that awakens basic values can enable us to transcend narrow self-interest and embrace the common good rather than reducing things to their lowest common denominator and negotiating factional interests.

I view politics from the vantage point of my own religious tradition—in particular from the perspective of the biblical prophets and the teaching of Jesus. But given the prominence of the religious right in contemporary American politics, any reference to the Bible prompts many to mistrust and suspicion.

Yet I believe the prophetic biblical tradition can serve as a fundamental alternative to both the limits of secular humanism and the oppressions of religious fundamentalism. The religion of the prophets can help us shape a politics of conscience.

As a foremost scholar of the biblical prophets, theologian Walter Brueggemann writes,

> After the best efforts of self-indulgent existentialism, technological positivism, revolutionary Marxism, and free-market ideology, we may yet discern that the covenantal discourse of the Bible, preserved as it is by [a] confessing community, is as close as we can come to a genuinely public language. That discernment can happen, however, only when it is unambiguously clear that the speakers and advocates of such covenantal discourse are not proselytizing or serving parochial ends—and that requires a self-emptying compassion.[3]

Such a voice, says Brueggemann, must be uncompromisingly bold but not sectarian,

> speaking the human agenda in a way that honors our social pluralism, in a way that touches our shared human requirements of love, mercy, justice, peace, and freedom. These are the property of no confessional truth and the monopoly of no confessional community.[4]

Spiritual and religious values should influence our perception of and participation in politics. But while religion belongs in the political world, religion and ideology are not good partners. Stephen Carter warns against reaching conclusions on political grounds and, afterward, finding religious justification for them, instead of letting genuine religious conviction shape honest political judgments.[5]

Perhaps the best test of the spiritual integrity of our political commitments is their predictability or unpredictability. Religious perspectives on political matters must not be predictable on the basis of prior ideological biases. We have seen enough of that on both ends of the political spectrum. For much too long, conservative evangelicals have been the Republican Party at prayer, liberal religious leaders have been easily confused with the left wing of the Democratic Party, and even grassroots religious peace and justice activists have not always distinguished themselves from the politics of other secular and solidarity movements. And, to be honest, most of us have fallen into such political predictability from time to time, especially during the height of the contentious Cold War years.

But this is a new time. It is a time when the spiritual nature of the many crises we face is increasingly clear to many people. The failure of ideology on all sides and the now-dysfunctional character of old political categories are also increasingly apparent. If discerned truthfully, religious faith will not be squeezed into predetermined positions of left, right, or center—or whatever new ones may emerge in the changing world of secular politics. At its best, religious perspective and conviction will transform categories by bringing independent moral values and social conscience to the public square.

New Openings

Emory University scholar-in-residence Eugene D. Genovese recently remarked on the subject of religion and politics. Genovese, a widely respected intellectual of the left, said,

> Liberalism is over. The Left is dead. Politics will be principally shaped by religious communities. The only question is, will they be repressive and totalitarian religious communities or lucid, progressive ones.[6]

In an equally surprising development, the progressive magazine Z declared in its January 1994 issue, "It is long past time that the American Left re-evaluated its judgment that religion is unadulterated superstition." The article goes on to describe the historically religious roots of today's progressive egalitarian movements and the radical character of Jesus![7]

Z's writer suggests that progressive Christian movements could be "the salvation of the secular left."

> Only a religiously based radicalism can succeed in winning a major sector of American sympathy.... The American people will not sacrifice their lives for a secular utopia that does not fulfill their emotional and spiritual needs. Although the American Left seems to have little awareness of its own religious vision, the American people do know what they want, what Jesus wanted, a universal community of peace, love, and justice sustained by the experience of a loving God.[8]

These are surprising and interesting developments. On the other side of the political spectrum, large evangelical groups like the relief and development organization World Vision and the student-focused Inter-Varsity Christian Fellowship are making strong connections between faith and social justice. Especially important is their commitment to confront racism with Christian opposition.

Despite the popular identification of the evangelical community with the religious right, social concern among evangelicals is growing with new energy and power, especially among the poor and the young. In many developing countries, congregations of poor evangelical and pentecostal Christians are providing new ferment for social justice. Across the old political spectrum, the possibilities for new forms of convergence are becoming more clear.

CONSERVATIVE AND LIBERAL RELIGION

When religion becomes conformed to the culture, it can no longer provide a reliable path to spirituality, and our public life loses its moral compass. The two dominant forms of religion in our time have failed to provide the spiritual guidance that might inform a politics of moral conscience. Both conservative and liberal religion have become culturally captive forces that merely cheer on the ideological camps with which each has identified. And religion as a political cheerleader is invariably false religion.

Conservative religion has become preoccupied with words and dogma. Correct religious language and doctrine have replaced an emphasis upon faithful living and action. A certain lifestyle is associated with conservative religion, but it reveals more about the cultural and political biases of its adherents than about the meaning of authentic faith. Personal piety has become an end in itself instead of the energy for social justice. Religious language has little or no connection to moral action in society.

In a bargain for power, some conservative religious leaders have aligned themselves with reactionary political elements, creating a particularly bizarre and frightening combination of religion and politics. In the most materialistic culture in history, conservative religion has produced a gospel of prosperity. In a society whose inequitable distribution of resources has become obscene, conservative religion has become a defender of the wealthy. Within the greatest military superpower in the world, conservative religion has become a primary advocate for extending American hegemony and a consistent defender of the nation's every war.

In an already divided and polarized society, the religious right has drawn even firmer boundaries. It has been a white religion, has fueled the backlash against women's rights, and has used blatant caricatures and attacks on homosexuals as highly successful fund-raising techniques. The confusion and rejection of Christian faith caused by this unholy alliance of religious appeals and right-wing politics are now pervasive.

Liberal religion has lost its spiritual center. It has become both reactive to conservative religion and captive to the shifting winds of the secular culture. Liberal activism has often lacked any real dynamic of personal conversion and, therefore, transformative power. With liberal religion, social action in the world can become severed from its roots in faith, producing a language and practice that seem more bureaucratic and ideological than spiritual.

Liberal religion has made its own pacts with political power and has aligned itself with the liberal power centers of the society. Often its "political correctness" reflects the values of liberal elites more than the authentic voice of the powerless, in whose name liberal religion often claims to speak. Reforming our language for the sake of, for example, racial and gender justice is important. But ideological conformity undermines prophetic integrity.

Polarized religious leaders have behaved much like the politicians they have been allied with. The leaders of the religious right were the virtual chaplains of the White House during the Reagan and Bush years. The conservative presidents were the headline speakers at evangelical events, and the television preachers enjoyed unprecedented access to political power, along with honored places at Republican national conventions.

After the Democratic victory in 1992, many conservative evangelicals virtually identified the Clintons with the Antichrist (seeming especially offended by Hillary's role and power). At the same time, liberal Protestant leaders glowed in their newfound access to the corridors of power. Former diatribes against the government were quickly toned down in favor of a much happier relationship on "the inside." Most religious leaders would rather be invited to testify before a Congressional committee or have breakfast in the White House than be arrested for protest outside on the street. With few notable exceptions, the involvement of both conservative and liberal religious leaders in politics has left the ground of a genuinely independent and prophetic political witness largely unexplored.

One wonders how a president or government might truly be served by dialogue with religious leaders that encourages a serious accountability to political morality and offers prophetic insight to open up new directions and options. One wonders, too, whether any president would really want such a dialogue. In biblical language, does King David ever really want to have a serious conversation with the prophet Nathan? Uncomfortable topics tend to come up, like the bombing of children in Baghdad, which presidents from both parties have been willing to do.

Yet, there are precedents for such a relationship. One thinks of the biblical stories of Joseph and Daniel, captive slaves whose wisdom commended them to foreign rulers. There is also the modern example of the relationship between Martin Luther King Jr. and Presidents Kennedy and Johnson. The civil rights leader proved a prophetic goad to these powerful presidents, even though they both sought to undermine or discredit his leadership.

PROPHETIC SPIRITUALITY

Prophetic spirituality is the alternative to the current manifestations of conservative and liberal religion. Much older than either of the contemporary religious options, the prophetic biblical tradition is rooted in the Hebrew sages, Jesus, and the early Christian community. Prophetic spirituality has found expression in virtually every renewal and reform movement in history that has sought to return to radical religious roots.

Many religious traditions have their prophetic streams. Jewish and Christian faiths play leading roles in the history of the West, and the recovery of the prophetic character integral to both of them has much to offer our present crisis. The contemporary but sometimes shallow New Age explorations of Eastern and indigenous traditions indicate the cultural hunger for spiritual experience. Various Twelve-Step programs and recovery groups offer much-needed spiritual resources as well. But changes in consciousness will not be enough, without a consciousness that changes the world. The recovery of a prophetic biblical spirituality could offer some unique possibilities in renewing our moral values and reshaping our political life.

For years now, the religious right has controlled the public debate on politics and morality. Conservatives have tapped into people's longing for a new emphasis on values in public life. But that longing is for alternatives much wider and deeper than the narrow interpretations offered by the evangelical right wing. The extremism of the religious right suggests that the only alternatives are either to become totally secular or to subscribe to religious bigotry. A moral vacuum is waiting to be filled. People are now searching for another way, one that takes seriously the fundamental question of values—a question that lies just beneath the surface of political discussion.

Over the last few decades, a real alternative in American religious life has emerged, unrecognized by the media. While the press has focused on the loud voices of the religious right and limited its field of vision to the conservative tenor of the last several years, a prophetic spiritual movement for social change has been steadily growing and is making a difference in the institutions of both religion and society.

This spiritual movement existed before the religious right burst upon the national scene with Ronald Reagan's 1980 presidential victory, and the more prophetic commitment it represents has grown ever since. It relates biblical faith to social transformation; personal conversion to the cry of the poor; theological reflection to care for the environment; core religious values to new economic priorities; the call of community to racial and gender justice; morality to foreign policy; spirituality to politics; and, at its best, it transcends the categories of liberal and conservative that have captivated both religion and politics.

The effects of this progressive spirit are being felt in virtually every constituency of the American churches and in the Jewish community. This spiritual movement reaches out in respectful partnership with other faith traditions beyond the religious mainstream of the society. And it invites a new dialogue between the religious and nonreligious about the shape of social and political morality. A renewed ecumenical community has the capacity to offer new visions to a society desperately in need of them, on the basis of what South African Archbishop Desmond Tutu calls "the spirituality of transformation." [9]

The Religion of the Prophets

When we take the biblical tradition seriously, we can easily discern the relevance and timeliness of prophetic religion to the conflicts and questions that daily bombard us. For example, the biblical prophets encourage us to be suspicious of concentrations of wealth and power; to mistrust ideological rationales that justify subordinating persons to causes; and especially to become sensitive to the poor, the disenfranchised, the stranger, and the outsider. The Bible radically relativizes all claims to ownership and domination of land and resources by asserting that "the Earth is the Lord's" and its abundance intended to be shared by all of God's children. As for democracy, the biblical view of the human condition suggests that power and decision making should be decentralized and accountable, not because people are essentially good but because we so often are not.

Had we been listening to the prophetic biblical tradition, we would have known that you can't have an economic system that leaves masses of people behind without engendering endless conflict. We would have known that growth and progress that abuse, exploit, and degrade the earth will eventually poison our lives and choke us to death. We would have known that we cannot deny human dignity to our neighbors because of their race, class, or gender without endangering our own souls. We would have known that a society can't place its ultimate security in weapons and technology, rather than in justice and integrity, without falling victim to the social theft of arms races and the perils of escalating violence. We haven't really been listening to the religious traditions to which we have given cultural lip service, and the logic of the social systems we have created instead is killing us.

A Sense of Community

Central to prophetic religious traditions is the idea of covenant. The moral requirements of relationship and community serve to correct our human tendencies toward individual selfishness and exploitation of our neighbors and the earth. Today the fundamental covenant that holds life together has been profoundly damaged. We have little sense of community with our five billion neighbors, scant knowledge of a harmonious relationship with the ecosystem, and, at root, little meaningful experience of our identity as the children of God. Our deep need is to find a way to connect. The broken relationships must be healed; everything now depends upon our making connections.

The broken covenant can be seen in my own Washington, D.C., neighborhood, just blocks away from the White House, where babies are born with AIDS and addicted to drugs; where children live without the basics of health care, education, housing, or family; and where the young are shot down in their own streets before they have a chance to grow up. We see it, not only in urban areas that have become war zones, but also in rural communities that are struggling to survive.

It's overwhelmingly visible in the so-called Third World, where the poor are suffering and dying almost beyond our capacity to count or care. Our denial of harsh realities ultimately denies our connection to our neighbor and any sense of a whole or holy life. Both at home and abroad, whole areas of the world and huge segments of humanity are forgotten.

A great yawning chasm has grown up between us, and we have likewise become alienated from the earth itself. The terrible separation threatens the fragile threads that connect us to each other and to the rest of creation. We can all feel the alienation. Our neighbor is unknown to us, and the only bond we have left is fear.

When politics loses its vision, religion loses its faith, and culture loses its soul; life becomes confused, cheap, and endangered. Nothing less than a restoration of the shattered covenant will save us. That will require a fundamental transformation of our ways of thinking, feeling, and acting. At the core of prophetic religion is transformation—a change of heart, a revolution of the spirit, a conversion of the soul that issues forth in new personal and social behavior.

Historically, religion has been a source of guidance for spiritual and moral values. Transcendence calls us to accountability and gives us a sense of meaning and purpose we are unable to find on our own. Without ethics rooted in transcendent reality, moral sensibility becomes merely a matter of shifting cultural consensus.

PROPHETIC IMAGINATION

We are suffering today not just from greed, injustice, and violence, but from a lack of imagination. For lack of vision, we are perishing. We need new visions and dreams; our future

depends upon fresh imagination. We do, indeed, find ourselves in an in-between time; the old order is passing away
and the new is begging to be born.

But what does that mean today? What is vision, anyway?
Webster's Dictionary says vision is "the act or power of imagination." [10] And it defines imagination as "creative ability,"
the "ability to confront and deal with a problem," and "po-
etic creation." [11] Imagination comes from "what is remembered" or from what has been experienced only in part, the
dictionary says. Oxford's says to imagine is "to picture"
something new, [12] and vision is "something which is seen otherwise than by ordinary sight" [13] — seeing more than meets
the eye.

What does that tell us? First, we learn that vision depends
on imagination—the ability to see what cannot be seen in the
present and, indeed, the capacity to picture a new reality. Vision requires (a) using more than ordinary sight, (b) being
rooted in a historical memory, and (c) building upon some
experience of what you are seeking to envision. Such vision is
indispensable to any society, but especially one in crisis, both
for problem solving and for creativity.

New social visions and dreams thus will be rooted in our
core values, derived from our religious and cultural traditions,
and rooted in the moral sensibilities we still possess and the
memory of basic values still in our collective consciousness—
even though that memory may be fading. Vision will depend
upon social innovation and will derive, in part, from those
places where new social experiments based on remembered
values are already occurring.

The alternative moral and political vision that our social
crisis requires is unlikely to come from the pinnacles of
power. Prophetic visions almost never do. The task of prophetic politics is most often left to faith communities and
movements of conscience working from the bottom up to
change people's lives and redirect a society.

A prophetic and inclusive spirituality could speak to the hunger among us for both personal and social transformation, and it could bring many people together. Such a movement must be pluralistic and nonsectarian, respectful of other faith and moral traditions, and open to meaningful cooperation. An independent spiritual voice for social justice and reconciliation is much needed now, and it is something the religious community could help provide.

Prophetic Politics

The good news is that such a voice can already be heard. This prophetic spiritual movement speaks the language of both social justice and personal responsibility. In economics, it takes us beyond the bottom line of profit or the stagnation of bureaucracy to an economic ethic rooted in the religious requirements of community. On the environment, this deeper biblical perspective transcends old notions of either exploitation or protection and proposes a theology of relationship to the earth.

Such a prophetic perspective sees racism and sexism as spiritual as well as social sins and calls for repentance. In foreign relations, it puts human rights over national self-interest and seeks alternatives to war as the familiar solution to the inevitable conflicts between nations. While standing as a much needed alternative to the theocratic impulses of the religious right, this new movement of religious conscience will, nonetheless, insist on the vital connection between politics and morality. In so doing, it will provide a social reservoir of what Walter Brueggemann has named "prophetic imagination." [14]

Over the past few decades, this spiritually based activism has become visible in religious efforts to end the threat of nuclear war, in congregations providing sanctuary to Central American refugees or building new houses for the homeless, in the creation of dynamic church-based coalitions for community organizing, and in religious efforts to save children, rebuild families, and renew the creation. In both cities and rural areas across the country, the number of spiritually based ventures and coalitions to heal and rebuild local communities is beyond counting.

After years of very limited results from institutional ecumenical dialogues, a vital ecumenism is emerging between people who have found one another while putting their faith into action. A new faith community has emerged in urban ministry centers, homeless shelters, and soup kitchens; in street protests and jail cells; on racial and ecological battlegrounds; in prayer and Bible study groups; and in diverse experiments in community and spiritual renewal. What has often been expressed as "prophetic protest" now has the capacity to be a vital source of "prophetic vision" as well. Out of religious values and moral concerns, new social and economic alternatives are emerging.

This movement of prophetic conscience is political without being ideological. Predictable and party-line politics is anathema to authentic prophetic witness. Refusing partisan politics may be one of the most important contributions of a prophetic vision. A truly independent religious, moral, and ethical perspective has much to contribute in shaping a new kind of politics, and we must make the nature of that contribution increasingly clear.

This new prophetic spirituality has yet to be named, but the media should move beyond old and inadequate labels to describe it. It draws evangelicals with a compassionate heart and a social conscience. It brings together mainline Protestants who desire spiritual revival and justice. It invites Catholics who seek a spirituality for social change. It includes African-American, Latino, Asian, and Native American faith communities who are working to shape a more pluralistic and just society. It has the capacity to bring Christians, Jews, Muslims, and other religious communities together in a dialogue and cooperation based on the respect and contribution of each one's particularities rather than on a bland religious reductionism. And it attracts those who, long alienated from established religion, are hungry for a personal and communal spirituality to undergird their struggle to live more justly.

Prophetic spirituality will always challenge the system at its roots and offer genuine alternatives based on values from our truest religious, cultural, and political traditions. Some potential constituencies from which such alternatives have already begun to emerge include the poor themselves as they become conscious of the causes of their oppression and organized in their efforts to change it; the religious community where the renewal of faith is perceived to have social and political consequences; artists and poets who are striking a new chord in popular culture; community leaders determined to renew the practice of democracy; and the increasing number of working and middle-class families who painfully experience the failure of the system's promises but reject demagogic appeals to scapegoat other victims. A different future will be constructed not by merely shuffling the elites at the top, but rather by transforming values and action from below among such people and their communities.

The politics we most need right now is the "politics of community." In that birthing process, a prophetic spiritual network—across the lines of race, class, gender, and region—can act as the midwife of new possibilities.

THE PROPHETIC VOCATION: LIVING "AS IF"

The prophetic vocation is to challenge the old while announcing the new. Like the prophets, we must call certainty into question. The biblical prophets always had a twofold task. First, they were bold in telling the truth and proclaiming the justice that is rooted in God. They named the idols that had led the people astray and unmasked their destructive reality. And they called the people to return to their true selves and purpose, to reject their false gods, and to remember who they were as the children of God.

But in addition to truth telling, the prophets had a second task. They held up an alternative vision; they helped the people to imagine new possibilities.

Solidarity activist Adam Michnik used to say, "We live as if there is political space." [15] In the worst years of the struggle for democracy in Poland, there was no political space. But by living as if there was, the Solidarity workers helped create that political space.

Today, we need those who are willing to live as if an alternative vision is possible. Even when the possibility of real change seems quite dim—and especially then—history needs people who believe that change is possible and are willing to bet their lives on it. That often takes a good dose of faith.

A number of transformations are now absolutely essential. In many places, such transformations are already under way. Together, they could turn us around and set our feet on a new path. They are central to the meaning of prophetic politics today.

Reconnecting personal values to political morality is the first step. Healing family life, asserting the covenantal character of our relationships, and rediscovering the preciousness of our children are all crucial for rebuilding our communities and reestablishing integrity in our public life.

Our addiction to materialism must be healed. We can be freed from the falsehood that the accumulation and consumption of things are the substance and measure of human life.

Our alienation from the rest of creation must be overcome. We can be converted from the idea that the earth belongs to us; we can live as if we are part of a creation that belongs to God. Our assumption that the world's created abundance is ours to use and use up, to own and divide, to exploit and destroy, can be replaced with the values of stewardship and equity.

Our ethic of profit can be transformed by an ethic of community as the foundation of our economic system. We can live as if social goods were more highly valued than consumer goods in measuring our quality of life.

We can squarely confront and repent of our sins of racism and sexism, correcting the oppression of people of color and women in our personal behavior, cultural attitudes, and social structures. By opening ourselves to a genuinely multicultural and gender-equal future based on justice and opportunity we will rediscover ourselves as a nation.

Genuine citizen participation can replace passive public polling as the defining practice of our political system. The dominant power of money over the political process can be broken and wealth removed as the primary key to government influence. The hold of media conglomerates over the flow of information and political debate can be exposed and public discussion opened to plural voices.

Our wasteful and destructive militarism can be reversed as we begin to place our security in domestic equity, international justice, multilateral cooperation, and the persistent negotiation of our inevitable human conflicts—not in weapons of technological destruction.

Finally, we will begin to see and feel the connections between us all and with the earth and come to understand that, one way or another, our destinies are irrevocably tied together.

We need a new vision today. We need vision to provide us with a feeling of purpose, an assurance of meaning, a way of bonding, and a sense of direction. Vision connects us to the past and points us toward the future, which is what gives the present its truest significance.

We need to regain our bearings and find the values that can hold people together, give us a common sense of purpose, and point the way forward. We need to remember where we've come from, discover who we are, and together decide where we're going.

We need to understand the connections between all the issues we face and the spiritual foundations that undergird them. We must begin to restore the covenant we've lost with our neighbors on this planet and with the creation itself. The vision we now require is nothing short of a new covenant. At root, we need to return to our spiritual identity as the children of God.

There is an alternative—the message of hope in a hopeless time. And we can live as if that new vision is possible.

Ordinary people can create the visions we need and put them into practice. We need more than new ideas; we need to build new communities at the local level. We can't be content to be better informed about the problems of the world; we must discover how our lives can make a difference.

The world will not change until we do; personal and social transformation are inextricably linked together. That is the wisdom of the spiritual and social movements whose legacies endure. New politics and new spirituality can only emerge together. We must now make that vital connection clear.

Prophetic spirituality can offer a vision for that transformation. Through stories and parables, instead of blueprints and ideologies, we hope to point the way toward a different kind of future.

We stand at a political crossroads, and critical choices must now be made. Those choices are at heart religious, insofar as they will reveal our most fundamental values and moral sensibilities. The road we take will determine the kind of people we will become and the nature of the societies in which we will live. In short, the decisions we make will decisively shape the quality of life for ourselves and our children's children. The Hebrew Scripture says it well: "I have set before you life and death, blessings and curses. Choose life so that you and your descendants may live." [16]

Part Two

The Broken Community

Chapter Four

═══

A Tale of Two Cities
The Division of the World

Twenty blocks from the White House, the doors of the Sojourners Neighborhood Center open early for the Saturday morning food line. Just before we open those doors, all the volunteers join hands for a prayer. Most of the volunteers come from the food line themselves. Mrs. Mary Glover, a sixty-year-old African-American woman, prays, "Lord, we know that you'll be comin' through this line today. So help us to treat you well."

Her prayer recalls the words of Jesus, "I was hungry and you gave me food. . . . As you have done it to the least of these, you have done it to me." Jesus inhabits the food lines in the shadows of the monuments to the world's leading superpower. This truth holds a key to finding our way back to one another.

The neighborhood I live in is called Columbia Heights, and it runs along 14th Street in Washington, D.C. It was the scene of the much-publicized, so-called riots following the assassination of Martin Luther King Jr. in the bitter spring of 1968. The "riot corridor," as the area is still called, even today bears the scars of the frustrated and angry violence that erupted when people's hopes were suddenly and brutally cut down. Burned-out buildings and vacant lots remain after more than twenty-five years.

One day several years ago, my sister Barbara was walking through the neighborhood with her five-year-old son, Michael. They were on their way to Sojourners' community-run day care center. Michael surveyed the scene on the block. Looking up at his mother with puzzlement, my young nephew asked, "Mommy, was there a war here?" It has become commonplace to refer to neighborhoods like ours as war zones. But few from outside ask or really reflect upon what it would mean to live your life in a place so named.

The empty shells of buildings, piles of rubble, and general devastation all around give the impression of warfare. Perhaps the eyes of a child can see what jaded adult vision quickly passes over or too easily accepts: there was and is a war here. It goes on every day, and the casualties are everywhere.

The people who inhabit this and similar neighborhoods in inner cities across America are not only neglected and ignored by political decision makers, they are war victims. They are wounded by a system that has ravaged their lives and their communities. It is no wonder that those who make it through refer to themselves as survivors. But many are not surviving. The forces that have made war on them are global and impersonal, but the consequences for the people here are very personal indeed.

A TALE OF TWO CITIES

My city, like cities around the country, is divided in two. The center of power that is Washington sits next to the disenfranchised in the District of Columbia. Everyone knows "official Washington" with its marble, monuments, and malls. But the "other Washington" has been off-limits to the blue-and-white tour buses and to the consciousness of the rest of America.

Here are substandard tenements instead of stately government offices. Here children play in rat-infested back alleys strewn with glass, trash, and syringes instead of running in beautiful parks. Here the only monuments are to neglect, indifference, and the stranglehold of entrenched racism on the city that proclaims itself a beacon of freedom to the world.

Here the homeless huddle in the shadows of the great houses of state power, trying to keep warm by sleeping on the grates that expel hot air from the heating systems of the Pentagon, the White House, the halls of Congress, and the Department of Justice. The wet heat combined with cold winter air can produce pneumonia, and the pattern of the iron grates can be seen on the burned flesh of the unfortunate who fall into a deep sleep. Those who work in government buildings from which the New World Order is run must literally step over the homeless as they go into their offices. The symbolism is obvious, and the everyday scene is a striking metaphor of the world economic order.

People stream to Washington, D.C., to exercise power, influence power, or just be around power. Everyone is intoxicated with the feel of it. The key word here is *access*. Access to power is what everyone is always fighting for in this town. Power, like money, becomes its own justification, a potent aphrodisiac. How you get it or what it is used for are beside the point; having power is what's important.

As power defines official Washington, powerlessness defines the other Washington. Here are the people who clean the hotel rooms, flip the hamburgers, and drive the taxis—if they have work at all.

Washington is the most powerful city in the nation, and yet D.C. is the most powerless, without control even over its own affairs and destiny. Considered by many to be a colony, the District of Columbia didn't obtain even partial home rule until 1974. To this day, District residents (more than 606,900 people[1]) have no voting representation in Congress, and all actions taken by the elected city government are subject to congressional veto. As the "last colony," D.C. symbolizes the relationship many other parts of the world have with official Washington.

The place I live has become a symbol for the places we all live today. Washington, D.C., dramatically exemplifies what the entire global economy has become—a tale of two cities. The bipolar structure of our stratified global city is reflected in hundreds of communities across the country and around the world.

The story is always the same. Everywhere now there is an upper city and a lower city; in some places it's more visible than others, but it's true everywhere and becoming more evident. On a world scale, the reality is overpowering. It is the central reality of our global crisis—foundational to understanding all our other problems. And yet it is the reality we still want to deny or simply choose to ignore. Increasingly, that will no longer be possible. To face up to the tale of two cities is rapidly becoming a political and moral imperative.

Invisible Tenants

One day a knock came at our front door. A woman from across the street was asking for help. "They're taking away our home," she said, "and everyone else has given up and left, but I want to stay and fight. Would you help my family?" Sojourners community had begun working on housing issues, so I said we would try. Little did I know what we were getting into.

We discovered that the woman's apartment building had been purchased by a real-estate developer to resell for a 100 percent profit. He was evicting all the present residents (who were poor but had faithfully paid their rent) and was planning to renovate the place for a new clientele of more affluent occupants. We had seen it before. The process is known as gentrification or the "back to the city" movement, and our neighborhood is under assault from the developers and speculators who envision a prosperous future that doesn't include the low-income people who have lived their lives here. Everyone involved in the process makes lots of money, except the poor; they lose their homes.

We decided to make a stand in support of a courageous woman and her family. We went to see the new landlord who, it turned out, was a professor of law at the Catholic University of America (I remembered that Jesus never trusted religious lawyers!). When I invited him to help us turn the building into a tenant-owned cooperative so the people could stay, he laughed in my face, saying, "I'm going to double my investment on this deal, and neither you nor anyone else is going to stand in my way."

Sometimes when you're not sure what else to do, it's good to have a party. So that's what we did; the night before all the tenants were to be evicted, we celebrated community ownership of that building. It was a great moment and a gala event, with music, balloons, children from the day care center, and people from all over the neighborhood turning up. Day care center classmates of the little boy whose family was about to be evicted carried a homemade sign saying "Let Ofon Keep His Home." The woman who began this struggle took a bottle of champagne and broke it over the side of the building, thus christening the place as a neighborhood-owned property. Of course, we had no legal right to claim this small apartment house for the sake of neighborhood people when it was being "developed" in a "legitimate" transaction.

A few of us had decided to stay in the building and support this woman who sought to resist eviction. We settled in for what was sure to be a restless night. I remember not getting much sleep, suspecting what was about to happen. Sure enough, early the next morning, long after the crowds and television cameras had departed, the building was surrounded by the police. We were arrested, handcuffed, taken away, and thrown into the District of Columbia jail for the weekend, I suppose with the hope that we would be rehabilitated.

On Monday morning, we were taken to the courthouse and met a zealous young public defender who wanted to take our case. I told him we were prepared to defend ourselves, but he was insistent. "At least just tell me what you did and why you did it," he pleaded. So I told him. As I spoke, the young lawyer's eyes got bigger and bigger. When I finished, he became very quiet and serious. The now subdued attorney looked at me with utter sincerity and said, "I think you should plead insanity! Anyone who tries to stop real estate speculation in Washington, D.C., must be crazy!"

We lost that building, and the young woman and her children moved in with us for several months until they found another place. But the battle for 2542 13th Street, NW, did help galvanize new moral forces in the city—especially among the churches—to confront the injustice of the housing crisis for the poor.

Witnessing the same thing happen to poor people so many times since, and in so many places, has been a cause for much reflection. When displacing people from their homes or their land becomes normal, and when efforts to stop it appear foolish and useless, something indeed has gone terribly wrong. In such a time, it seems that some prophetic foolishness or insanity is called for.

Even the name, Washington, D.C., tells the tale of two cities. The white residents and professionals who run the federal capital live in Washington. The black residents who are the city's vast majority (66 percent)[2] are from D.C., the District of Columbia. This capital of the so-called free world is still virtually a segregated city, especially in housing, schools, and social interchange.

The forces of housing gentrification and real estate speculation are slowly pushing black and Latino residents into more overcrowded neighborhoods or out of the city altogether. Inadequate ghetto housing is being transformed into upscale dwellings with prices too high for any of their former inhabitants.

Invisible Poor

I recall a moment of clarity, only a few weeks before the 1988 presidential election. I was driving home from work through the streets of Washington, D.C., listening to a discussion on the radio about the lackluster fall campaign. The panel of experts, of both Democratic and Republican persuasions, was trying to determine why no substantive issues had emerged in the electoral contest between the nominees of the two major parties.

In the end, they all more or less agreed that the lack of sharp political debate in 1988 was due to the fact that there were no pressing issues to discuss. These commentators (all white, male, national-level journalists) concurred that the nation was experiencing "good times." In such a positive climate of peace and prosperity, they postulated, substantial political differences—much less the clash of ideological perspectives—tended to be muted.

As I arrived home, the words of the experts flooded my mind: "We are living in good times; there are no real issues to discuss." Standing there in the street for a few moments, I looked around at the obvious signs of a community fighting for its very survival—and losing.

Then it dawned on me: we just don't exist here. Neighborhoods like mine, and their counterparts in every American city, simply do not count in the minds of the political analysts and decision makers.

During the presidential election of 1992, a recession focused attention on the suffering of the middle class, and the Democrats promised tax breaks to relieve the pressure and gain votes. The missing issues in this campaign, especially those related to our cities unraveling, pointed again to the need for a larger vision. Columnist Charles Krauthammer remarked before the election that he almost never heard the word *poor* in the debates or during the campaign.[3] The candidates appealed more to middle-class insecurity.

As political commentator Cokie Roberts points out, the politicians know that the middle class vote more than poor people.[4] The people who live in my neighborhood simply don't matter to the discussion and are not factored into the debate. It's as if the poor just don't exist. We still wait for political leadership that will directly assault the poverty that now imprisons 35 million Americans;[5] most of the suggested remedies to poverty are based on different versions of the trickle-down policies of recent years that have proved to be such a disaster for the poor.

A TWO-TIERED ECONOMY

Revealing paradoxes exist on almost every level of life in Washington, D.C. Housing costs are among the highest in the country, as are the rates of homelessness.[6] Infant mortality is at third-world levels in the same city with more lawyers and real estate developers than any other.[7] Black youth unemployment is at least 60 percent, while young white professional couples with two incomes search for investments.[8] Scholastic Aptitude Test scores for D.C. public school students are 100 points below the national norm.[9]

Nineteen million tourists spend 2.4 billion dollars here each year,[10] while the D.C. jail runs out of money for plastic cups and toilet paper. The downtown hotel business is booming, while more and more women and children move into the city's shelters or onto the streets.

Washington's affluent suburbs are rated among the most desirable places to live in the nation,[11] while the death rate in black D.C. increases due to a lack of good health care and nutrition.[12] Young white men pay some of the highest college tuition rates in the country at local universities, while their black counterparts are nine times more likely to be the victims of a homicide.[13]

Washington, D.C., is a microcosm of the dynamics that

now govern the world order, and the current drug war brings all these contradictions into sharp relief.

In our neighborhood, children as young as eight years old wear beepers on their belts so that drug dealers can call when a drug run has to be made. It is safer for the dealers to use children for their drug runs, because detection and punishment are less likely.

Young people can make more money in a day or a week than they ever dreamed possible. Thousands of dollars are available to them in the dangerous and illegal drug trade— much more than they can make in the uncertain, part-time, minimum-wage employment of the legal economy. And many are taking the dangerous option.

No one knows the exact numbers, but an extraordinary percentage of D.C. youth are involved in drug trafficking. As in the source countries such as Colombia, income from the drug trade has become a livelihood for the poor. It is, in fact, the only real market in the "market economy" in places like Colombia and Columbia Heights. In the high-stakes atmosphere of drugs and money, life becomes cheap indeed; in Colombia now, it costs only forty dollars to have someone murdered. From Colombia in South America to Columbia Heights in Washington, D.C., poverty sets the stage for tragedy, and the drama of drugs simply carries out the executions.

In the current economic and cultural environment, it becomes very difficult for young people to "just say no to drugs." In effect we are telling them to be content working part-time at fast food restaurants and pursuing the American Dream as best they can. In a declining economy, the better jobs and brighter future we want to promise inner-city children are just not there.

Meanwhile, the images that assault them daily—through television, movies, and popular music—all tell young people that their very worth and status as human beings come from how much they possess and consume. Fancy clothes, new cars, a nice house, and lots of gold around their necks become the aspirations of inner-city youth. In that, they are no different from most Americans.

The crucial difference is that these inner-city youth are virtually denied legal access to the alluring attractions of American consumer culture. They are blocked out by an economy that has no room for them, their dreams and hopes for the future denied.

In Washington, D.C., members of what are often called in the media the permanent underclass can pick up the paper any day of the week and read how conscious the political leaders, just a few blocks away, are of their plight. The *Washington Post* "Style" section on September 27, 1991, reported on two political dinners held the previous night by each political party.[14] The White House affair to honor the king of Morocco was a typical state dinner, replete with stars from the worlds of entertainment, sports, big business, and politics. The guests dined on a menu of "medallions of salmon in champagne jelly and caviar sauce, cushion of lamb in tarragon, and cold pumpkin soufflé," before all sang "God Bless America."

A few miles away, at the Sheraton Washington Hotel, the Democrats had their own party, at 1,500 dollars a plate. One senator joked that when he was growing up, he played with blocks like other boys, "but mine were called 48th Street and 49th." All the presidential candidates for the next election were there, talking about feeding the hungry, while they dined on "poached fillet of salmon with saffron cream on seasoned greens, . . . grilled fillet of beef tenderloin served on seasoned spinach with Gorgonzola cheese, and white and dark chocolate terrine topped with crème anglaise with raspberry coulis." The performance of the rich and powerful of both parties, with regard to the poorest in the land, has been similar.

TWO GLOBAL CITIES

Like Washington, D.C., the rest of the global system is now run by a two-tiered economy. At the top is a highly lucrative and booming sector of managerial and professional elites, and at the bottom is an increasingly impoverished population that services the high-tech economy but whose labor and even consumption are less and less needed.

The fact that absentee landlords own most of the property in both America's urban and rural poverty centers and in third-world countries is a clear signal. So is the fact that the poor in both places do have resources, but the resource flow is overwhelmingly out of those places to wealthier areas and countries. The fact that in both the First and Third Worlds, whole communities and sectors are now being excluded tells us something about the direction of the global economy. Whole populations are now simply defined outside of the economic mainstream. And to be shut out of the global economy means to be consigned to death. Like Jesus' parable of the rich man and the beggar Lazarus, millions and millions of God's children are now shut outside the gate.

The Refuse of the Affluent

I recall sitting in the office of Bishop Antonio Fortich, one of the most courageous and respected church leaders in the Philippines. His poor parishioners on the island of Negros were caught in the crossfire between the military and insurgents in a situation of great oppression. Farmers had lost their land to feudal families and foreign agribusiness and were struggling to survive. Military and paramilitary forces had declared war on opposition voices, some of whom were church people. Outside the office where we were talking, the wall was riddled with bullet holes from a recent attack. "If you are working for the poor," said the bishop, "you are [considered] a subversive."

That night I met with a survivor of one of the recent massacres by the military. A young father and catechist in his Christian community, he cried as he told me the brutal details of the night he lost his wife and three young children.

Out in the countryside, I visited poor rural communities where the people gather for Mass in outdoor chapels around makeshift altars with simple statues of Mary, flowers in plastic glasses, and candles in empty Coke bottles. With violence threatening all around, one congregation reflected on Jesus' words from the beatitudes, "Blessed are those who are persecuted for righteousness' sake." The moderator, a woman, responded, "We are not greater than our master. He also suffered, and we are to follow in his steps." I learned that all who attend such Masses of the basic Christian communities are suspect by the military.

We traveled from village to village during the rainy season, and mud was everywhere. Most of the dwellings are made from grass, bamboo, and pieces of wood, with dirt floors and roofs that leak when it rains. Inadequate diet and sanitation cause malnutrition and terrible health problems. From the clotheslines hang garments that are little more than rags. Smiling but clearly undernourished children wear T-shirts sporting "He-Man," "Ghostbusters," and "Have a Nice Day."

Another sign of the ironic and painful connections between the two global cities made a particularly poignant impression upon me. On the walls of many of the poor households I visited were cut-out pages from magazines—glossy advertisements of assorted products and luxury goods. Especially striking were the pictures of food—lavish meals and gourmet dishes—in humble dwellings where there was hardly anything to eat. An updated version of Marie Antoinette's famous quote before the French Revolution might be, "Let them eat pictures."

My last morning in the Philippines was spent in Bagong

Barrio, one of the poorest sections of Manila. It is a factory area, where the workers are terribly exploited and the problems of high unemployment, crowded and substandard housing, increasing crime, and drugs abound. It reminded me of home.

As we walked the back alleyways, we saw people—sometimes whole families—washing plastic. Bags, scraps, and Styrofoam containers are carefully scrubbed, bundled up, and sold to factories that recycle the material. If you work all day washing plastic, you can make twenty pesos, about one dollar.

The scene was another parable of the global system: men, women, and children—the poor of the earth—washing the refuse of the affluent world. In too many places like this, the grim reapers of hunger, disease, and poverty are carrying out a silent holocaust that seldom makes the evening news. In our global economy, a figure of forty to sixty million deaths each year is now accepted as normal.

A World of Contrasts

Gandhi said, "Poverty is the worst form of violence." [15] And the poverty is simply overwhelming in many places we call the Third World, where the poor are suffering and dying almost beyond our capacity to count. The United States spent the 1980s further redistributing wealth from the poor and working class to the rich. Those at the top reaped a bonanza of excess and self-indulgence, while in the world's poorest places 35,000 children die every day for lack of the simplest things like clean drinking water and basic nutrition. [16]

That figure takes on a more dramatic meaning when we realize it would be a number approximately equal to filling 100 jumbo jets with 350 infants and children each and then watching one crash every 14 minutes. [17] In the meantime, a small elite travels the world in first class.

In *Millennium: Winners and Losers in the Coming World*

Order, French economist Jacques Attali describes a chilling picture of a global economy divided into two classes of people.[18] The first group are "rich nomads," who are extremely mobile and whose resources give them access to virtually anything on the globe. The second are "poor nomads," denied any land or place to call home, trapped in the abandoned sectors of the world economy, and having access to almost nothing. Neither will experience any real sense of community with the rest of God's children and, especially, will have no relationship to each other. The rich nomads are, of course, a small elite; the number of poor nomads continues to grow.[19]

In a chilling article in the *Atlantic Monthly* entitled "The Coming Anarchy," Robert D. Kaplan describes a future global scenario of growing polarization, population explosion, resource scarcity, and the disintegration of governmental authority into a lawless "road warrior" culture of chaos and crime.

> I got a general sense of the future while driving from the airport to downtown Conakry, the capital of Guinea. The forty-five-minute journey in heavy traffic was through one never-ending shanty-town: a nightmarish Dickensian spectacle to which Dickens himself would never have given credence. The corrugated metal shacks and scabrous walls were coated with black slime. Stores were built out of rusted shipping containers, junked cars, and jumbles of wire mesh. The streets were one long puddle of floating garbage. Mosquitos and flies were everywhere. Children, many of whom had protruding bellies, seemed as numerous as ants. When the tide went out, dead rats and the skeletons of cars were exposed on the murky beach. In twenty-eight years Guinea's population will double if growth rates go on at present rates. Hardwood logging continues at a madcap speed, and people flee the Guinean countryside for Conakry.[20]

Kaplan describes global environmental breakdown and the rising tide of crime and violence as the "revenge" of the poor and nature.[21]

The author quotes the University of Toronto's Thomas Fraser Homer-Dixon as claiming that future wars will arise from such polarity and scarcity.

> Think of a stretch limo in the potholes of New York City, where homeless beggars live. Inside the limo are the air-conditioned post-industrial regions of North America, Europe, the emerging Pacific Rim, and a few other isolated places, with their trade summitry and computer-information highways. Outside is the rest of humankind, going in a completely different direction.[22]

Kaplan concludes, "We are entering a bifurcated world."[23]

It was precisely when such polarities of extravagant wealth and crushing poverty became institutionalized and rationalized that the prophets of the Bible would thunder the judgment and justice of God, calling the people to repentance. But who will be the Jeremiahs today?

In Manila, I watched as Filipino boys and girls stood in the streets getting baths from their mothers, who poured water over their heads and out into the road. Eyes shut tight, they grimaced just as do kids getting a bath all over the world. As the children stand naked in their squatter barrio, anxiously shutting their eyes to keep the soap from stinging, they look as vulnerable as their position at the bottom of the world economic order has made them. In Brazil and other poor countries, paramilitary squads have now begun to target and murder the street children in an effort to "clean up the cities."[24]

When Brazilian archbishop Dom Helder Camara came to visit Sojourners Community in 1977, he wanted to take a walk through the neighborhood. A little man in a long black robe, the charismatic Nobel Peace Prize nominee drew a lot of attention. But he seemed to feel right at home, smiling and waving comfortably to people we passed on the street. He asked about the real estate market. As I described how the poor were being displaced, he nodded sadly and said it was the same back home where he lived in northeast Brazil.[25]

Standing Side by Side

Throughout the world, wealth and poverty stand side by side. First and Third Worlds are separated, not by oceans, but by city streets. Just outside of Capetown, South Africa, is a squatter camp ironically named Free Ground. It isn't free at all. Those who reside there paid rent to the Pretoria government for the privilege of living on what is nothing more than a pile of sand. Here the poor were just dumped. The shacks they live in were by law only four meters square—a limit imposed by the white government.

A woman came out of a shack to greet us. As we talked, she recounted how she had been pushed and pushed—always on the move, as so many black people have been in South Africa. "We have no jobs. We have no food. We have no water. We have nothing." She looked down at the ground, became very quiet, and then looked up at us again. "We are at a dead end." That night another nearby squatter camp was bulldozed by the government. The displaced people came to Free Ground, and another family moved into the shack of the woman we had just met.

It was only two minutes by jeep to another place, called Marina De Gama. A white area, this neighborhood is full of huge, stunning homes—no limit here on the size of houses. Beautiful green lawns stretch in every direction. Luxury automobiles are parked in each driveway, and the backyards of those magnificent residences look out on a human-made lake where pleasure boats tied to docks are gently swaying in the breeze.

This is the First World and the Third World standing side

by side, just two minutes apart. I had seen poverty like that before and also such extravagant wealth. But I had never seen them so close together. Here the two cities of the global economy live in stark proximity—the one literally killing the other for the sake of its own wealth and privilege, the other suffering and dying just out of sight of its oppressors. Free Ground and Marina De Gama are, indeed, a mirror in which we can see ourselves.

First and Third Worlds live side by side in many cities in our own country. Connecticut Avenue, in Washington, D.C., is a beautiful, tree-lined street of restaurants, hotels, shops, offices, and parks—at the heart of the global economy. Just six blocks away is 14th Street, NW, teeming with poverty, drugs, and violence—as much on the margins of the world economic order as squatter camps and shantytowns elsewhere. You can walk the dirt paths of the Palestinian refugee camps of the West Bank in the afternoon and eat dinner at a posh cafe in West Jerusalem, under the watchful eyes of heavily armed young Israeli soldiers.

From the glass towers of Wilshire Boulevard to the barrios of East Los Angeles, from Seoul's Olympic Conference center to South Korea's urban sweatshops, from Sydney's beautiful harbor to Aboriginal homelands in the Australian outback, from the media headquarters on famous Fleet Street to the housing flats in immigrant East London, from Managua's Inter-Continental Hotel to the rural town of Jalapa on Nicaragua's northern frontier: the tale of two cities is evident everywhere I've been.

Even midsized American cities such as Rockford, Illinois, Portland, Oregon, and Burlington, Vermont, now have problems that differ only in degree from the South Bronx, Detroit, Chicago, and Washington, D.C. And roving bands of youths in West African slums now name their ravaged urban districts "Chicago" and "Washington."

I hear the same story and see the same patterns in all these places. Invisible boundaries separate us and make us oblivious to each other's suffering and pain. We are divided from one another, and our division is the defining story of our modern world.

The South African woman from the shack in the squatter camp spoke prophetically when she said, "We are at a dead end." Unless we recognize that, we have a troubled future ahead. The logic of the global system we have inherited has run its course and come to a dead end.

THE GREAT RAGE

A great chasm separates those who benefit from the world economic order and those who are victims of it. Now out of the canyon of our great human divide a violent rage has emerged; and we are in danger of simply being overcome by it.

For a long time, neither the extremes of wealth and poverty nor the racial polarization in Washington, D.C., were well known beyond the beltway, the highway encircling the metropolitan area. But suddenly in the 1980s, my city began making national and international headlines—not as the center of culture and power but as the "murder capital" of the nation.[26] Quickly the media cameras so used to turning away from the other Washington focused their attention on neighborhoods overrun with drugs and guns. D.C. became famous. National news magazines did cover stories that spoke of the "two Washingtons," [27] while nervous local officials rushed to assure anxious tourists that the killing was limited only to "certain parts of the city."

Our Columbia Heights neighborhood became the murder capital of the murder capital for several years, according to the District Office of Criminal Justice Plans and Analysis.[28] The killings increased on the streets where we live, occurring, as they say, very close to home. At a meeting in the Sojourners Neighborhood Center, one local resident asked, "What does it mean to live in the most murderous neighborhood in the most murderous city in the most murderous nation in the world?"

Today the violence continues and is still increasing. Every time I go out to speak about it, I have new stories—painful stories, often involving children whom we have watched grow up or whose families and friends we are close to.

Three children waiting for their school bus were the victims of a random shooting in the middle of the day. A friend walking down the street found himself in the middle of a gun battle between two children and had to duck into a storefront to save his life. More and more people are getting caught in the crossfire. In our neighborhood, it's quite easy to be at the wrong place at the wrong time.

The shooting goes on both day and night. I remember one day the shots rang out on a Sunday afternoon. A young man was making a phone call at a sidewalk telephone when someone pumped seven rounds into him from an automatic weapon. The murder occurred right outside the Sojourners intern house. Our newest group of volunteers had been there just two weeks. All but one of them were home, and they were among the first to see the lifeless body through their living room window. The police went through the now common routine and, eventually, took the body away. Afterward, longtime Sojourners Community member George Gentsch came out with a pail of water and scrubbed the blood off the sidewalk as a sacrament to the young man. His action was a metaphor for "urban ministry" today.

In 1983, I traveled to the war zones of embattled Nicaragua on the first team of a project known as Witness for Peace, a church-based effort to support the victims of the war and end the senseless violence. In a refugee resettlement camp, I met a thirteen-year-old boy named Agenor, who made a lasting impression on me. His baseball cap, tattered shirt, and beat-up tennis shoes reminded me of the kids who run up and down the streets of my own neighborhood, except that this slender Nicaraguan boy carried a heavy automatic weapon on his back. He was a member of the citizens' militia, defending against attacks from the U.S.-backed contra forces who were terrorizing the local area. As I returned home, Agenor's face, with his searching brown eyes and shy smile, was etched in my memory.

I met Eddie on the street the day I got back. He also was thirteen at the time. While telling Eddie about my trip, I had a terrible thought. If the U.S. government escalated the war in Nicaragua and eventually sent American troops, Eddie—a young black man from a poor family with few other options—could be among the first to go. I remembered the pattern from the Vietnam War.

In that moment, I imagined the awful possibility of Eddie and Agenor meeting on some Nicaraguan battlefield, raising their guns to shoot each other, and one or both being killed. The great ideological confrontation between East and West could come down to Eddie and Agenor killing each other— two young men, one black and one brown, dying in the name of a global conflict between two white superpowers. Instead of that horrible picture, I tried to imagine Eddie and Agenor playing baseball together.

Eddie didn't die on a Nicaraguan battlefield, as I had feared. Eddie died several years later on the streets of his own neighborhood. He became for a few hours the latest victim and the newest statistic in the city's epidemic of violence.

Eddie was always a fun-loving, if mischievous, kid with a quick smile and eyes that were big and alive with exciting possibilities. He used to hang out in our houses and some-times swipe apples. Eddie knew we would give him an apple, but the thrill of sneaking one was the appeal. Growing up in a poor family, Eddie succumbed to the allure of the rewards from drug trafficking, and it eventually killed him. He was never a kingpin, just another kid with big eyes for a better life.

One month after Eddie's death, we were all gathered in church on Sunday morning. During the intercessions, the news was announced that another young man, Anthony, had been killed a few nights earlier. I watched faces around the room grimace in pain and the tears begin to flow. Anthony had been a student at our community's day care center many years earlier. We knew his whole family.

After the service, Martha, who had been Anthony's teacher, flashed with anger. "He was such a sweet and sensitive boy," she said. "It's this whole violent system!"

After church, I found myself in a funeral home, viewing the body of a handsome, vital young man, now cold and dead. Anthony's grieving mother and brothers and sisters were all there, but I could hardly think of anything to say.

We miss Eddie's smile and Anthony's gentle spirit. A young girl in our Neighborhood Center program misses her seventeen-year-old brother who was machine-gunned to death by another seventeen-year-old, just three doors down from my front door.

In a striking scene from the powerful 1991 film on gang-related violence in Los Angeles, *Boyz N the Hood,* several young African-American men are sitting out on a front porch the night after one of their companions is killed. One laments the focus in television news on wars and violence in other parts of the world — "all these foreign places." His friends ask why they don't come down to the hood and tell people the truth about what's going on there. He sadly replies, "Either they don't know, don't show, or don't care about what's going on in the hood." [29]

Vincent Harding, noted author and historian of the civil rights movement, made a trip to West Germany in 1989, where he led retreats for black American soldiers. Many told

Harding they were reenlisting in the Army to keep from coming home to their own neighborhoods, where they were afraid of being killed. Young African Americans were deciding to stay in the military to save their lives.[30]

I remember an evening of particular poignancy that opened up my own understanding. Vincent and Rosemarie Harding were visiting Sojourners Community on this occasion, shortly after we had lost another young friend to a senseless act of street violence. Vincent and I stayed up late into the night, reflecting upon the event. The great chronicler of the freedom movement began to weep, and from deep within his soul an anguished cry arose: "A whole generation of us is being destroyed!"

At that moment, I understood more clearly than ever before why our society was allowing the deadly carnage to continue. I realized that for most Americans who are white and middle class, it is not a whole generation of "us" that is being lost. Rather, it is "them." And we tell them what we think of them in clear messages every day: They aren't important, they don't count, they don't exist.

The fundamental connection that tore at Vincent's heart is simply not felt. I understood, at that midnight hour, that until Vincent Harding's lament becomes our collective cry, there will be no end to the terrible violence.

SEEING THE CONNECTIONS

In various communities around the world, more and more people are seeing the connections between the two cities. Salvadoran priest Jon Sobrino is one of these people. On November 16, 1989, six Jesuit priests, along with their housekeeper and her daughter, were brutally murdered in their home at the University of Central America in San Salvador. El Salvador's U.S.-backed military committed the crime. Jesuit theologian Jon Sobrino, whose absence from home during the attack surely saved his life, had been a member of that community for fifteen years. Away in Asia at the time, Sobrino came to Washington, D.C., just three weeks later. When he visited Sojourners, the renowned liberation theologian reflected on the meaning of the martyrdom of his fallen colleagues.

The Jesuits were murdered because they exposed the "gigantic cover-up about the world," Sobrino said.

> [The] world wants to cover up death. . . . The killings of the six Jesuits—and of so many other people—is a revelation of something which is usually hidden. What they reveal is the truth of El Salvador, of the Third World, and of the whole world.[31]

What the Jesuits brought to light was the tale of two cities; and they were killed for it. Said Sobrino,

> This world which gives death to so many millions of people also lies about it. It tries to ignore death very consciously; even worse, it uses euphemisms to cover death up. . . . [The Jesuits] unmasked the lies—the efforts to cover up the scandal. . . . El Salvador is not just a terrible anecdote in present history, it's one case among many that show the kind of world we live in.[32]

An unusually candid ad in a business magazine one year later demonstrated Sobrino's earlier insight. It read,

> Rosa Martinez produces apparel for U.S. markets on her sewing machine in El Salvador. You can hire her for 33 cents an hour. . . . Rosa is more than just colorful. She and her co-workers are known for their industriousness, reliability, and quick learning. They make El Salvador one of the best buys. . . .[33]

Brazil's Dom Helder Camara and El Salvador's Jon Sobrino sensed the connections. The more time I spend in the most forgotten and forsaken places around the world, the more I feel the connections, too. We must allow these connections and contradictions to begin to change our understanding.

As I've suggested before, our view of the world is largely shaped by what we see around us every day—by what we can touch, feel, taste, see, and smell. We all like to believe that our opinions on most matters, especially social and political questions, are formed by our ideas and principles, the things we have learned, and the concepts we have studied. But in reality, our perspective is primarily shaped by our experience—what we see when we get out of bed in the morning. We search for a moral perspective that might open our eyes, soften our hearts, and change our ways. That may require that we sometimes change our location.

Time to Look and Listen

The prayer that was described at the opening of this chapter by Mary Glover goes to the heart of the problem. She knows what it is to be poor and she knows how to pray. Mrs. Glover normally offers the prayer because she is our best pray-er. She prays like someone who knows to whom she is talking. You can quickly tell that Mary Glover and God have had a conversation going for many years.

First, she gives thanks for the gift of another day. She prays in gratitude, "Thank you, Lord, for waking me up this morning, that the walls of my room were not the walls of my grave, and my bed was not my coolin' board." Just before the doors are opened and the people pour in for their food, she always prays the words that profoundly conjure up the teachings of Jesus: "Lord, we know that you'll be coming through this line today, so help us to treat you well."

In Matthew 25, Jesus says, "for I was hungry and you gave me no food, I was thirsty and you gave me nothing to drink, I was a stranger and you did not welcome me, naked and you did not clothe me, sick and in prison and you did not visit me." [34]

In this Gospel scene of final judgment, the people seek to excuse themselves. They say, "Lord, when was it that we saw you hungry or thirsty or a stranger or naked or sick or in prison, and did not take care of you?" [35] They say, in effect, "Surely you don't mean us, Lord. We never saw you in distress; and if we had, you can trust that we would certainly have done something about it. We just didn't know it was you, Lord. Had we known it was you, at least we would have formed a Social Action Committee."

Then Jesus says to them, "Truly I tell you, just as you did not do it to one of the least of these, you did not do it to me." [36] Jesus is here asking, "How much do you love me? I'll know how much you love me by how you love those who are the most vulnerable." He is putting himself in their place. The Son of man, as he is described in this scene, is taking the place of the poor, forgotten, and lonely of the earth. He is telling us simply: What we do to them, we do to him. That is a revolutionary religious idea.

From the inner city of Washington, D.C., to black townships in South Africa, to rural barrios in Central America and the Philippines, to all the forgotten and neglected places in this world, we find the Mary Glovers who help us to find the face of God and the path back to one another. It is their voices we must hear, their sorrows and their hopes that must intrude upon our lives, their pain and their faith that can help us understand our own.

In the cries and prayers of the poor, we will hear the spiritual call of our time. Though most today would consider the idea foolish, the point of this Gospel passage is that our future is with the poor; our destinies are tied together, one way or another. Despite the many noises of this society that distract our attention, assault our minds, and harden our hearts, we have a very real stake in one another's lives. And the circumstances of the most vulnerable among us are always the best test of our human solidarity with one another.

The Spiritual Connection

Building a new sense of solidarity, however, will require our going beyond the ideological frameworks of the left and the right. Liberal ideas of expanding individual rights and entitlements don't go deep enough and run up against financial and cultural resistance. The more radical left notions of class warfare will not provide the solutions we need in an increasingly polarized world. Similarly, conservative calls for individual initiative, unrestricted business enterprise, and trickle-down economics have utterly failed to bridge the enormous gaps between the rich and the poor. The right has failed to generate the moral imperative to challenge an unjust status quo; indeed, the right has provided its most vigorous defense.

The crisis of the global economy is, at root, a moral one; and mere political arguments and solutions will prove inadequate. We need to find and feel a connection to one another, and only such a spiritual connection will yield new and creative steps toward justice. Here is where central spiritual imperatives, drawn from our religious traditions, could provide pivotal insight at this critical moment.

We begin with the fundamental insight of *imago dei*, the image of God. Most of the world's great religions teach that humankind and every human being is created in the divine image. That most foundational premise gives each person an equal and sacred value.

At the heart of our problem is the painful truth that the affluent believe their children are more important than the children of the world who are now starving to death. The religious assertion that those children are also sacred means that they are just as important as our own children and must be treated that way. It is a spiritual imperative that we have ignored, and the consequence is our own spiritual poverty and moral deterioration. There is a cost to disregarding moral values, and we are now reaping the social and cultural disintegration resulting from our spiritual disregard.

The radical assertion of the image of God in every human being lies at the heart of our best religious traditions and is the insight that could convert and renew our hearts and minds. What would it mean to fashion a global economy and conduct our politics as if every human being had equal and sacred value? Would that not create a fundamental challenge to all our present systems and operating assumptions? Only a renewed consciousness of the worth of each and every one of us can provide the beginning of a new politics of community that could bring us together. To create such a new consciousness will be a formidable spiritual and political task.

The politics of community will also require a more profound understanding of the meaning of justice. Both liberal and conservative notions of justice are based on widely assumed and well-established Western doctrines of individualism. Justice is rooted in individual human rights for both the right and the left. But such an individualistic idea of justice is now failing us in the midst of a global crisis that cries out for a new and deeper sense of connection and community.

Here again, religious insights can help us. In the Hebrew Scriptures, one finds the more holistic concept of *shalom* as the best definition of justice. It is a deeper and wider notion than the securing of individual human rights. The vision of shalom requires us to reestablish "right relationships." It is a call to justice in the whole community and for the entire habitat. Shalom is an inclusive notion of justice extending even to the rest of God's creatures and whole of the creation. Restoring right relationships takes us further than respecting individual rights. It pushes us to begin to see ourselves as part of a community, even as members of an extended but deeply interconnected global family, and ultimately as strands in the web of life that we all share and depend upon. The biblical vision of shalom could be a basis for a new politics of community and the social healing we so need.

Soon we will come to see that making the spiritual connections between the two cities is not only a spiritual imperative, but also a spiritual joy. I am frequently reminded of the joy and satisfaction which come from making that connection in our own little neighborhood center and in the countless numbers of places I have the opportunity to visit around the world.

In places like the Open Door Community, in Atlanta, Georgia, those whose backgrounds are worlds apart are finding the joy that comes from making a new world together. Murphy Davis and Ed Loring were both seminary professors who now spend their lives in a community of hospitality and justice for the poor, which includes Atlanta's homeless street people. On Sunday nights, when Murphy gets out her guitar, everybody sings together in a service that unites those who were never intended, in this world, to worship God together. But they do, and every time I am there I experience a little bit of heaven right in the midst of our still-divided earth. Communities like the Open Door provide us both a sign and a promise.

But to find and fashion a new politics of community we must first confront the obstacles and idolatries that stand in our way.

Chapter Five

———

Fire in the Sky
The Heat of White Racism

In the spring of 1992, the nation was interrupted by a wake-up call. The verdict in the trial of the police officers who assaulted Rodney King and the subsequent explosion in the city of Los Angeles carried the clear message that the problem of racism has not been solved.

Ironically, I was watching a rented video of *Blade Runner*[1] the evening the Rodney King verdict was announced. I had never before seen this futuristic film that some commentators have called a popular-culture text for our times. It depicts a high-tech polarized society characterized by social chaos and random violence in a smoldering urban environment. Chilling images of skies thick with smoke and a horizon ablaze with the bright orange of countless fires played against my dark bedroom walls. The movie was set in Los Angeles.

I heard the news of the Simi Valley jury's decision to acquit the police officers who savagely beat King, and I turned to the networks for analysis and the community's response. What I saw was as startling as it was eerie. The television images of Los Angeles burning were indistinguishable from the ones I had just seen in the apocalyptic film.

GROWING UP WHITE IN DETROIT

Painful memories rushed into my mind and heart. In the summer of 1967, my hometown of Detroit exploded into a city at war with itself. As the Kerner Commission would later describe, Detroit, like the rest of America, was divided into "two societies, one black, one white—separate and unequal." [2] Growing up white in Detroit, I had no exposure to black people, but for an occasional glimpse on a downtown bus or at a Tigers baseball game. What I was told about black people was based on the stereotypes so common in white culture.

Troubling Questions

As a teenager in the 1960s, I felt the tension and hostility that pervaded the conversations among whites whenever the subject of blacks, race, the city, or crime would come up. People that I knew to be otherwise kind and loving would be transformed, uttering vicious words of intolerance and fearful hatred.

I wanted to know why. Why did whites and blacks live completely divided from one another? Why did most whites seem prosperous and most blacks poor? Why didn't I know any families who sometimes went without a meal or had loved ones in jail, when I heard that black families had those experiences? And why didn't we go to church together? What created the fear? I was persistent in taking my questions to my parents, teachers, and friends, but I soon discovered that no one could or would answer them.

Hoping that the church might provide some answers, I asked, "What about our Christian faith? Doesn't God love all people?" I reminded them of the song we were all taught in Sunday School as children: "Jesus loves the little children, all the children of the world. Red and yellow, black and white, they are precious in his sight. Jesus loves the little children of the world." I asked why we sent missionaries to Africa but didn't have any contact with black people, or even black churches, in our own city.

I was told that we were all better off separated. Some even used the Bible to undergird their argument, citing a distorted interpretation of the Genesis story in which Noah curses the descendants of his son Ham. Other whites said that blacks were happy with the way things were. "They" had their ways and places to live, and "we" had ours. There should be no problem. And if they had problems, they probably deserved them; after all, they were lazy, had too many children, and were dangerous, or so I was told.

Some people told me that asking these questions would only get me into trouble. That proved to be the only honest answer I ever got in the white community. It didn't take long to realize that I wasn't going to get the answers I was looking for from white people. So I decided to make my way into the inner city.

A Pilgrimage

I started by seeking out black churches. As I asked my questions, a whole new picture of the world began to emerge. Black Christians made time in their very busy lives for a young white kid who was full of questions and who had come to visit them in the inner city. They were extraordinarily patient and receptive, never patronizing and always compassionate. They must have been smiling inside at my questions, which had such obvious answers, but they never let on. My pilgrimage into the black community opened up a whole new world and would affect the rest of my life.

The simple, self-justifying worldview of my childhood and my church, in conflict with my growing awareness of racism and poverty, caused mounting havoc in my teenage years. I was shocked at what I saw, heard, and read; I felt betrayed and angry by the brutal facts of racism. Worse, I felt painfully implicated.

As my involvement intensified, I went further into the black community. I found opportunities for interaction and dialogue, especially with young black workers and students. Over several summers, I took jobs in small factories and on custodial and maintenance crews. The young blacks I met were much more angry and militant than the black Christians I had come to know, and they provided me with a new education.

These were Detroit's manual laborers and unskilled workers, who worked hard for little money. They had no future in the system, and they knew it. The goods of a consumer society were dangled in front of their eyes like carrots on a stick, but they were systematically shut out of the good life.

Never having the opportunity for a decent education or good job, they lived in ghetto apartments and houses overflowing with parents, brothers and sisters, grandparents, and friends who had no other place to stay. Most were at home on the streets and had become tough at an early age in order to survive.

Dramatic Answers

Butch was typical of the militant young men I came to know. We worked together as janitors the summer before I went off to Michigan State University. Our lives were as different as the destinations of our paychecks. Mine went into a savings account for college; his went to support his wife, mother, and all his sisters and brothers, who lived together in a small house in one of Detroit's worst neighborhoods.

My job became a school in political understanding, and Butch was a ready commentator and tutor. He was very savvy—about the streets, the job, Detroit, and even international politics. His education came from his own life and from the pages of the perpetual sequence of books he kept tucked in the back pocket of his khaki janitor's uniform. His experience of oppression and his reflections on it were turning him into a political revolutionary.

That job gave us an opportunity to spend many hours together, often when we were both on elevator duty. Elevator operators are required by law to get periodic breaks, because going up and down all day without a respite makes one's head spin. Mine was already reeling with all the thoughts and ideas Butch and I talked about. We had many of our best conversations in the elevators, as I spent all my breaks in his elevator and he spent his in mine.

Butch and I talked about everything: our backgrounds, our families and neighborhoods, our churches, the police, and our hopes for the future. We were two young men, one black and one white, growing up in the same city of Detroit; but it seemed we had grown up in two different countries.

Eventually, Butch invited me to his home to meet his family. I felt deeply honored and was eager to go, but every time I asked him to write directions to his place, he would change the subject. Finally one day, I handed him pen and paper and made him write out directions. Awkwardly Butch began to scribble on the paper, and I realized the reason he had hesitated was that he could barely write. I was embarrassed at my own insensitivity.

That small incident was very significant to me. I went home that night and both cried and cursed. I could not believe that someone as bright as Butch had hardly been taught to write, and I was furious at a system that had given me so much and him almost nothing, simply by virtue of our skin color. By accident of birth, I had all the benefits and he had all the struggles.

I will never forget the night I went to Butch's house. It was a formative experience for me. Butch's younger brothers and sisters were up in my lap from the beginning, their eyes sparkling at a newfound friend. The older ones, with more experience of racism in a white society, were distrustful at first, suspicious of what a white man was doing in their home. It's a common pattern I've experienced many times since. But after several hours, everyone began to open up.

Butch's mother made the most lasting impression on me. She was a lovely woman, gracious and warm, so anxious for me to feel at home. Like my mother in so many ways, she was primarily concerned about the health, happiness, and safety of her family. Her love for Butch was obvious. Having lost her husband, she regarded Butch, her eldest son, with pride and joy. Butch's love and respect for his mother were clearly evident.

But I could also see how fearful she was of his growing anger and militancy. She, just like my mother, was afraid that her son's political views would get him into trouble. It wasn't that she disagreed with him, but she was afraid he might be hurt.

She told me about her past, her experiences in Detroit, and her hopes for her family. Butch's mother had a way of looking into your eyes and speaking right to your heart. I knew that I was hearing the honest reflections of a proud woman who had somehow kept her family together through the difficulties of growing up black in Detroit.

The Policeman Is Your Friend

Butch's mother recounted a history of poverty and violence, especially at the hands of the police. I was stunned by what she said about the Detroit Police Department. She told of countless times that her husband or one of her sons had been picked up on the street for no apparent reason, taken down to the precinct, verbally abused, falsely accused, and even beaten.

When she went down to the police station to find out what had happened and try to bring them home, she was often assaulted with vile and profane language. The police would tell her that they would "take care of" her husband or son, give her man what he deserved, and that she'd better "get her ass on home" or she was going to get the same treatment.

I remember how my insides began to hurt and my eyes welled up with tears as one by one every person in the room told me stories of how they or close friends had been abused by the police, mostly for the crime of being at the wrong place at the wrong time, and for being black. I had never heard such things before, but I knew they were telling the truth.

Butch's mother told me what she taught her children about the police. If they ever got lost, they were to look out for the police. When they spotted a cop, they were to duck into an alley, crouch under some stairs, or hide behind a corner. When the policeman passed by, it was safe to come out and try to find their way home themselves. "So I tell my children," she said, "to watch out for the policeman." At that moment, the familiar words of my own mother flooded my mind: "If you are ever lost, look for a policeman. He will help you find your way home. The policeman is your friend." It was a pivotal moment, after which I looked at things differently.

If education is to learn to see the truth and to know the world as it really is, then my education began when I got to know black people in Detroit. They showed me the other America, the America that is unfair and wrong and mean and hateful, the America that we white people accept. But they taught me about more than racism. They taught me about love and family and courage, about what is most important and what it means to be a human being. In listening to the black experience, I discovered more truth about myself, my country, and my faith than by listening anywhere else.

THE PERCEPTION GAP

My mind came back to the images of Los Angeles on my television screen. It was all happening again.

That Sunday morning, after the Simi Valley verdict, ABC's *This Week with David Brinkley* showed dramatic footage of a burning Los Angeles. Then it showed 14th Street in my own inner-city neighborhood of Washington, D.C. Brinkley was trying to show what happened here in the violent eruptions of 1968 and how so much has never been rebuilt. The veteran journalist asked helplessly why this keeps happening.[3]

Most Americans, black and white, were appalled by the verdict in the trial of the police officers who brutally beat Rodney King. After seeing the videotape, shown repeatedly around the world, many whites reported they were stunned and thought the decision unfair. But the pain went much deeper in the black community because the wound already existed. One African-American man in my neighborhood summed up the feelings I heard over and over again: "This is another declaration of war against us."

The talk and images of war and war zones continued throughout the days of violence and destruction, with comparisons to Beirut and El Salvador. The tremendous gap in perception between most white and black people about the meaning of the violence in Los Angeles points to the virtual chasm between what political scientist Andrew Hacker describes as the "two nations" of this country.[4] I heard no one condone the violence; even gang members and others involved told me they didn't regard it as any solution. But conversation after conversation dramatically revealed the gap of comprehension.

On the streets of Los Angeles during the violence, a young white soldier in the National Guard told a reporter, "I've got a fifteen-month-old son, a beautiful wife, and a lot to look forward to. I'm not going to risk everything I own by being a little careless out here. I think that's the way we all feel."[5] He felt very sad at the destruction but really couldn't understand it. The key phrase was "everything I own."

During a night of violence in Los Angeles, a police officer and a young black man stood next to each other, watching a building burn to the ground. The officer asked, "How do you feel to see this place in flames?" The young man's answer flashed with rage. "You know what, man? The f—— heat and steam comin' from this building ain't no worse than the heat and steam comin' from my heart. . . . That's just how I'm burning inside. You don't have to believe it, you don't have to listen to me, you don't have to understand." [6] It's time we tried.

Then-President George Bush said he too was stunned by the verdict and promised a federal investigation, but he spoke most strongly of "criminals," "thugs," "murderers," and "mob violence." One recalled Bush's election campaign and the Willie Horton rhetoric. When presidents use racial fears and stereotypes to get elected, white jurors feel justified in using them, too. When the nation's top political leader demonstrates the emotional resolve to "do whatever is necessary to restore order" but not the passion to establish racial and economic justice, white suburbanites who constitute the majority of voters get the message. In the wake of Los Angeles, a hunger for racial justice again becomes a moral criterion for political leadership.

Some startling new statistics from the nation's capital came out shortly after the Los Angeles events. [7] The new study showed that 42 percent of black men in Washington, D.C., were either in jail, awaiting trial, or on parole. It further revealed that 90 percent of African-American men in the city would be arrested at some time in their lives. The United States already has more people incarcerated, in numbers and per capita, than any country in the world—costing more, per prisoner per year, than a Harvard education.

When I was first sent to the D.C. jail for actions of nonviolent civil disobedience, I noticed the jail intake cards were already filled out. Piles of cards had certain words previously handwritten in: Color of hair—Black. Color of Eyes— Brown. When my turn came, the guards had to cross out those words and substitute "brown" hair and "blue" eyes. Clearly, this facility had been constructed for men and women of color. Recently, a former head of three state prison systems predicted a vast network of prison camps for poor black and Latino men that would leave the inner cities empty of all but single women with children in more and more desperate poverty.[8]

After Los Angeles, many were again asking why the urban violence occurs. The answers will not be found until we better understand the dynamics of how both racism and rage function today and the impact of marginalized people on our social structures and spiritual values.

Low-Intensity Riot

Several weeks after the Los Angeles events, a friend wrote to me, saying, "Watching the painful images of Los Angeles in flames caused me to think of your community, always living in the middle of a low-intensity riot." The image has stuck with me. We have seen wars of low-intensity conflict in places such as El Salvador, South Africa, and the Philippines. But what is happening all the time in South Central L.A., inner-city Washington, D.C., and in countless other urban cauldrons of human suffering across America can, in truth, be termed a low-intensity riot.

The "riot" is already taking place for literally millions of people and has especially devastated the lives of the children who inhabit our cities. As we saw again in Los Angeles, it only takes a spark to escalate to high intensity. When the explosion comes, the preferred term on the street is *rebellion*.

Violence does not solve any problems, but it does get attention. In America, violence is about the only thing that makes us see the poor or even remember that they exist. Is there really any doubt that it once again took burning, looting, and wanton destruction to focus the nation's attention on the cities and the huge numbers of poor and desperate people who are crowded into America's abandoned urban wastelands? The Los Angeles rebellion broke the long, frightening silence in both the media and the highest levels of national political leadership about the disintegration of life and society—something that has become the norm of existence in vast inner-city territories.

After the riots, the media were full of compelling stories about the destructive consequences, particularly for the young, of living without education, jobs, health, home, security, respect, hope, and any promise for the future. Politicians who have had little or nothing to say about the cities and the poor were blaming each other for the problems.

The truth is, something is terribly wrong in our country, and America has just accepted it. As a nation we have condoned the injustice, tolerated the suffering, and ignored the consequences. The majority of Americans have simply looked the other way and made sure their security is assured. There is more than enough blame to go around; the question is who will take responsibility.

Historically, violence has drawn public attention but not resulted in the action necessary to change prevailing conditions. In the last several decades, the eleven commissions that followed the eleven periods of "urban disorders" have documented the problem in great detail, but the sustained political will for change has not followed. I dusted off my old, well-worn copy of the Kerner Commission Report, issued six months after Detroit exploded in the summer of 1967. A re-reading made it clear that no new information was coming to us from the events in Los Angeles. It is also clear that we are now witnessing the unraveling of America. Short of a profound change in national direction, this unraveling will continue and become more brutal.

As we have said, the prophetic vocation always has two dimensions—truth telling and pointing to an alternative vision. In the wake of the events of Los Angeles, it is imperative that we take up the prophetic vocation immediately, before it is too late.

Truth Telling

Let's start with some truth telling. When a black man can be beaten fifty-six times in eighty-one seconds by four white police officers, and a jury can be convinced that the officers were only protecting themselves, the deepest pathologies of America's racial past and present are deeply implicated in the judicial decision. There was no question that Rodney King was brutalized; the issue was whether it mattered. The first verdict, in effect, told every black American that it did not. The subsequent outpouring of personal stories of mistreatment and discrimination against African Americans of all social classes demonstrates the absolute and persistent reality of racism on every level of American life and society.

It is time for white Americans to step forward and address what Dan Rather referred to during the rioting as "America's problem."[9] Those who say they care must stop leaving the task of addressing racism to black people.

For white people, a prophetic interrogation of personal attitudes, social structures, and cultural and religious institutions to reveal and remove racism is long overdue. There is no more important test of white integrity than to act to heal the scars that slavery and racism have left on this society. And white guilt isn't enough; it passes too quickly. Rather, white responsibility to attack the root causes of racism is what is most needed. A black-and-white partnership must be formed to diagnose the disease and perform the radical surgery that alone can save us. But like any disease, to fight it we must first understand it.

THE DISCOVERING OF AMERICA

The United States of America was established as a white society, founded upon the near-genocide of one race and then the enslavement of yet another.

That statement has always generated an emotional response. Some say it's outrageous, some say courageous. But it is simply a statement of historical fact. People's reactions to it are instructive and revealing. The historical record of how white Europeans conquered North and South America by nearly destroying the native population and how they then built their new nations' economies on the backs of kidnapped Africans whom they turned into chattel are facts that cannot be denied. Yet to speak honestly of such historical facts is still to generate great controversy.

The storms Christopher Columbus encountered on the voyage that landed him on a Caribbean island on October 11, 1492, were probably moderate compared to the tempests that accompanied the 1992 quincentenary of that pivotal journey. The blasts came from all sides, which made both moral and political navigation difficult during what became a highly symbolic and confrontational year.

It once seemed easy. All American school children learned the simple rhyme, "In fourteen hundred and ninety-two, Columbus sailed the ocean blue." But the color of the Atlantic proved to be less important than the colors of the many peoples whose destinies would be altered forever because of this epoch-changing event.

Of course, the real question is, who discovered whom? Christopher Columbus was, after all, quite lost when the *Niña, Pinta,* and *Santa Maria* arrived in the so-called New World. It has been rightly pointed out that Columbus didn't know where he was going, didn't know where he was when he got there, and didn't know where he had been when he returned home. What he did know was what he wanted—wealth and power, gold and slaves for himself and his royal patrons. One contemporary descendant of the indigenous people who welcomed Columbus and his men says that the native people's subsequent problems stemmed from a "lax immigration policy." [10]

The rhetoric during 1992 was high and heated, and what some thought might become a teachable moment quickly turned into a high-stakes ideological conflict. What was the fight really about?

Few dispute the historical facts of the European conquest of what would come to be known as "the Americas." The violence and brutality instigated by Columbus and carried on by subsequent "explorers," "pioneers," and "settlers" can no longer be hidden. Even a cursory reading of the famed Italian sailor's diary indicates his unashamed glee at how easily these indigenous people could be subjugated and this new land exploited.[11]

Columbus's royal Spanish benefactors couldn't have been more pleased. Along with their monarchical cousins, they built empires and established modern Europe through the resources stripped from these vast, new, unexpected territories. The "new" world provided the "old" with an outlet and opportunity for expansion, conquest, and renewing itself. From the beginning, what occurred was nothing less than the rape of one world and people by another.

The consequences for the native peoples who inhabited the conquered lands were, of course, catastrophic. Through a combination of military campaigns and disease-borne extermination, the "Indians" suffered a holocaust. The near-destruction of the indigenous population and the insatiable greed of the conquerors led to the second great evil in founding the nations of the Western Hemisphere—the slave trade. Kidnapped Africans made into property died in the middle passage by the millions, as did their Native American brothers and sisters on their own land. Africans who survived were forced to endure one of the most cruel forms of slavery in human history.

America's Original Sin

These founding events of the American nations are not just historical. They also have theological and spiritual meaning.

The systematic violence, both physical and spiritual, committed first against indigenous people and then against black Africans was, indeed, the original sin of the American nations. In other words, the United States of America was conceived in iniquity.

Whatever else is right about America cannot and does not cover over or erase that original sin. The good things about this country and the reasons many have come here need not be denied or dismissed, but the brutal founding facts of nationhood cannot be erased. Like any sin, this one must be dealt with, not only for the sake of our integrity but also because the legacy of that original history is still with us. An American future worthy of its best ideals depends on our honestly coming to terms with our origins and their continued influence.

Our history has affected us all in profound ways. It still shapes our national experience and obstructs the fulfillment of our professed values. Its face is dramatically revealed in the continued devastation of native, black, and other communities of color; in the legacy of benefit still enjoyed by most white people; and in the fear and anger felt by many whites facing shrinking economic realities and the temptation to scapegoat racial minorities.

The nation's original sin of racism must be faced in a way that we have never really done before. Only then can America be rediscovered.

What Has Changed and What Has Not

But for most white Americans, racism is not a welcome subject. After the brief racial crisis of the sixties, white America, including many of those involved in the civil rights movement, went on to other concerns. Also, the legal victories of black Americans in that period, as far as most white Americans are concerned, have settled the issue and even left many asking, "What more do blacks want?"

Federal courts have more recently interpreted civil rights legislation—originally designed to redress discrimination against black people—as applying to the grievances of whites who believe affirmative action programs have gone too far. In addition, popular racial attitudes have changed to some extent, as attested to by opinion polls and the increased number of black faces appearing in the world of sports, entertainment, the mass media, and even politics. After all, *The Cosby Show* was the highest-rated TV series in the country, and Jesse Jackson ran for president.

Indeed, in the two decades since the passage of momentous civil rights legislation, some things have changed and some things have not. What has changed are the personal racial attitudes of some white Americans and the opportunities for some black Americans to enter the middle levels of society. (The word *middle* is key here, insofar as few blacks have yet to enter into the upper echelons and decision-making positions of business, the professions, the media, or even the fields of sports and entertainment, where black "progress" has so often been celebrated.) Legal segregation has been lifted off the backs of black people with the consequent expansion of social interchange and voting rights, and that itself has led to changes in white attitudes.

What has not changed is the systematic and pervasive character of racism in the United States and the condition of life for the majority of black people. In fact, those conditions have worsened. Racism has survived the end of legalized segregation. To uproot it, we will need a deeper understanding than we have had before.

THE SYSTEM OF RACISM

Racism originates in domination and provides the social rationale and philosophical justification for debasing, degrading, and doing violence to people on the basis of color. Many have pointed out how racism is sustained by both personal attitudes and structural forces. Racism can be brutally overt or invisibly institutional or both. Its scope extends to every level and area of human psychology, society, and culture. Racism is the ocean we swim in and the air we breathe.

Prejudice may be a universal human sin, but racism is more than an inevitable consequence of human nature or social accident. It is a system of oppression for a social purpose. Racism is prejudice plus power.

In the United States, the original purpose of racism was to justify slavery and its enormous economic benefit to whites. The particular form of racism, inherited from the British to justify their own slave trade, was especially venal, for it defined the slave not merely as an unfortunate victim of bad circumstances, war, or social dislocation but rather as less than human, as a thing, an animal, a piece of property to be bought and sold, used and abused. Ancient and tribal cultures often had slaves, but they were usually prisoners of war who became servants and were still thought to be human beings.

Under the British and American systems, the slave did not have to be treated with any human consideration whatsoever. Even in the founding document of our nation, the famous constitutional compromise defined the slave as only three-fifths of a person. The professed high ideals of Anglo-Western society could exist side by side with the profitable institution of slavery only if the humanity of the slave was denied and disregarded.

The heart of racism was and is economic, though its roots and results are also deeply cultural, psychological, sexual, even religious, and, of course, political. Due to two hundred years of brutal slavery and one hundred more of legal segregation and discrimination, no area of the relationship between black and white people in the United States is free from the legacy of racism.

The most visible and painful sign of racism's continuation

is the gross economic inequality between whites and blacks and other people of color. All the major social indices and statistics show the situation to be worsening, not improving. The gap between white and black median family income and employment actually widened in the decade between 1970 and 1980, even before Ronald Reagan took office. And the subsequent twelve years of the Reagan and Bush administrations brought what felt like an economic plague to the black community; black unemployment has skyrocketed, and the major brunt of slashed and gutted social services has been borne by blacks and other people of color, especially women and children.

All this has particularly affected black youth, whose rate of unemployment climbed above 50 percent in many urban areas. The very human meaning to such grim statistics can be seen in the faces of the kids in my inner-city neighborhood. They know they have no place, no future, and therefore no real stake in this country. As one commentator put it, society has ceased to be a society for them. Alcohol, drugs, poverty, family disintegration, crime, and jail have replaced aspirations for a decent life and a hopeful future.

The economy itself enforces the brutal oppression of racism, and it does so invisibly and impersonally. In the changing global economy, manufacturing jobs are lost to cheaper labor markets in the Third World or to automation while farm labor becomes extinct; both historically have been important to black survival. In the new high-tech world and service economy, almost the only jobs available are at places like McDonald's.

As we have already described, we now face a two-tiered economy: one a highly lucrative level of technicians and professionals who operate the system, and the other an impoverished sector of unemployed, underemployed, and unskilled laborers who service the system. That people of color are disproportionately consigned to the lowest economic tier is an indisputable proof of racism. The bottom levels of the global economy have a role to play in servicing the top. And the bottom rungs on the economic ladder are filled with people of color just trying to hang on. Even when educational and employment levels are equal, persons of color consistently suffer a wide gap in income and security when compared to their white counterparts.

The existence of a vast black and brown underclass, inhabiting the inner cities of our nation, is a testimony to the versatility of white racism thirty years after legal segregation was officially outlawed. The problem nobody dares to talk about is the fact that no one intends to include the children of our inner cities in the economic mainstream. They are not being educated, nurtured, matured, cared for, or discipled in their hearts, minds, and bodies because they are simply not in the plans of those charting the future. That is the heart of racism in the 1990s.

The Growing Barriers of Class

The pain of economic marginalization is made worse by the growing class distinctions within the black community itself. Middle-class blacks, having taken advantage of the legal gains of the sixties, have further distanced themselves from the poor black population. Never has the class and cultural split in the black community been so great. In Atlanta, Chicago, Washington, D.C., and other cities, a black elite prospers and lives an entirely different social existence, not in proximity to but in full view of an increasingly resentful and angry black underclass.

In Washington, D.C., subway routes follow class and racial lines, carrying middle-class commuters around downtown, through gentrified areas of the city, and out into the suburbs—avoiding black and Latino ghettos. The buses running along the affluent white and black "gold coast" of 16th Street are new and air-conditioned, while just two blocks away, old, hot, and broken-down buses run along the infamous 14th

Street corridor through a major black ghetto. All this exists under a black city government.

To be fair, the increase in black political power over municipal governments has given black political leaders all the problems of modern urban life, including inadequate city budgets and little real power or leverage to change the national policies and priorities that create the problems in the first place. Nevertheless, transcending the growing barriers between a relatively affluent middle class and the impoverished underclass is one of the most important and problematic challenges facing the black community.

The cold economic savagery of racism has led to further declines in every area of the quality of life in communities of color—health, infant mortality, family breakdown, drug and alcohol abuse, and crime. The majority of black children are now born to single mothers; 45 percent of black and 40 percent of Latino children live in poverty.[12] A primary cause of death for young black men today is homicide; and nearly half of all prison inmates in the United States are black males.

Despite landmark court decisions and civil rights legislation, two-thirds of black Americans still suffer from education and housing that are both segregated and inferior. Such conditions, along with diminishing social services, lead to despair, massive substance abuse, and criminality, and the fact that this reality is still surprising or incomprehensible to many white Americans raises the question of how much racial attitudes have really changed.

Racial Backlash

In the face of such structural oppression, the deliberate rollback of civil rights priorities and programs during the Reagan and Bush years became even more callous. Conservatives in power have continually "played the race card," which has helped reinforce racial polarity in American political life after the important gains of the 1960s. White politicians have won votes by appealing to racial backlash and hatred. The most prominent example is former Klansman David Duke's political appeals, which cannot be as easily separated from those of his more respectable conservative brothers as the latter would like to think. Republican presidential candidate Pat Buchanan defiantly promised at the 1992 Republican National Convention to "take back" cities like Los Angeles, "block by block." Who is taking back what from whom?

I remember hearing a National Public Radio report of three African-American schoolgirls in New York State who were waiting for the bus one morning, when they were attacked by a group of white boys who beat them and then painted their faces white. The resurgence of such overt forms of white racism and violence, as exemplified by incidents in Howard Beach and Bensonhurst, New York; Forsyth County, Georgia; rural Wisconsin; and so many other places is foreboding and exemplifies how the alienation and discontent of poor whites are displaced and expressed against blacks or Native Americans instead of at the system that oppresses them all and has always sought to turn them against each other.

STRATEGIES FOR CHANGE

The strategies for how people of color must confront and finally overcome the ever changing face of white racism in America must always originate within those communities themselves. White allies have played and can continue to play a significant role in the struggle against racism when the autonomy and leadership of people of color are sufficiently present to make possible a genuine partnership. But an even more important task for white Americans is to examine ourselves, our relationships, our institutions, and our society for the ugly plague of racism.

Whites in America must admit the reality and begin to operate on the assumption that ours is a racist society. Positive individual attitudes are simply not enough, for, as we have seen, racism is more than just personal.

All white people in the United States have benefitted from the structure of racism, whether or not they have ever committed a racist act, uttered a racist word, or had a racist thought (as unlikely as that is). Just as surely as people of color suffer in a white society because of their color, whites benefit because they are white. And since whites have profited from a racist structure, whites must try to change it.

To benefit from domination is to be responsible for doing something about it. Merely to keep personally free of the taint of racist attitudes is both illusory and inadequate. Just to go along with a racist social structure, to accept the economic order as it is, just to do one's job within impersonal institutions is to participate in racism.

Racism has to do with the power to dominate and enforce oppression, and that power in America is in white hands. Therefore, while there are instances of black racial prejudice against whites in the United States today (often in reaction to white racism), there is no such thing as black racism. Black people in America do not have the power to enforce that prejudice.

We must not give in to the popular temptation to believe that racism existed mostly in the Old South or before the 1960s or in white South Africa. Neither can any of our other struggles against militarism, environmental destruction, hunger, homelessness, or sexism be separated from the reality of racism.

Repentance: Turning Around

Contrary to what many critics charge, delving into the issues raised by the 1992 quincentenary is not a matter of just feeling guilty, engaging in "America bashing," romanticizing native peoples and Third World cultures, or giving the left a boost. Instead, it means exploring the meaning of repentance—the real meaning of the word. *Repentance* means far more than feeling sorry. The biblical meaning of *repentance* is "to turn around." It means to change your course and your behavior by heading in a new direction. Many people regarded 1992 as "a time for turning." Among some Lutherans, a phrase emerged: "Remember, Repent, Renew."

After the Los Angeles rebellion, an angry African-American street organizer in another city said to me, "There's no hope from any of the politicians. The liberals are bankrupt, and the secular left is nowhere. The only hope we have is from an awakening of the churches, because the issues now are flat-out spiritual."

In spiritual terms, racism is a perverse sin that cuts to the core of the religious message. From a Christian perspective, racism negates the heart of the gospel and the reconciling work of Christ. It denies the purpose of the church: to bring together those who have been divided from one another.

The gospel tradition says the only remedy for such a sin is repentance, which, if genuine, will always bear fruit in concrete forms of conversion, changed behavior, and reparation. While religion has often been distorted to serve the unholy cause of racial division, every authentic portrayal of our religious traditions rejects that message and holds forth the vision of an antiracist society.

Though the United States may have changed in regard to some of its racial attitudes and allowed some of its black citizens into the middle class, white America has yet to recognize the extent of its racism—that we are and always have been a racist society—much less to repent of its racial sins.

And because of that lack of repentance and, indeed, because of the economic, social, and political purposes still served by the oppression of people of color, systemic racism continues to be pervasive in American life. While constantly minimized by white social commentators and the media, evidence of the persistent and endemic character of American racism abounds.

The religious community must, of course, get its own houses in order. The church, for example, is still riddled with racism and segregation. The exemplary role of the black church in the struggle against racism offers a sharp indictment to white churches, which still mostly reflect the racial structures and attitudes around them.

The religious community still has the capacity to be the much-needed prophetic interrogator of a system that has always depended upon racial oppression. The spiritual imperatives remain clear. The nation desperately needs examples of social and spiritual communities where the ugly barriers of race are finally torn down to reveal the possibilities of a different American future.

In a divided and violent world, a religious community behind the walls has no future and should be allowed to die. In its place, a new community of faith must be constructed, one that cherishes our diversity, finds unity in the common quest for justice, and helps lead a visionless nation through the troubled waters of confusion and division toward the shores of a multicultural and pluralistic future. The notion of a white America must also die so that the colorful mosaic of expanded horizons for all of our peoples can come to birth. On that day, America will finally be discovered.

Guilt and Responsibility

Guilt is not the issue; responsibility is. The limits of white guilt are clear. It usually doesn't last, and either it paralyzes people or quickly runs out of steam. White Americans should not feel guilty for the facts of their birth and heritage; both should be honored and celebrated. But white Americans must take responsibility for the legacy of benefit they have inherited by acting to dismantle racism and helping to create an anti-racist and multicultural future.

The official Columbus commemoration activities that various government and civic organizations planned for 1992 revealed no recognition of the real history. It's not that they denied it; they just ignored it. This is the real revisionism, not the attempt to tell the true story, but the effort to suppress it. As Native American leader Winona LaDuke said, the "callous rewriting of history"[13] was at the heart of the official quincentenary celebration.

REDISCOVERING AMERICA

Just as we were about to enter the fateful year, a new controversy erupted in intellectual circles, on university campuses, and in media debates—the "PC" issue, *PC* referring to "political correctness." Conservatives charge that a left-wing ideological assault is occurring against all things Western, white, male, or traditional, especially in various university curricula and academic discourses. They accuse a radical "totalitarianism" and "fundamentalism" of trying to take over, usually in the name of a "politically correct," rigorously enforced "multiculturalism" and often using the Columbus symbolism as a jumping-off point to attack America and the values of "Western civilization."

Is there truth to the charges? Undoubtedly. Human nature being what it is, efforts to redress injustice and rectify imbalances can often lead to excesses, sometimes even creating new injustices. That new ideologies can arise in response to established ones, and themselves become stifling or repressive, is hardly news, nor is the fact that secular or religious zealots can sometimes take themselves or their ideas too seriously.

But the PC controversy must not become a new smoke screen to cover up historical facts and continuing injustice. The PC critics run the danger of minimizing whatever Native Americans try to say to us, whatever blacks and other Americans of color want us to remember and repair, and what many white Americans see as an opportunity for positive self-examination and change.

The point is hardly to blame Columbus for every atrocity of the West since his first voyage. While Columbus seems to have been a pretty unsavory character, even by the standards of his own time, his personal significance and influence were not terribly decisive. He just happened to be at the wrong place at the right time.

The real issue is the social paradigm and economic order that the Columbus event set into motion and the fact that it has dominated all of our lives and, in particular, the lives of marginalized peoples for the past five hundred years. There is, in fact, no new world order; we are still being governed by an old one whose economic, political, philosophical, environmental, and especially spiritual roots can be traced back to the conquest and colonization of the Americas.

What are the values of that social order? What is their relationship to people of color, to the earth, to technology, to the economy, to security, and to so many other vital questions that now face us? Most important, can the values and structures of the old social paradigm carry us into the future? If not, what must we do?

These questions are the real challenges that were posed by the quincentenary year of 1992, and they have nothing to do with who is or is not politically correct.

The success of the American experiment depends on our remembering the past, transforming the present, and altering the future. How can we forge a genuinely pluralistic nation where everyone's dignity, contributions, and aspirations can be respected and even nurtured?

All the great social movements that succeeded brought people together. Almost all the social movements that failed did so because the powers that ran the social order succeeded in dividing people from one another, most often by the use of racism.

The best thing about America is our diversity. It is our greatest national strength and not our greatest problem. After

Los Angeles exploded, the tearful Rodney King asked a pro-phetic question: "Why can't we just get along?" Learning to live together and drink from one another's wells of culture and tradition promises an exciting future for America. A fail-ure to do so portends a scenario of growing racial polariza-tion and bitter conflict.

When Columbus landed on these shores five hundred years ago, America didn't need to be discovered. Today it does.

Chapter Six

Pattern of Inequality
Exploiting the Sisters

We've learned that the division of the world into rich and poor will only be overcome when those in the privileged sectors join in the effort to reconnect the "two cities" of the global economy. Likewise, we've confronted the fact that those who benefit from racism are responsible for dismantling it. Now we turn to the issues of sexism and the exploitation of women. Here too, those who have been served by the inequality of power between men and women have a particular role to play.

Men have profited from their dominant role in the family and society, as have the rich from the world's structural arrangements, and as have white people from systems that support their privilege and power over people of color. The same principle that applies to the other issues we have discussed also applies to the challenge of gender justice: to benefit from oppression is to be responsible for it. The time has come for men to move from a posture of reaction, defensiveness, and guilt, to a pro-active initiative on behalf of genuine equality between women and men.

Some are already doing so and are finding the new benefits that come from relinquishing privilege based on injustice and aligning ourselves with the movement toward justice. While the empowerment of the poor, people of color, and women is absolutely central to that movement, so is the responsibility that must be undertaken by those on the other end of society's hierarchical chasms. The assumption of new rights is only half of the movement necessary for change. The other half is the assumption of rightful responsibilities, especially on the part of those who have benefitted unjustly. For men, taking responsibility for gender justice and equality is not only for the sake of women, but also for the sake of our own integrity and healing. That is the point and power of redemption.

One of the most powerful insights of contemporary women's movements is the fact that women are more than just victims of sexist oppression; they also have the power within them to change their lives and the world. But it is still painfully apparent that the structures of male supremacy still function to victimize women. Oppression and violence on the basis of gender and sexuality are at the heart of some of the world's worst contemporary horrors.

Sexual Labor

Olongapo was once a small fishing village of a thousand people in the Philippines. That was before the United States Naval Base at Subic Bay was established adjacent to it. "Subic," as the base was called, was the largest in the Western Pacific and home to the U.S. Seventh Fleet. Almost overnight, sleepy little Olongapo was transformed into a honky-tonk city of 250,000 people, with more than 500 nightclubs, bars, and restaurants to service American military personnel. Olongapo also became the largest brothel in the world.

Just one aircraft carrier could bring 6,000 sailors to Olongapo. Waiting for them were 16,000 "hospitality women." Most were from poor and rural provinces, and they had answered advertisements for waitress jobs that promised good money. But their hopes for better lives turned into living hell as the young women quickly became captives in the clubs owned by American, Australian, Chinese, and local Filipino businessmen.

Living in barracklike facilities, the women never even saw

the profits made from their prostitution. They received only minimal room and board, along with the constant threat of violence. With no money to return home and no other livelihood, most of the women felt trapped and learned to survive as best they could. Subic's base gate literally opened onto the strip of nightclubs and bars. The cooperative relationship between the naval base and the Olongapo brothel was blatantly clear. This violation of the Filipina women was sanctioned by the U. S. government.

I visited Olongapo in the summer of 1988, four years before the eruption of Mount Pinatubo forced the closing of the Subic Naval Base. "The entire economy of Olongapo is based upon sex," one local official told me. The deeper truth was that it was a system based upon power—the power of men over women, and the profitable character of that system of male domination.

The consequences for the women were catastrophic. Tens of thousands of women endured daily sex with strangers for years. Sexually transmitted diseases were common, and, through U.S. service personnel, AIDS may have been introduced to the Philippines, according to the report of one navy doctor. A number of women had already been infected by 1988, and some had given birth to HIV-positive babies. Of course, unwanted pregnancies and abortions were rampant. The women had little protection from the high levels of male violence against them, and many stories circulated about women, some hardly more than young girls, who had died from the physical abuse of their "customers."

That young American navy doctor got into trouble with his superiors for doing research into navy-related sexually transmitted diseases and AIDS problems and trying to protect the women's health. Fearing negative publicity, the navy threatened the doctor with a court-martial, and he was finally discharged, said church workers with whom I spoke.

Brenda Stoltzfus was a young woman working with the

Mennonite Central Committee in the Philippines. She began to visit the city of Olongapo. There she saw the plight of thousands of young Filipina women who had become trapped in a lifestyle of oppressive and dangerous subjection to the endless line of sailors who regularly docked at Subic.[1]

On her own, Brenda began to go to the bars and brothels. She would buy the time of the young women, as the sailors did, and just talk to them. Brenda became a very welcome face—a safe and comfortable friend to talk with. Not deterred by the dangers, obstacles, and threats she encountered, Brenda persevered.

The eventual result was a women's center that offered refuge, support, and many health and human services for the Filipina women. Through that center many women regained their lives. Because of Brenda's initiative and the courage of the women who together started the center, a real alternative to an abusive and violent system came into being. No longer just victims, the women, through their community, found their humanity restored. As in any authentic movement toward liberation, these women began to experience the transformation of moving beyond their status as victims to assuming a primary role in overcoming their oppression.

I met Glenda and Myrna, two Filipina women who worked in the bars and had become involved in the women's center. Like most of the hospitality women, Glenda and Myrna first arrived in Olongapo when they were only fourteen or fifteen. They came seeking a better life and found a nightmare world instead. They shared the dream of many hospitality women to marry a U.S. serviceman and be taken to the United States. According to the Mennonite volunteers I talked with, 72 percent of such marriages fail, and, of course, the dream never materializes for the vast majority of these Filipina women.

The sailors off the ships were often little more than boys themselves. Glenda and Myrna took us on a tour of the bars one night. Under the bar marquee announcing "Welcome

U.S.A. Kittyhawk," eighteen-year-old American men met fifteen-year-old Filipina women in a high-stakes sexual system of money and power run by wealthy men. Bodies, hearts, minds, and souls were all devastated in the process.

When the Subic Naval Base finally closed, I heard many reports from Olongapo businessmen and politicians lamenting how much "the economy" would change. But I heard few words spoken about the shattered lives of the thousands upon thousands of women who were so systematically exploited. They didn't have the power to make their voices heard.

Rape Camps

I thought of those women I met in Olongapo when I first heard about the rape camps in Bosnia and Croatia. In the bloody conflicts of the former Yugoslavia, tens of thousands of women were being destroyed by men at war. Elizabeth Holler Hunter of Sojourners visited the war-torn land and heard the stories of some of the survivors. Women raped multiple times each day were forced to remain in the camps until they became six or seven months pregnant.

Later, two Croatian Franciscans came to visit Sojourners. These veteran priests wept as they told about pregnant sisters in Franciscan convents who had been raped by soldiers. In July of 1993, Ms. magazine reported that many of the rapes and murders in the camps were filmed. It is possible, suggested the article, that those films would be sold to the worldwide pornography industry.[2] Here was the ultimate promise of pornography—the degradation, brutalization, and killing of women—not with actors and actresses, but with real women.

A Catholic sister who was working with rape survivors spoke with Elizabeth Holler Hunter in Zagreb. "A young woman of sixteen came to us in a horrible psychic state. She was suicidal and on the brink of losing her mind because she had been forced to witness the murder of her father, mother, grandfather, and grandmother. She was spared only to be brutally raped many times before being released." [3]

After learning the stories of many survivors, Holler Hunter reported, "Mothers have been forced to watch as their young children were raped, and the children forced to watch as their mothers were attacked. In rape camps and elsewhere, accounts indicate that some women were raped fifteen to twenty times each day. Those who resisted were killed in front of other women; many were destroyed by the physical and psychological violence and died. Survivors report having spent four and five months being tortured this way.

"It is expected that thousands of the women will give birth to children conceived as a result of rape. One woman reported that this was an explicit purpose of the abuse. She said that once pregnant, they were held in the camps until abortion was not an option. Then they were put onto buses and sent out into areas not occupied by the Serbs. On the bus, the woman said, the Serb fighters wrote, 'Croatia, we are sending you little Chetniks.' " [4]

A Pattern

Some would say such examples are extreme. But they are only terrible examples of a pattern—a pattern of violence that continues to dominate the relationship between men and women. In a comprehensive anthology entitled *Violence Against Women*, coeditor Elisabeth Schüssler Fiorenza charts the pattern of violence in its frightening breadth and brutality:

The list of abuse is endless: child pornography, sexual harassment in schools and jobs, sex tourism in Asia, Latin America, and Africa, trafficking in women, sexual and domestic bondage, gender-specific violations of human rights, lesbian bashing, right wing neo-Nazi terror against women, mutilation and stoning of women on grounds of infidelity, restriction of movement and exclusion from the public sphere, Purdah in its various forms, sati in India, sexual assault in the workplace, rape in war and peacetime, women refugees and displaced persons, maids and migrant workers, illiteracy, poverty, forced prostitution, child prostitution, wife bartering, female circumcision, eating disorders, psychiatric hospitalization, battered women and children, incest and sexual abuse, homelessness, silencing of women, negation of women's rights, HIV infection through husbands, dowry death, isolation of widows and older women, abuse of the mentally ill, emotional violence, cosmetic surgery, cultural marginality, torture, strip search and imprisonment, female infanticide, witch burning, foot binding, rape in marriage, date rape, food deprivation, serial murder, sado-masochism, genital mutilation. . . .[5]

One can hardly finish the list without becoming overwhelmed and sick at heart. Such horror and barbarity is so difficult to read, much less imagine, especially for men. But the painful truth is that the list of cruelties is far easier for women to imagine. As Schüssler Fiorenza points out, these are "multifarious forms of violent attacks against women just because they are women."[6]

She goes on to describe the intimate character of such violence: "Most women around the world are murdered in their homes by men with whom they have shared daily life. In the U.S. nine out of ten women murdered are killed by men known to them; four out of five are murdered at home."[7] Schüssler Fiorenza documents the enormous percentages of women in cultures around the globe who experience violence and abuse and reports that "in the U.S., battering is the single greatest cause of deadly injury to women. Its impact is greater than muggings, car accidents, and rapes combined."[8] She concludes that "the most dangerous place for Western women is not the street but the privacy of the home." [9]

The newly named incidences of date rape and acquaintance rape are increasing at many universities. Attitudes reported among the young men committing these crimes suggest that they believe they have a "right" to sex, and when the women refused, they just took it.

Women of every race and social class are subject to violence, every day and in every neighborhood in America. Even wealth and privilege do not finally protect; to be a woman is to be at risk. The rates of rape and violence against women are not going down but are, in fact, increasing and have reached almost epidemic proportions in the United States.

Schüssler Fiorenza describes how the news media seldom reports the extent of violent crimes against women, and the culture still carries the subliminal message that women victimized by such violence must be somehow to blame. "Worse, the victims themselves often have internalized such guilt." [10]

Sexism and Advertising

When sexuality is used to promote and sell almost everything in a consumer society, sexuality itself becomes a cheapened commodity. When sexuality is separated from the integrity of personal relationship and the covenant of commitment, people are reduced to sexual objects that can be readily purchased, used, and abused for the sake of power. And women suffer the most in the imbalance of power.

For example, there is a direct connection between the blatant use of women and sexual imagery to sell beer to young men, and the attitudes of those young men toward women. Joyce Hollyday writes in *Sojourners* about the beer industry's practice of using sex to sell its product. Her report serves as a case study of how such commercial messages reinforce and fuel the patterns of sexual harassment and abuse of women.

It used to be that guys out camping, talking around a campfire about their day in the wild and drinking Stroh's Old Milwaukee beer, could say, "It doesn't get any better than this." But, say you parachute in a few gyrating, blonde, near-naked women known as the Swedish Bikini Team. "It did get better," the guys say now.

If it got better for the men, Hollyday reports, it certainly did not get better for the women, especially those employed by the Stroh's bottling plant in St. Paul, Minnesota. Five of these women, on November 8, 1991, filed lawsuits against the company for its "sexist, degrading" advertising campaigns, including the commercial using the bikini team and posters of nearly nude women in provocative poses. The plaintiffs charged that these ads helped to encourage sexual harassment on the job at Stroh's.

Hollyday reports on the complaints detailed in the suits. They included:

> repeated subjection to lewd comments and behavior, un-wanted physical contact, and instances of intimidation. The women have been grabbed and touched, had lies spread about their personal lives, had their toolboxes sabotaged and air let out of their tires in the parking lot, been told to get "women's jobs," and been subjected to displays of condoms and obscene pictures.... One poster hanging inside the bottling plant, according to the women, lists 13 reasons "Why Beer Is Better Than Women," including "After you have had a beer the bottle is still worth 10 cents" and "Beer doesn't demand equality."

The women said they were threatened with physical assault for reporting sexual harassment. Their suit named twenty-five male employees who they said either perpetrated harassment or did not use their power as supervisors to stop it.

The plaintiffs intentionally linked their company's advertising to its treatment of women in the workplace. Said Jean Keopple, the only female machinist at the plant, "When the company as a whole is treating women as sexual objects, as body parts, it . . . sends a message to the employees." The company, in other words, gives "a big stamp of approval" to sexual harassment. The lawsuits broke legal ground in connecting advertising to workplace practices.

In addition, the lawsuits challenge the assumption that beer cannot be sold without exploiting women's sexuality.

> As Tom Pirko, a beverage-industry consultant, put it, "You still basically have one iron-clad attitude in the brewing industry, which is that you cannot sell beer effectively unless you sell it to young men, and you can't sell beer effectively to young men unless you use sex." When asked if beer could be sold without sex-heavy advertising, Pirko answered, "It's probably a moot question. No one's ever really tried." [11]

THE STRUCTURE OF SEXISM

But the real issue between men and women is not sex, but the inequality of power. Most men would state their opposition to at least the most extreme forms of violence against women, and virtually all the established institutions of the society claim their outrage as well. Indeed, the extreme cases of violence against women are often used to turn the light away from the more prominent and everyday realities of oppression based on gender. What most still will not admit is the pattern that underlies and fuels the violence. The name of the pattern is patriarchy—the subordination of women to men. It is a structure of domination. And like the division of the world between rich and poor and the institutional character of white racism, sexism is also systematic, with clear social purposes.

In male-dominated societies, the imbalance of power be-tween men and women is deliberate—it is a system of both control and exploitation. As long as the differential of power between the genders is so great, various forms of violence and abuse will continue. When women earn only two-thirds the pay of men for the same job, when they are subject to sexual harassment on those jobs, when key social and religious insti-tutions still refuse to grant half the population full dignity and equality, or when women must also bear the disproportionate weight of responsibility for child rearing, the power imbal-ance persists. The American Association of University Women reports that girls are still widely discriminated against in America's classrooms.[12] The socialization of patriarchy begins at an early age.

In the two-tiered world economy, women around the globe are overwhelmingly on the bottom of the social and economic order. Study after study now documents the "feminization of poverty," as women and their children become the most at-risk populations. The biblical concern for "widows and or-phans," as usually the poorest of the poor, rings with a con-temporary clarity. The abandonment and exploitation of women by men and by the structures controlled by men is still the modern reality all over the world.

In Washington, D.C., again, the two-tiered social pattern is clear. The riveting spectacle surrounding Anita Hill's testi-mony during the confirmation hearings for Supreme Court nominee Clarence Thomas revealed that pattern once again. As a conservative and career-oriented lawyer working for Clarence Thomas, Hill was hardly a champion of the op-pressed. Yet she became a powerful symbol for many. The national controversy surrounding her allegations concerning Thomas opened up the whole question of sexual harassment to national discussion.

But perhaps even more dramatic was the scene itself. It was a parable of image and truth. The picture of a solitary black woman confronting an all-white male panel of Senate inquisitors made an indelible impression. The fact that the Senate Judiciary Committee represented the nation's most important governing body of one hundred senators—ninety-nine of whom were white and ninety-eight male—was lost on no one, especially women. At the highest levels of political leadership, the structure of power was undeniably male. That media image prompted several women's Senate and House campaigns the following election year, making a small dent of change but hardly altering the pattern.

At the other end of the power equation in the nation's capital, the pattern is much the same. In the District of Columbia, the majority of women are poor. They do the domestic work, not only for their families, but for the whole society. Poor women are the ones who clean up the messes made in a patriarchal system—from the hearing rooms that hold the senators to the hotel rooms that house the VIPs to the homes that suffer the chaos of poverty and social disintegration. Here, too, women are abandoned by men who father their children and beat them up when they get drunk. Young girls in the ghetto are socialized into the traps of teenage pregnancy and welfare dependency. Older women are generally the ones who try to keep life going, despite lacking the resources to do so. Those strong women become the glue holding families and communities together.

Like the system of racism, which dehumanizes both oppressed and oppressor, sexism too is a system that imprisons both women and men. Women are subject to the structures of male power, while men are socialized and squeezed into the requirements of maintaining that structure in ways that diminish their own humanity and possibilities.

In the last chapter, we described white racism as America's original sin. Ironically, the language of original sin has been used for centuries to oppress women. It is a clear case of religion being used as a tool of oppression. Male interpretations of the Genesis creation story have often blamed Eve more than Adam for bringing sin into the world. As punishment, women have been assigned a subordinate role to men. In a sexist system, men regard women as sources of temptations and dangers. Women's natures, bodies, and relationships are perceived to be a threat. Therefore, the control of women becomes a central male priority and has been the dominant characteristic of patriarchy from the earliest times.

The desire for control is expressed not only individually and culturally, but also institutionally—just as in racism. As with racism, the property laws and practices in regard to women reflected the patriarchal pattern. Like slaves, women were made into property themselves—male property. Slaves were constitutionally considered three-fifths of a person; white women were also excluded from the promise of "life, liberty, and the pursuit of happiness," for they had no legal personhood apart from their husbands or fathers.

Today when social, economic, political, and religious institutions still deny the full expression of the rights and gifts of women, both women and the society are blocked from fulfilling their promise. And when men are denied the full expression of their humanity in relationships and family life, the society is governed by an exceedingly narrow, one-dimensional perspective.

Backlash

Clearly, some of the recent increases in violence against women are a backlash against the gains made by the women's movement in recent decades. In reaction against small changes in the gender order, a full-blown political, cultural, and religious backlash is now under way. Led by the political and religious right, the attack on feminism has reached outrageous proportions. Famed conservative talk show host Rush Limbaugh rails almost daily against the "feminazis" who he claims are responsible for many of our cultural and social problems. While only a small minority of separatist feminists have made their cause into an ideology that blames men for everything wrong in the world, the backlashers paint all feminists with that unfair brush. And Susan Faludi, in her book *Backlash: The Undeclared War Against Women,* contends that a concerted effort is being put forward to blame feminism for "every woe besetting women." [13] Another observer suggests, "Feminists have alternately been accused of hating men and of wanting to be just like them." [14]

The religious right bears a particular responsibility for the climate of fear being fomented against women. In 1992, Pat Robertson, whose Christian Coalition raised over 13 million dollars to elect so-called pro-family candidates, sent a letter to supporters in Iowa, where the voters were considering a state equal rights amendment. Describing feminism as a "socialist, anti-family political movement that encourages women to leave their husbands, kill their children, practice witchcraft, destroy capitalism, and become lesbians," Robertson sought to raise more money for his cause. [15] What the Limbaughs and Robertsons fail to take responsibility for is the way that verbal violence and hate talk are the precursors of physical violence.

THE BATTLEGROUNDS: FAMILY VALUES, ABORTION, AND HOMOSEXUAL RIGHTS

The context of gender, sexuality, and family issues has become the pitched battleground for raging political and cultural wars. Gender politics has produced many of the most pressing issues in contemporary national debate. But it must also be said that many of our society's most controversial subjects are simply thrown into the discussion of "women's issues," even when they do not exclusively or primarily have to do with women. That feminism must bear the weight of all these controversies is certainly unfair and indicates the way that women continue to be demonized in relation to many issues that affect us all. The controversies around family values, abortion, and homosexual rights are hardly just about women. Yet that is the context in which they most often arise. Because it is in the context of gender questions that these political/cultural battles are most often fought today I include the discussion of them here. They are not principally about women. They are about all of us.

The Value of Family

The rhetoric of family values has become especially pernicious. The need for rebuilding disintegrating family systems is now abundantly clear, as is the presence of both male and female role models in the lives of children. But the code language of family values is often a cover for a return to the patriarchal structures of the past. Male control seems to be the underlying issue, not healthy family values or the well-being of children. Indeed, conservative family advocates often support the very things that are destroying families—policies that gut jobs, ignore the health-care crisis, deny family leave, flex-time, and accessible day care.

On the other hand, liberals have not often advocated for the strong family life that our unraveling social order most needs. Women's rights have been the concern of the left, while the right speaks only the language of male-headed nuclear families. Again, our polarities impoverish us. The impasse cries out for new and more balanced approaches to family life, alternatives that create just, whole, and healing environments. Restoring the integrity of family, marriage, and parenting is indeed critical now, but in each case doing so in a way that ensures the dignity and equality of women is absolutely essential.

Abortion

At *Sojourners,* we have anguished over the question of how to editorialize about abortion. From our founding, we have advocated for the rights and equality of women. Also from our inception, we have upheld the sacred value of human life, drawing from our religious roots and our commitment to nonviolence. These two values—the rights of women and the sanctity of life—have become the antagonistic poles of our public discourse.

The most familiar media image today of the battle over abortion is a shouting match outside of an abortion clinic. With signs that scream "Abortion Is Murder" and "Keep Abortion Legal," two protesters stand nose to nose, yelling in each other's faces. The voices are so strident and loud, one cannot make out what either is saying.

It's time to tone down the rhetoric and listen to the legitimate concerns of each side. The level of passion and hatred being engendered has already led to the murders of doctors by inflamed anti-abortion gunmen, and the reaction on the other side has prompted dangerous legal decisions to stifle dissent. Both sides must stop labeling the other as either "baby killers" or "woman haters."

Absolute support for unrestricted abortion on demand should not be a litmus test for authentic feminism. Such a view denies the existence of a growing number of feminists, especially in religious, African-American, and Hispanic communities, who are concerned about abortion. Some women favor a consistent ethic of life, which views threats posed by nuclear weapons, capital punishment, poverty, racism, patriarchy, *and* abortion as parts of a seamless garment of interconnected and interwoven concerns about life's sacred value.

Similarly, to defend women who must often make painful and lonely decisions about abortion is also to choose on behalf of human life. Backing women into desperate corners by criminalizing desperate options is not a good answer. Poor women, lacking the resources of their more affluent sisters, would be especially at risk from dangerous illegal abortions.

We need answers that speak to the concerns of both sides. To find those answers, we will need to seek some common ground between the opposing positions, which, thus far, both extremes have been unwilling to do. As long as the rights and dignity of women and the sacredness of human life are posed as conflicting choices, we will continue our escalating confrontation.

Feminist Shelley Douglass laments the lack of conversation between people who hold opposing views on abortion. Instead of trying to find common ground, she says, people seem more interested in labeling one another.

> When I'm in a room with progressives from the Left, my stomach knots up as soon as abortion is mentioned: In the next breath will certainly come the phrase "Right-wing evangelical fascists." The same thing happens in more conservative groups, where a mention of abortion will evoke the promiscuous New Age conspiracy. What happens to a person like me, caught between slogans?

Douglass believes abortion is "almost always a moral wrong," and she arrives at that conclusion through reasons that are both feminist and spiritual. "I have mixed feelings about making laws about abortion," she writes, "either enshrining it as an inalienable right or forbidding it under any circumstance."

> I think people like me bring insight to the issue because we see and suffer with the question on all sides: The answers are not as clear-cut as either side wants to believe. When those who occupy the middle ground are silenced, it becomes impossible to forge a workable compromise.[16]

Perhaps the "workable compromises" we need may come from the conversations that *are* beginning to occur across ideological lines, mostly among women looking for more thoughtful and human alternatives to the present debate. They represent the hope expressed by Joyce Hollyday that we will not

> give up on creating a world where there is justice for women and children, where there is sexual responsibility, where men share responsibility for the children they father. . . . At the heart of this position is an understanding that we need to build a world in which women and men are equal and children are cared for—a world, as others have put it, in which abortion is unthinkable.[17]

Homosexual Rights

In Colorado, Oregon, Cincinnati, and, potentially, dozens of cities and states around the country, voters are confronting referendums on the question of gay and lesbian rights. In many places, the conservative activists of the religious right have successfully framed the issue as "special rights" for homosexuals. Gay and lesbian people and their supporters have fought back to protect their "equal rights" to housing, employment, and public accommodations. Most people will vote against special rights for any group or individual if that is how the question is framed, but the contested ordinances, when closely examined, concern the fundamental civil and human rights that are supposed to be guaranteed to every American under the Constitution.

Nevertheless, the right, again under the banner of family values and the leadership of famed television preachers, has launched a national campaign. The hate-mongering homophobia has been fierce. Most of the leaders of the religious right have found antihomosexual rhetoric to be their most successful fund-raising tactic. Jerry Falwell has launched a new fund-raising effort decrying "the homosexual takeover of America" and has vowed an all-out effort against homosexual rights.[18]

In what has become an ironic symbiotic relationship, some of the more extreme gay rights activists, in groups like ACT UP, have responded to the conservatives with tactics of outrageous social parody and guaranteed-to-shock public behavior. Some observers have suggested that each group depends on the extreme antics of the other side to justify its own cause.

In this controversial battle over gay rights, issues of sexual morality, family stability, cultural breakdown, and even theological interpretations have all been passionately discussed. In the name of these important issues, appeals are made to oppose gay and lesbian rights. But rebuilding strong families will not be accomplished by denying civil and human rights to people because of their sexual orientation. Our family instabilities have other origins. And the lack of healthy sexual ethics in our culture can hardly be blamed on gays and lesbians. To deny fundamental human rights to a group of people is to violate the core of professed theological integrity. Cultural breakdown is real, but it does not easily submit to simplistic slogans aimed at somebody else. Homosexuals have become the convenient scapegoat for society's unresolved social and moral crisis. After the successful passage of the antigay amendment in Colorado, an outbreak of hate violence against gay and lesbian people immediately followed.

Regardless of the positions religious and other groups may take regarding larger social and moral questions, the bigotry, intolerance, and violence being carried out against gay and lesbian people involve fundamental issues of justice and require a forceful and definitive response. Again, those in the middle on this question can play a decisive role.

Jim Rice reports in *Sojourners* how some other religious leaders have responded to that challenge:

Some church leaders have refused to yield to hate-mongering and homophobia, regardless of their own moral qualms about "homosexual behavior." Cincinnati's Catholic Archbishop Daniel Pilarczyk condemned the anti-gay rights initiative, saying, "It is not right to mistreat persons or to be legally able to mistreat persons on the basis of their homosexual orientation." The Catholic Bishops of Florida issued a statement in October (1993) saying that past discrimination against gays and lesbians justifies laws forbidding it, such as laws that include "sexual [orientation] as a category protected under the hate-crime statute(s)." [19]

Other evangelical Christian leaders, such as sociologist and popular preacher Tony Campolo, have taken great heat for firmly defending civil rights for gays and lesbians. On this issue, too, the decibel level of the discussion must be reduced on all sides, and a more compassionate and creative dialogue begun. Given the high visibility of certain Christian groups in this debate, Rice highlights the particular responsibility of the churches for countering this mean-spirited assault on human dignity. He directs his challenge "to those who have raised biblically based arguments against gay and lesbian involvement in sexual relationships—predominantly in the evangelical and Catholic branches of the church—but who stand for social action on behalf of human rights." The church cannot afford to be neutral, he asserts. "It's time to stand up and be counted." [20]

Given the level of backlash being directed especially at feminists over these and other controversial public issues, the work women and men are doing for equal justice will take more and more courage. Women are threatened, tortured, and killed every day around the world because of their struggle to change the oppressive conditions of their lives and indeed, just because they are women.

LEADERSHIP AND STRENGTH

The backlash against feminism and the dramatic increase in violence against women give ever greater significance to an authentic commitment to genuine equality between women and men. The leadership role of women in our society is absolutely essential to its renewal. Without gender equality, the society simply cannot and will not be changed.

In 1888 Elizabeth Cady Stanton made a speech to the International Council on Women. More than one hundred years ago, she expressed her hopes for women's liberation and the next generation:

> We who like the children of Israel have been wandering in the wilderness of prejudice and ridicule for forty years feel a peculiar tenderness for the young women on whose shoulders we are about to leave our burdens.... The younger women are starting with great advantages over us. They have the results of our experience; they have superior opportunities for education; they will find a more enlightened public sentiment for discussion; they will have more courage to take rights which belong to them.... Thus far women have been the mere echoes of men. Our laws and constitutions, our creeds and codes, and the customs of social life are all of masculine origin. The true woman is as yet a dream of the future.[21]

While Stanton's optimism went largely unfulfilled in the next generation, her identification of the whole social order being "of masculine origin" was right on the mark. The women's movements of our day, no less than that of hers, have challenged that core reality. New values and changes in consciousness always precede political change. The most recent wave of feminism began in the 1960s and is an example of how a change in consciousness can accomplish enormous results.

In every area of the society, women have challenged male assumptions, interpretations, and power. Changing roles within both the family and the workplace have opened up new opportunities and possibilities for women (and for men) and have also produced whole new sets of questions and tensions. Yet the dominant institutions of the society have not yielded to more than a selective assimilation of mostly professional women, leaving the poor and, especially, women of color on the outside of most of the progress. In most social, economic, and religious institutions today, the inclusion of women is still more of a concession than a commitment.

Today, feminism is not one movement but many. It represents many streams of thought, insight, and approach growing out of diverse experiences and constituencies. Maria Riley writes in *Transforming Feminism,* "Feminism as we understand it today is a rich and complex blend of ideas, histories, and ideological perspectives." [22]

The most powerful visions of feminism call for the transformation of the society, not just the winning of individual rights. One of the modern movement's founders, Gloria Steinem, puts it well:

> The real opposition comes when you say, "I'm a feminist, I'm for equal power for all women," which is a revolution, instead of "I'm for equal rights for me," which is a reform. . . . We don't just want to have a piece of the pie. We want to make a whole new pie. [23]

The Womanist Voice

One of the most promising sources for a transformative, strong, and responsible feminism comes from the womanist movement among our African-American sisters. First coined by Alice Walker, in her book *In Search of Our Mothers'*

Gardens,[24] the term *womanist* refers to a feminist approach that seeks to integrate the dynamics of race, gender, and class. Womanist voices emerge from the life experience of the oppressions women of color have endured for generations. Emilie M. Townes, writing in her anthology *A Troubling in My Soul: Womanist Perspectives on Evil and Suffering,* says a womanist perspective

> . . . arises from a deep concern to address the shortcomings of traditional feminist and Black theological modes of discourse. The former has a long history of ignoring race and class issues. The latter has disregarded gender and class. Both modes of discourse have begun to address these internal flaws.[25]

Many women today are calling for an integrated feminist approach that values the life experience and contributions of all women. Womanist testimonies have added a great deal to our reflection about how independent but closely related structures of domination in this world can be more deeply understood and resisted.

Delores Williams, in *Sisters in the Wilderness: The Challenge of Womanist God-Talk,* claims that "very few if any discussions of patriarchy give full attention to women's oppression of women."[26]

> *Patriarchy*—as a term to describe black women's relation to the white (male and female) dominated social and economic systems governing their lives—leaves too much out. It is silent about the class-privileged women oppressing women without class privilege. It is silent about white men and women working together to maintain white supremacy and white privilege. It is silent about the positive boons patriarchy has bestowed upon many white women, for example, college education; the skills and credentials to walk into jobs the civil rights movements obtained for women;

in some cases the *choice* to stay home and raise children and/or develop a career—*and* hire another woman (usually a black one) "to help out" in either case.[27]

This does not mean, she continues, "that most women in male-centered societies have unlimited choices; they do not." Nor does it mean that white women should no longer use the term *patriarchy*, for it may well apply to white women's relations to the men governing their world.

But for *patriarchy* to be inclusive of black women's experience in white society, there needs to be discussion between womanists and feminists about the revision of the term. Black and white women need to become conscious of the negative effect of their historic relations. When this is clearly seen and anticipated, perhaps white feminists will become more conscious of the ways in which their life-work perpetuates the oppressive culture of white supremacy. Then womanists can perhaps desist in questioning the sincerity of white feminism about the liberation of *all* women.[28]

A particular insight of feminist movements is that reflection should grow from experience. Abstraction, which has often been preferred in male-controlled systems, too easily distances us from people's real struggles and can become a cover for oppression. Thus the emergence of feminist thought and action from women of color is a significant development.

A fundamental principle we have been working with is that the truth of a society is best known from the bottom. The insights and energy we most need to transform the social order will often come to us from those who have been marginalized. Therefore the experience and perspective of all women is essential; and the testimony of those women who have survived the "double jeopardy" of racism and sexism will be most instructive.

In the beginning of her book, Delores Williams tells her own story and what she has learned from it. She praises a perspective that goes beyond the language of personal rights to include concern for the wider community, the survival of families, and the defense of children. In the upbringing given her by black women, personal responsibility and social justice walked hand in hand.

Faith has taught me to see the miraculous in everyday life: the miracle of ordinary black women resisting and rising above evil forces in society; where forces work to destroy and subvert the creative power and energy my mother and grandmother taught me God gave black women. Ordinary black women doing what they always do: holding the family and church together; working for the white folks or teaching school; enduring whatever they must so their children could reach for the stars; keeping hope alive in the family and community when money is scarce and white folks get mean and ugly. I discovered that this miraculous "resisting and rising above" has *for generations* been many black women's contribution of faith, love, and hope to the black family, to the church and to the black community of North America.... More often than not, they accounted for their perseverance on the basis of their faith in God who helped them "make a way out of no way." The courage and perseverance of these everyday black women shaped a model of faith and social behavior passed down to generations of women in the community and church.[29]

Sisters of the Summit

Again, the stories emerging from the streets and the bottom of our society may offer the greatest hope for change. The gangs provide another case study.

Street gangs, like the society around them, are very patriarchal. Despite the involvement of women as sisters, girlfriends, and members, gangs have been perceived from within and without as a "guy thing," with men running the show. As we prepared for the Gang Summit in Kansas City, the role of women from the gangs began to grow. When we arrived for the meeting, almost a third of the participants were female, much higher than had been predicted. But at the outset of the weekend, it was clear that the male leaders thought the "sisters" were there to be seen and not heard.

The sisters were not prepared to accept such a role any longer. In a dramatic and liberating moment, all the women walked out of the room to meet together—a ritual of feminist empowerment that has been the source of new beginnings all over the world. They returned with a statement. They were prepared to take responsibility alongside, and not behind, their brothers.

The "Sisters of the Summit Statement" read:

We are the mothers, the sisters, the girlfriends, and the gang bangers. We have to stand beside you, not behind you if we are to grow together.

We must be equal participants. We must be able to speak up without being condemned or silenced. Our agenda is the same as yours.

As women we have always known violence. It is gang banging and police brutality, but it is also domestic violence, rape, child abuse, and poverty.

We insist that women are appropriately represented on any advisory group or board of directors developed out of this summit.

We are our best resources. No amount of money in the world can accomplish what the strength, intelligence, and love in this room can. We have to pool our skills.

The most important issue is that we work together. We love you and support you. Our effort is one.[30]

From that moment on, the summit was changed. Young brothers were being schooled by their sisters and were, for the most part, willing learners. No one could deny the authority of the women's experience, and nobody challenged their participation again. Could their suffering prove instructive and redemptive?

Several young women from the streets spoke to the change that was needed. Blanca Martinez, Director of Nuestro Centro, a gang, drug, and dropout intervention program in Dallas, spoke of her experience at the Gang Summit:

> It was strengthening to me. I had a lot of barriers in my life to point that I should have been a statistic, or even dead. But because a lot of people cared, I worked myself back into the community. These kids have that same potential and can reach it if they're encouraged and have their basic needs met. . . . The way women came together was a growing experience for our men. They not only saw us as mothers, as sisters, as daughters—which we are. They also began to see us as spiritual leaders. They began to see us as effective partners rather than just in our traditional roles. You could never take those roles away from us. But there were many times when it was the women who influenced, motivated, and encouraged a lot of things to happen at that summit.[31]

Najma Nazy'at, a young community organizer working with street youth in Boston, spoke about the common bond of suffering between black men and women and the strength that comes from unity:

> Black women in this country are dying like young black men are dying. Everybody's saying, "Save the black man." I work on the street. I'm watching the sisters' side, too, but in a different way. I watch sisters get four and five abortions by the time they're sixteen. I watch sisters

carry guns. I've seen women gangs. I was on the street doing all of that negative stuff, too.

It can't be that we're only fighting for the black man. We have to fight for black people—men, women, and children—because we are all dying.

The sisters coming forward and saying that was very powerful. We made ourselves a priority, which black women and Latina women, a lot of times, don't do. In the women's caucus, we got to do the talking, we got to show our fears, we got to cry. I thought that should have happened in the general summit.

The men are crying the same tears that we're crying, they're feeling the pain that we're feeling. We know what's happening to the brothers. They also needed that time to share and cry, but because of the way men socialize, we didn't even deal with that. This hurt me, but we know it's there.

Also, the older sisters were really helpful in saying, Yes, the struggle is ours; yes, we have been involved and not ignored. It was powerful to know the strength of women, and that our strength is relevant. Sometimes in our communities that's downplayed. So if you see these women out in the forefront, it's important.[32]

Marion Stamps, a longtime community organizer from Chicago's notorious Cabrini Greens projects, was one of the older activists at the Kansas City meeting. She talked about the evolution of male and female roles at the summit:

Certainly the people at the summit represent the very fabric of the grassroots community. It was very significant for the brothers to work out for themselves some of the problems they have created for the community.

It was very clear from the onset there had not been any participation in leadership from sisters. There were no sisters sitting at the head of the table, there were no statements coming from sisters, there was no introduction of sisters participating in the summit. This is typical in any organization nowadays unless it is a women's organization.

I think it is very clear to us as women that we must constantly struggle for our rightful voice when it is a predominantly male situation. The brothers make a serious mistake when they do not include women in the planning and organizing as it relates to development in our communities. Because first of all, we are the ones who give life; without us, there would be no them. I'm sure they could use the same argument, but the bottom line is women of color hold up three-fourths of the world. We are not to be ignored or patronized.

How we perceive the situation is going to be different than the brothers because it has nothing to do with that macho piece. It has nothing to do with muscle. It has to do with brains and our hearts. A lot of times that's the excuse the brothers use not to do with us—that we're too easily manipulated, that we make decisions based on how we feel instead of what is politically correct.

When the sisters walked out of the meeting and called a caucus among themselves and put together a prepared statement, the brothers had to deal with us in relation to leadership.

My training is to determine who can get the job done, whether male or female. That's the kind of training that the brothers will have to have. There's a basic education that has to take place in terms of the history of struggle of black and poor people in this country.

A lot of those brothers don't have that history; they come from the street, but they don't come from struggle. The education that we learned in the civil rights movement must be integrated in the development of this peace summit.

The brothers had to do one thing before we even talked to them about peace. They first had to apologize to the African-American community—specifically the sisters and the babies—for all the pain and suffering they have caused us. We demanded they publicly apologize to us. Once they did that, the nonbelievers changed their perspective. The same kind of thing needs to be done on a national level.[33]

When asked about the bonding that took place between the older and younger women, Stamps replied, "Oh, that was powerful! One of the younger sisters said in the women's caucus that she did not know what it was like to be around stronger, positive black women. If she'd had a strong mother, she was almost sure that she would have taken a different role at the summit." She continued,

There was so much love in that room. We shared concrete experiences together, and it was obvious that the youngsters in that room needed to understand that we didn't get to where we are as elders without going through some hard times ourselves.

It was very clear that we have not put forth the effort to address the concerns of the young sisters. We made a commitment that would not happen again, and since we've been back in Chicago, we've met every Thursday as a collective group of black women, pulling in sisters from the streets and reading about Ruth and Esther in the Bible.

It's like a political education process we are going through. They can see the love is real and didn't start with us. We are able to love sisters because we know that from the inception of womanhood, sisters have loved us. We are strong because sisters loved us. You can understand if you know how these nations [gangs] function and the way they treat women, that there's going to be some changes, some serious changes.[34]

Voices for Change

All over the world today, women are at the center of the most creative projects in social service and community building, racial reconciliation and economic justice, religious life and theology, political action and alternative models. They have begun workers' cooperatives, cottage industries, human rights organizations, and mothers' coalitions to end violence. Urban women create neighborhood solidarity when no one else does so; suburban women form support circles for victims of sexual and domestic abuse; rural women sustain the viability of family farms. Professional women have risen to push against the glass ceilings of corporate America. Black and Latina women have fought both racism and sexism and provided the spiritual energy for transformation. Religious women have labored in the "brotherland" of their churches and congregations to seek equality in ministry, to reimagine feminine images of God, and to restore the vitality and integrity of faith.

Former sharecropper Fannie Lou Hamer became the mother of the civil rights movement in Mississippi and challenged the very seat of power at the 1964 Democratic National Convention in Atlantic City. With her husband in prison, Albertina Sisulu became the spiritual leader of Soweto and demonstrated the power of the old South African warning, "You have struck the woman, you have struck the rock!" Dorothy Day founded a movement of radical faith and social compassion out of the Great Depression and from the foundation of a most unlikely place—the Catholic church. The women of SOSAD in Detroit, the mothers of the disappeared in Argentina, and the widows of Belfast have organized against the senseless violence destroying their families, communities, and countries.

Countless other women, lesser known but no less courageous, have assumed leadership in the church, the community, and the struggle for justice, even when no one expected or asked them to. Together, they confront a disbelieving world of men with the bold challenge of Sojourner Truth, "Ain't I a Woman!"

The many stories and voices of women in this country merely reflect what is happening in various places around the globe, where women are usually in the middle of the events that are transforming local communities and the world.

What about the Men?

Just as the reality of racism confronts white people with their privilege and responsibility, so the persistence of sexism challenges men to their own conversion and transformation. If relinquishing white privilege is required for racial justice, then the relinquishing of male privilege will be necessary for gender justice. For men, there are everyday examples of the overt and subtle kinds of privilege that will have to be given up: the privilege of having masculine pronouns stand for all of humanity; the privilege of having the bulk of the decision-making power in churches and social and political institutions; the privilege of being listened to with more deference than is given to women; the assumption that maleness is the norm and femaleness is "different," etc.

Because the issues of gender are so intimate and close to home, the obstacles to change are sometimes most difficult. Male control and privilege run deep, not only in our social and cultural institutions, but in our personal psyches and behavior. Most of us as men are used to having our own needs and goals come first, even in relationships with women we respect and love. It's a deeply ingrained habit of mind and heart that is very hard to break.

As with racism, change generally comes through developing honest and mutual relationships, where new dynamics are finally made possible with patience and perseverance. We men will be converted through listening to our wives, lovers, mothers, sisters, friends, colleagues, and co-workers. Only by coming to see the world through their eyes will we have ours opened. Through the women with whom we live and work, we will come to understand justice, faith, and even power in more inclusive ways.

Men conditioned to value hierarchy, independence, and control can learn to incorporate new leadership styles of sharing decisions, forging relationships, and building consensus. Over time, family environments, community circles, and workplaces can come to feel like safe places for both women and men as they try to work out their identities, commitments, and vocations.

What is lost in patriarchy is not only the full contribution of women, but also the essential and intended relationship of women and men. The creation of male and female was meant to be for more than equality; it was for partnership. Our battles between the genders are still over equality, and they are critically important ones. But equality means more than sameness, and it is only a prerequisite for partnership. Our differences and similarities will continue to be better clarified; but the promise of gender partnership is enormous, and we have yet to fully explore its possibilities.

The bonding between women that is at the core of the women's movements is a necessary step. So is the forging of trust and accountability in the circles of male companionship. Each gender finding its true self may be a beginning to coming together in ways that are more just, healing, and creative. In the relationships between men and women, listening will be the path to learning.

After so much oppression and distortion in the gender relationship, partnership will be a large challenge, indeed. Healing the broken bonds between us will not be easy. For the healing of their own lives and the social fabric, women must claim their power to choose their own destinies and exercise power in new and creative ways. Men, too, can find healing in the process of relinquishing the control that limits the development of women but also restricts the deeper dimensions of their own humanity. Feminist theologian Rosemary Radford Ruether says that one of the most important developments now occurring is among men who are learning what it means to take mutual responsibility for the raising of their children.[35]

Both men and women need to learn the responsible use of power—power that is shared and offered in service of justice. To share power is the essence of partnership; to channel it in service of others is to find power's redemption. A new and dynamic partnership between men and women could teach us the lessons about power that both genders need to learn. Gender partnership is essential to social transformation.

Prophetic Feminism

A friend and feminist who touched my life and community was Virginia Earnest, who died in 1993 of cancer at the young age of forty-one. A woman of spirit and power, a builder of community, an artist, a friend of many, a partner to Rob, and a mother of Anne and Jake, Ginny was the kind of woman who makes a deep impact on people's lives.

She was an articulate and committed feminist. Through her insight, perseverance, encouragement, and constant challenge, we all were invited to deepen our commitment to feminism in both word and deed. In 1988 Ginny wrote on the spirituality and politics of feminism. She understood the need for a new kind of gender politics and knew that would require a deeper spirituality. Ginny represented "prophetic feminism"—one persistent in its call for both equality and community. I quote her here extensively in conclusion because of the wisdom of her words and as a tribute to her legacy.

The feminist axiom says that the personal is always political. The unique contribution that women of faith can make to feminism is the insight that the personal and political are always essentially spiritual. The demands of feminism—in both our personal lives and in the culture at large—are too great to suggest simply reforming the status quo or making a few adjustments. Feminism is a movement toward radical change and transformation. Its actualization demands conversion, and conversion is always a spiritual issue requiring spiritual force.

We Christian feminists find ourselves in a paradoxical position. We stand within a tradition that has been and continues to be oppressive, yet holds within its life and teaching the seeds for our empowerment and transformation. Both the wisdom and the prophetic writings in our scriptures give us images, instruction, and encouragement for our conversion. Our faith centers on the person of Jesus, who came to demonstrate a different way of being human. Central to the life and teachings of Jesus was the message of liberation—the good news of God's new order where the mighty are brought low and the humble exalted. . . .

Our vision for liberation has to be deeply rooted in responsible analysis of gender, ethnic, and class oppression so we don't climb out of our ghetto by standing on someone else's back. We live in a society, and beyond that in a world, in which all the "isms" are interdependent, and it is difficult to get at one without tripping over another. It is tempting to over-simplify our analysis in order to achieve clarity, but the cost of doing so is high. We need to find ways of talking about our experience that do not create hierarchies of oppression or deny other people's experience.

When we choose a lifestyle of alienation and anger, we will simply become more alienated and angry beyond our choosing. It is also true that anger, when recognized and channeled, can be a positive and powerful force for change. Liberation must always contain in its promises the possibility of healing and personal wholeness. Therefore, it must always hold open the possibility of reconciliation.[36]

Elizabeth Cady Stanton said, "The true woman is as yet a dream of the future." So is the true man.

Chapter Seven

I Shop, Therefore I Am
Wounded Hearts, Wounded Earth

The British Airways steward announced that the in-flight movie would be *Chariots of Fire*.[1] "Is that the only one?" I asked. "We are also showing *Gandhi*,"[2] he replied. "Where do I have to sit to see it?" I responded. "I'm sorry, sir, but *Gandhi* is only showing in first class." The irony seemed to escape him.

Air travel is mostly a middle- and upper-class mode of transportation. On long journeys spent in planes, passenger lounges, and shuttle buses, one can hear a good sampling of the conversation among people of the more affluent classes. In listening, I've discovered that the overwhelming majority of the talk is about consumption: where we ate last night and where we will eat tonight; which hotel we will be staying in; what was our last vacation and what is the next one planned; where the best shopping can be found.

On a flight home several years ago, I found myself on an airport shuttle bus with other travelers. Two handsome young white couples were having a loud conversation about their favorite restaurants around the world. Many of the rest of us would have preferred not to listen, but the close quarters left us no choice. Finally, one of them exclaimed in praise of his favorite place, "It's just a wonderful restaurant—two can spend 300 dollars for dinner in your shorts!"

At my destinations the conversation is much different, often about survival: Where will our next meal come from? How can we keep the rain out and the children dry? Where can we find water clean enough to drink? Will we ever have any land to call our own?

Again, where is the connection?

OUR MODERN CREDO

The credo of modern consumerism screamed at me from the bumper sticker: "I Shop, Therefore I Am." This contemporary version of Descartes's old maxim, "I think, therefore I am," momentarily took my breath away, with its stark truthfulness about our materialistic age. The same week I saw the bumper sticker, another murder occurred in my neighborhood—this time over basketball shoes.

In many cities across America, it has become quite common for kids to shoot each other for fancy athletic shoes, leather jackets, or some other desirable possession. The bumper sticker declaration of the central meaning of our time struck me as far more brutal than humorous, when at the bottom rungs of the consumer society, children of the inner cities are killing each other for a pair of sneakers.

A Culture of Consumers

Consumption is the thing that everyone, both the rich and the poor and everyone in between, seems to care most about. Our culture has managed to commercialize (and trivialize) almost everything. Not only does consumption define the culture, materialism has become the culture in America. Our possessions have come to possess us, and we ourselves have become almost wholly objectified as consumers and markets by the scientists of Madison Avenue. The entirely economic definition of life that shapes our society, without question, has cheapened our human existence. The result is a culture that is losing its very soul.

The problem is not that the young people haven't learned our values; it's that they have. They can see beneath our social and religious platitudes to what we care about most. Our great cultural message comes through loud and clear: it is an affluent lifestyle that counts for success and happiness. Yet we sometimes seem startled when the young really take our consumer values to heart and lose their hearts in the process.

In truth, we have become an addicted society. Many of our psychological therapists and healers who work with substance abusers have concluded that the whole social context in which we live today is an addicted one. Drugs and alcohol are not our only addictions. In the inner city of Washington, D.C., the money that comes from drugs is another addiction leading to violence.

That addiction—the addiction to materialism—is fed every hour of every day in this society. And it is not only legal to feed that addiction, it is the whole purpose of the system. It is our reason for being as a people—to possess and consume.

The images dance before us every waking moment. They attract, allure, and create desire; they awaken the greed and covetousness of our worst selves. Our children are glued to the television screen, and the beat of incessant consumption pounds in their ears. At every level of the life cycle, our hopes and fears, vanities and insecurities, aspirations and appetites are carefully researched and mercilessly exploited. Our many addictions are systematically created, creatively cultivated, and constantly manipulated.

Everything has a sponsor now. Every moment of every day is brought to us by somebody who wants to sell us something—most of which is demonstrably harmful to us or useless for a meaningful and satisfying life. The beginning of consumer wisdom is to understand that we have become part of the merchandise. Consumers are now what are bought and sold.

Celebrities as Leaders

For the most part, America no longer celebrates leaders, only celebrities. What is a celebrity? A celebrity is somebody who wants to sell you something and get famous and rich by doing so.

The celebrity competition was stiff in the 1994 Super Bowl ads. There was Shaquille O'Neal rapping and slam-dunking for Reebok; Chevy Chase getting canceled again in a Doritos ad; Mike Ditka coaching the tired old football game between Bud and Bud Lite beer bottles; Michael Jordan and Larry Bird shooting baskets from outer space to sell Big Macs; Michael Jordan and Steve Martin selling Nikes (Michael has become our most promiscuous huckster); Bo Jackson running down a skyscraper for Lipton Tea; and, of course, Dan Quayle selling wavy Lays Potato Chips.

Pepsi got a chimp to drive a Jeep down the beach (the highest rated commercial, which showed that anyone can become a celebrity) and had Cindy Crawford change into Rodney Dangerfield after a month of Pepsi deprivation. I don't believe Jimi Hendrix would have done a Super Bowl commercial, but former Woodstock performers Country Joe Macdonald and John Sebastian did their Super Bowl bit for Pepsi in a mock anniversary of the famous music festival where all the sixties protesters have grown up and sold out. Now they are celebrities again.

Television ads bring more fame and money than what the celebrity was initially famous for. Advertising equals more recognition equals more money equals celebrity status and cultural influence. It's a great system for developing cultural leaders. The list of those who have become advertising celebs now includes Ray Charles selling us Diet Pepsi, Candace Bergen persuading us to switch to Sprint, Karl Malden making us feel more secure with American Express cards, James Earl Jones hawking phone books, and Bill Cosby feeding Jell-O pudding to children. Do they really need the money?

I Shop, Therefore I Belong

Our shopping malls have become the temples, shrines, and communal centers of modern America. An advertisement on D.C. Metro buses reads "I was saved at Potomac Mills" and displays a large picture of a dollar bill. George Washington smiles down upon observers, presumably over the terrific savings he has just incurred while shopping at the large discount mall. Malls combine every conceivable kind of store with movies, restaurants, video arcades, exercise clubs, and, more recently, condominiums so you never even have to leave home. The total-environment mall may be the best archetype of our advanced consumer culture.

Consumerism offers us its own sense of community. Magazine articles seriously suggest that a sign of global community is that we can travel all over the world and find the golden arches of McDonald's. Ads for Coca-Cola feature young people of every race and nation all singing in joyful chorus, with a bottle of Coke in every hand, while the now world-famous Coca-Cola signs rise over the misery and death of squatter camps and shantytowns around the globe.

The issue here is deeper than greed and selfishness. Material consumption—buying and possessing things—has become the primary way of belonging in America and around the world. If we can't buy, if we can't consume, we simply can't belong.

I once saw a newspaper column announcing a new, simulated car phone. For five dollars you can buy a piece of plastic that looks like a car phone. It doesn't work, but from outside your car in the parking lot, it looks like the real thing. The motivation for such a product isn't greed, it's belonging.

Perhaps our shared cultural values reflect the emptiness of our situation most of all. Television rules the popular culture, and advertising dominates television. Television has become the principal vehicle for promoting consumerism. It is the message of the medium. Consumption has become our highest social value and purpose. In fact, material consumption is the only universal form of social participation that Americans have left. Everything else has been either marginalized or completely coopted by the frenzied desire for things.

Consumerism as Citizenship

Citizenship itself has been replaced by consumption. Shopping has become our great collective activity, and consumerism has invaded and even usurped our civic life. People feel they no longer have the power to change their communities or their nation, only to make choices among products. Political participation has waned dramatically, just as the rituals of consumption have come to dominate more and more of our social life. Politics has become a spectator sport, as sports have become totally subjected to the power of money and advertising.

We don't participate in the debate over ideas, the formulation of public policy, and the construction of the social order. Instead we shop. Our consumer voting is merely among the endless goods and gadgets offered to us, and democracy has been reduced to the freedom to decide among forty brands of toothpaste.

News has more and more become entertainment, fed, of course, by advertising. Network news superstars host "TV magazine" shows with an array of mindless and titillating topics that would have thoroughly embarrassed many of their journalistic predecessors. And even our political voting feels more like shopping for candidates, who have been packaged and sold by the same methods and people who bring us everything else.

THE RIGHT TO OVERCONSUME

Much of the crime overtaking our society stems directly from the values of an utterly materialistic culture combined with the observation of many youth that the rich and powerful (both people and nations) generally take what they want and get away with it. More and more are concluding, "If they can, why can't I?"

Advertising tells us not just that all these things are wonderful to have, but that "you deserve it." Material acquisition has been made into a human right, without which life is empty and meaningless. Ironically, the reverse is true. The portrayal of overconsumption as a deserved right has emptied human life of meaning and turned us into increasingly violent creatures. When people are told on their televisions that they deserve all the goods of American life and then are denied their attainment, more and more resort to just taking the stuff.

Yes, we are suffering a crisis of values. However, the charge of lack of values is normally addressed to those on the bottom of society, to inner-city youth and young perpetrators of street crime. We often hear political candidates speak of a criminal class that must be locked up. However, since the United States has more persons incarcerated, in proportion to its population, than any nation on earth,[3] it might be time to ask why. Clearly, we are suffering from a profound erosion of moral values. But where does it come from?

In an April 1989 series of articles entitled "At the Roots of the Violence," the *Washington Post* described the unwritten code of conduct of the drug dealers in their own words: "Never back down.... Be willing to kill or die to defend your honor.... Protect your reputation and manhood at all costs...." The drug dealers who live by this code are known on the street as soldiers. A reporter asked one of them why they are always so ready to shoot. "I guess it's greed for that money," was his answer. The *Post* then commented on the code of the streets, saying, "It is a way of behaving that flies in the face of traditional American values."[4]

The Roots of Overconsumption

Was the reporter right? What have been the values reflected in American foreign policy? What code of ethics governs the wars of Wall Street? How does the enshrinement of greed and the glorification of violence every day on television sets and movie screens shape our cultural values?

What message does society give young people every day about what is most important in life? Have they not been convinced, like most other Americans, that status and success come by way of material acquisition? Does it matter anymore how people in America get rich?

With great danger to themselves and others, these children of the poor are pursuing the same glittering materialistic dream as others in the quickest and perhaps only way they see open to them. Isn't there an irony in highly paid entertainers and professional athletes, as the role models, encouraging young black children to reject the big money they can make in the drug traffic and settle for minimum wage?

When the government launches its war on drugs, it takes careful aim to avoid the deeper causes of the problem, then shoots volleys that fall far short of addressing even the symptoms. Critics cry out for more money to be spent on the symptoms, while they ignore the underlying causes and corruptions of drugs.

On ABC's *Nightline,* after a presidential speech on the drug crisis, two incarcerated drug traffickers at D.C.'s Lorton prison spoke prophetically. One said, "I think we've witnessed in the past a great devastation in this whole country because of a certain materialistic ideal or materialistic approach to things. And it's not the answer. We need moral training." Another spoke of the attraction of "the gold bracelets" and "the big cars." The inmates at Lorton agreed that the combination of the two—a systemic economic injustice and an insatiable lust for material possessions—is indeed the formula causing the death and destruction.[5]

Frustrated Desire

We simply must stop continually pumping the moral pollution of rampant consumerism into the heads and hearts of the young; as long as we continue to do so, we have no right to be shocked when they behave as selfish materialists. By creating the desire for affluence, then blocking its satisfaction, we are fueling a combustion engine of frustration and anger. We can no longer exclude whole communities from the economic mainstream, relegate them to the peripheries, tell them in a thousand ways that their labor and their lives are not needed, abandon their social context to disintegration and anarchy, and then be surprised when those communities erupt.

When there are no ethics at the top of a society, it's likely there will be none at the bottom either. Our urban children have inherited our values. The violent carnage of our inner cities is the underside of a consumer society that uses violence as entertainment. Looting is a crude shopping spree reflecting a system that loots and pollutes the rest of the world.

When the kids on the street during the Los Angeles riots said of looting, "Everyone was doing it," they didn't just mean their neighbors and friends. The savings and loan ripoff bankers are looters, too, as are the military contractors who always run over budget and the Wall Street inside traders, merge makers, and takeover pirates.

I remember the names invoked by the young men who tore Detroit apart in the mid-sixties—Franz Fanon, Stokely Carmichael, and Malcolm X. Theirs was a highly politicized violence of rising expectations in a global revolutionary environment. Today, young gang leaders and drug dealers invoke different names: Ivan Boesky, Michael Milken, and Lee Iaccoca. They are not heroes but role models: "They got theirs, now I'm going to get mine."

We are witnessing a nihilistic violence of rising despair in a global environment of dividing walls and polarized extremes. Indeed, it is time to take a strong stand against the criminal behavior of looting, all the way from the top to the bottom.

The children of the inner cities may be uneducated, but they aren't stupid. They know they've been left behind. They know there's no room for them. Many feel little investment or stake in the future. And they are enraged.

Trickle-Down Violence

The painful violence of the rejected and exploited always exposes a twisted mirror image of the dominant society. It's quite uncomfortable to see ourselves and the values of our culture in the skewed reflection of our children's frustrated rage. But if we refuse to hold the mirror up to ourselves now, the reflection is just going to get worse.

Despite the promises of politicians and economists, it is painfully clear that wealth does not "trickle down" from the rich to the poor. When the rich are getting richer, the poor are generally getting poorer. But while wealth doesn't trickle down, violence does. The trickle-down theory of violence is being verified on the streets of virtually every neighborhood in this country in an epidemic of violent crime that is seemingly out of control.

In my former hometown of Detroit, a new phenomenon was born in the late 1980s. They called it "carjacking" in the Motor City. When you stop for a traffic light or get out of your car at a gas station or parking lot, someone confronts you, puts a gun to your head and tells you to give up your car or you'll be killed.

On a visit with my family in Detroit, I was told that more than three hundred cars had already been taken in the few weeks since carjacking began, and six people had been killed for resisting. Sure enough, within several months, carjacking had come to Washington, D.C., and was the latest crime epidemic across the country.

Television and radio talk shows were full of people's anxiety and lots of advice about how to protect yourself. But almost nowhere were the roots of the problem of violent theft explored. The idea of taking what you want (and using whatever means are required to do it) has become common practice among the rich and powerful as well; it has been the operative behavior of American foreign and military policy for many years.

Playing by the rules, working hard, acting fairly, and respecting the rights and lives of others have been characteristics of neither Wall Street nor the Pentagon. The lack of such values at the top of a society is a fact not missed by those on the bottom. It is particularly hard to convince cynical young people to do things the difficult and right way, when many of their society's most successful people and companies, and even their government, routinely do things the easy and destructive way.

A report on National Public Radio told of a seventeen-year-old young woman on trial in Milwaukee for shooting another teenage girl to death because she refused to give up her leather jacket. The girl's lawyer said she was a victim of a "cultural psychosis" — the environment of violence that prevents children from knowing right from wrong.[6]

It may be more fruitful to look for some of the causes of our crime problem in the leveraged buyouts, insider trading, and junk-bond peddling that made the fortunes of our most successful financial giants while creating banking crises and ruining the economy. Could it be that the law-and-order rhetoric of the 1980s had less effect on the national spirit than the frenzied greed in high places showcased during the "getting mine" decade? Might we better understand our cultural acceptance of violence by looking to the military leaders who casually spoke of "eliminating the enemy" on video-game-like radar screens or presidents who boasted about "kicking ass" in Middle East wars? Maybe we should scrutinize the advertisers who sell sex and use sex to sell everything else in order to find the causes of rising violent crime against women, for women are used in the mass media as objects to be consumed.

Our Material World

At root, we might examine the reality of our material world: in our consumer culture, things have become far more important than people. Indeed, people themselves have been turned into things to be used and abused in a society where everything and everyone is a commodity to be bought and sold. The commodification of human life is the moral framework upon which our materialistic system has been built. It is that whole system that inevitably produces the amorality we now suffer.

The proverb quoted earlier, "Where there is no vision, the people perish," can be translated in slightly different ways. Another translation says, "Where there is no prophecy, the people will cast off restraint."[7] The bitter meaning of that sentence has become painfully clear to me now, right in my own neighborhood. When vision is lacking, people quickly degenerate into their worst selves and begin behaving in violent and destructive ways.

Martin Luther King Jr. recognized the intimate connection between our materialism and all our other problems more than a quarter century ago, when he wrote that as a nation we must undergo a radical "revolution of values."

We must rapidly . . . shift from a "thing"-oriented society to a "person"-oriented society. When machines and computers, profit motives and property rights are considered more important than people, the giant triplets of racism, materialism and militarism are incapable of being conquered.[8]

Nearly three decades later, we have yet to address the spiritual crisis that our worship of things has produced, and we are reaping the violent consequences.

THE WOUNDED EARTH

The Aboriginal leader took his food and walked some distance away from the small crowd that had assembled for lunch at a community site run by the indigenous people in western Australia. He sat alone on the ground and began to eat his meal. I followed the tribal elder out onto the dusty red earth, where he invited me to sit with him. We had been speaking earlier about the life of the community there, the projects the people were undertaking, and his determination to pass on a way of life to the young. Now he began to talk about what it means to be an Australian Aborigine.

He reached down and put his hand on the ground beneath us. "The earth is our mother," he said. Then, putting his hand on his chest, he continued, "I can feel the earth in my bones, in my flesh, and in the blood moving through my body." Our lives depend on the earth, he told me, and we also must depend on each other. "That's why we share what we have with one another. There is no one here who goes without. We would not let that happen."

Relationship to the earth and a sharing of resources are at the heart of Australian Aboriginal spirituality. And that spirituality is still alive, despite the genocidal consequences of two hundred years of white settlement. One finds it most clearly in the grandfathers and grandmothers who provide community leadership by telling the stories of the "dreamtime" before white settlement, thus passing on the memory and traditions of the Aboriginal people to the next generation.

The grandfather with whom I sat told me that Aborigines are a spiritual people and their spirituality is essential to life itself. Without it they would surely die. It seemed to him that most white people have a very different spirituality.

His observation was strikingly revealed in that morning's Australian newspapers. There on the front page was a picture of George Bush sitting in his golf cart and ordering American troops to the Persian Gulf over his mobile phone. The contrast between the two leaders could not have been more stark.

I was in the middle of Australia in August 1990, when Saddam Hussein's Iraqi army invaded Kuwait and sparked the chain of events that eventually led to the Gulf War. I stayed up very late one night in Australia to hear President Bush speak live to the American people in his first speech after the crisis began.

During the hour before his address, while I waited nervously, Australian television aired a documentary on the environment, specifically the growing dangers to the earth's ecosystem from global warming trends and pollution caused by the industrial world's massive dependence on fossil fuels, that is, oil. I then watched George Bush tell the American people that we must be prepared to go to war to protect the supply of oil. Nothing less was at stake, said the president, than "our way of life."

It was a very vivid and frightening picture, in the middle of the night and halfway around the world, of my own nation—addicted to a way of life that is slowly killing us. In all the coverage and commentary about this crisis over oil, few ever really asked the most important question: What does the oil fuel?

The Economic Earth

What the oil fuels is a global economic system of massive consumption at the top and massive misery at the bottom, a system we know is doing incalculable damage to the natural order in which we live. Consuming a grossly disproportionate share of the world's resources, the West suffocates in its own affluence, while even within the wealthy nations, more and more people are abandoned to poverty. The United States, with only 6 percent of the world's population, still consumes 35 percent of the earth's resources. And the distribution of those resources within the United States has become visibly obscene.

The world economic order is not only unjust, it is also unstable, as the Gulf War demonstrated. Even getting rid of the Saddam Husseins does not remove the underlying instability in the Middle East. The truth is that the West itself has helped to create the situation in which we now find ourselves. Western colonialism and the thirst for oil drew up the map of the Middle East to the point even of carving out the borders of all the Arab states embroiled in present-day conflicts.

Kuwait and Saudi Arabia were established to ensure a continual supply of cheap oil for the West. Oil-rich states are run by corrupt and brutal elites who abandon their own people, crush all opposition, fight among themselves for wealth and power, live in incredible opulence, and invest their untold fortunes in the West, while Arab masses live in poverty and resentment. The feudal oil sheiks have proven quite willing to cut favorable political deals with their colonial benefactors, humiliating Arab pride and inciting Arab nationalism.

And sometimes, as in the case of Saddam Hussein, the greed and ambition get out of control and threaten the oil contract, which is the bottom line of the relationship to the West. The West arms all the Middle Eastern states (and has thus flooded the entire region with sophisticated weaponry), plays them off against one another, generally ignores their abuses (including Iraq's many past horrors), changes alliances as quickly as shifting desert sands, and seeks to manage events with no consistent principle except our insatiable thirst for oil. The U.S. commitment to restore a Kuwaiti royal family that has suppressed every democratic impulse in that country—and to defend a Saudi monarchy with one of the more dismal human rights records in the world—suggests that we are making the world safe more for feudalism and gas guz-zling than for democracy.

The High Price of Oil

Clearly, what the United States cared most about during the Gulf crisis was oil. The United States was willing to pay a high price to secure continued access to oil on our terms. The price of the Gulf War included over a hundred American lives and as many as 100,000 Iraqi soldiers and civilian casualties. The price included risking the potential use of chemical war-fare and even tactical nuclear weapons.

The genuine fear and concern of many Americans over the prospect of losing loved ones in the sands of the Arabian Pen-insula was caused by something far deeper than a so-called madman in Iraq; it was the direct consequence of "reaping what we have sown." The easy success of the war quickly covered over the deeper questions that it had begun to raise.

"The bugle from the Middle East," wrote columnist Ellen Goodman, "sounds an unhappy wake-up call."[9] We are con-fronted with soul-searching questions that simply will not go away. What are we most willing to sacrifice—a way of life based on massive overconsumption, or the lives of young Americans and other peoples it may take to keep it going? How many cents on a gallon of gas are equal to the human cost of so many potential deaths? What are we ready to risk—changes in our lifestyle or the prospect of endless future confrontations?

Are we ready to make the critical choices to opt for less dependence on oil, for energy conservation, and the shift to safer, more reliable, and renewable sources of fuel for the sake of the earth and our children? Are we prepared to begin a serious dialogue about what a more equitable and sustain-able global economy might look like? Or are we prepared to again bomb the children of Baghdad, or somewhere else, if necessary, to protect "our way of life"?

Farmer and poet Wendell Berry reflected at the end of the Gulf War:

> We must recognize that the standards of the industrial economy lead inevitably to war against humans just as they lead inevitably to war against nature. We must learn to prefer quality over quantity, service over profit, neighborliness over competition, people and other creatures over machines, health over wealth, a democratic prosperity over centralized wealth and power, economic health over "economic growth." . . . If we want to be at peace, we will have to waste less, spend less, use less, want less, need less. The most alarming sign of the state of our society now is that our leaders have the courage to sacrifice the lives of our young people in war, but have not the courage to tell us that we must be less greedy and less wasteful.[10]

The Cry of the Heart

We have already spoken of the pain and violence of life at the bottom of a global economy defined by the tale of two cities. But we can also see the problem at suburban shopping malls, where the human heart is slowly dying because of our failure to recognize that we were created for more than consumption. At the upper end of the world's hierarchical chasms, the affluent drown in loneliness and anxiety, and their children wander aimlessly in a society in which there is always more to buy but nowhere to find meaning. These are the spiritual consequences of our separation from one another and from the earth. The anxiety and despair of affluent cultures is a direct result of their unjust relationship to impoverished peoples and nations. Again, the principle holds true: we are inexorably linked together.

Underneath the noisy chaos of our consumer culture, the constant rush of media images that define our reality, and the relentless pressure of a lifestyle that demands our very souls, do we even hear the cry of the poor? And beneath their cry, can we hear the cry of creation itself? At the deepest level, can we even hear the cry of our own hearts?

The conservatives say the problem is a breakdown of values; the liberals say the cause is poverty. They are both right and both wrong. Our value structures have broken down. The most basic understandings of simple decency and respect can no longer be taken for granted. May Sarton, introducing John LeCarré's *The Russia House,* says, "One must think like a hero to behave like a merely decent human being." [11] We have entered an amoral era, where notions of right and wrong, which were once commonly held assumptions, are gradually slipping away.

THE SPIRITUAL MIRAGE

I've made several pilgrimages to the Nevada desert, to the site where all U.S. nuclear weapons are tested. Even before dawn one can feel the heat of the desert while walking the gravel road toward the place where, for more than four decades, the government has conducted dress rehearsals for nuclear war. Little is there but sand, desert brush, cacti, and a few lizards.

The stark landscape stretches in every direction as far as the eye can see. By 8:00 A.M. it's hot, and the senses begin to feel deprived. Everything is barren in the desert, and thoughts come alive where there is nothing to distract. It's easy to understand why the prophets often went to the desert to think, pray, and wait for a new word to be spoken.

A religious delegation walks to Camp Desert Rock, where, forty years earlier, American soldiers were deliberately exposed to atomic radiation to test the effects of the bomb. Huge craters are still visible as ugly scars in the desert from years of above-ground testing. Now it's all done below ground, but the explosions still shake the earth. On this particular day, a small group of spiritual pilgrims has come to mark the fortieth anniversary of the first atomic bombing, on the Japanese city of Hiroshima.

Just a few miles away stands the city of Las Vegas, a vivid embodiment of the glittering dreams of materialism. The luxury, gambling, food, sex, entertainment, and, most of all, money, are there in all their gaudy display. To this unlikely desert playground people stream from all over the world to bask in lights that are brighter than the brightest dream of material success and pleasure. Here the hungry and thirsty come. Las Vegas: the great mirage in the desert.

Las Vegas is a caricatured symbol for a culture that is full of mirages. It's what modern advertising is all about—the skillful promotion of mirages. Desert mirages appear to be water, which is desperately needed. But they are an illusion—a trick of sun, heat, and sand. When you see a mirage, you head toward it, moving faster and faster, until finally, you plunge headlong right into it! But all you get is a mouthful of sand.

Advertising is the false spirituality of materialism, promising what it can never deliver. Even the slogans of advertising sound religious, using the language of ultimate concern: "Buick, Something to Believe In"; "Miller Beer—It Doesn't Get Any Better Than This"; "G.E., We Bring Good Things to Life." Television images of young, beautiful, sexy, successful people enjoying the best of life surround almost every product—and you can be just like them, suggest the ads. If you just drink this beer, use this toothpaste, drive this car, wear this perfume, or buy these jeans, this can be your life, too. Is this not the essence of idolatry—a misdirected form of worship?

But these promises are an illusion, a mirage that is very dangerous. All of life has been reduced to consumption. We sacrifice our souls for the mirage of glittering images, and all we get is a mouthful of sand. We have run after mirages in the desert, and now the desert is in us.

On this subject Jesus was quite clear:

No one can serve two masters; for a slave will either hate the one and love the other, or be devoted to the one and despise the other. You cannot serve God and wealth. Therefore I tell you, do not worry about your life, what you will eat or what you will drink, or about your body, what you will wear. Is not life more than food, and the body more than clothing? Look at the birds of the air; they neither sow nor reap nor gather into barns, and yet your heavenly Father feeds them. Are you not of more value than they? And can any of you by worrying add a single hour to your span of life? And why do you worry about clothing? Consider the lilies of the field, how they grow; they neither toil nor spin, yet I tell you, even Solomon in all his glory was not clothed like one of these. But if God so clothes the grass of the field, which is alive today and tomorrow is thrown into the oven, will he not much more clothe you—you of little faith? Therefore do not worry, saying, "What will we eat?" or "What will we drink?" or "What will we wear?" For it is the Gentiles who strive for all these things; and indeed your heavenly Father knows that you need all these things. But strive first for the kingdom of God and his righteousness, and all these things will be given to you as well.[12]

In such Gospel wisdom is the beginning of the more relaxed and balanced perspective we will need to place material things back in their proper place and restore the rightful priority of human life, relationships, and the integrity of the whole natural order.

Another bumper sticker I've seen is the one that reads, "Live Simply, So Others May Simply Live." That slogan gets close to the heart of things. We are all connected. As long as some can talk only about their materialism, others can talk only about their survival.

One of the most urgent personal and social qualities needed in our present political crisis is compassion. Compassion means a radical empathy for all those who suffer under present arrangements. This means suffering in all its forms, including both the oppression of the world's poor and marginalized majority, and the spiritual and psychological disintegration of the affluent minority because of that very oppression.

The internalization of oppressive values is one of the most decisive causes of both the alienation of the affluent and the self-destruction of the poor, and it is dramatically illustrated in the violent inner-city neighborhoods of America. We now witness the tragic irony of growing numbers of people in the middle classes gripped with the recessionary fear of falling down the social ladder, while simultaneously experiencing the personal and family consequences of the empty and competitive values of a materialistic society. We are afraid of losing what is already killing us.

THE COST OF CHANGE

The creation and all its abundance is good. It is meant to be both shared and enjoyed. But our overconsumption has damaged creation, our materialism has corrupted our hearts, and injustice has wounded our souls. The violence we do to one another, either through unjust structures of international trade and finance or through street crime, is the moral consequence. And change will be costly.

We need a citizens' movement against overconsumption. The best way to resist the materialistic values of a consumer society is simply to withdraw our participation from them and find alternative ways to live that are more creative, healthy, life giving, and even fun. That will not be an easy task, but it is possible, especially with the support and energy that can be generated by people doing it together. It is already occurring in diverse places, where the excesses of affluence, concern for the environment, and a desire for justice have created both disaffection and a hunger for new patterns of resource use. People are finding new ways to meet their legitimate needs, ways that don't destroy the earth, their global neighbors, their children's moral characters, and their own humanity in the process.

Alcoholics Anonymous and related groups for various other substance abuses have become a spiritual home and haven for many recovering people. As a recovering friend of mine puts it, "A.A. is not for people who want to keep from going to hell, but for those who have already been there." The standard introduction of a member goes like this: "Hi, my name is Bill, and I'm an alcoholic." To which the whole group responds with acceptance, "Hi, Bill!"

Perhaps we need to learn from the successful principles of Alcoholics Anonymous and have meetings that begin, "Hi, my name is Bill, and I am a materialistic overconsumer." It sounds funny, of course, but accepting of our mutual problem would make it possible for the process of healing and recovery to begin. The issues involved in our destructive overconsumption are more than political; they go to the spiritual core of our identities and needs.

Out of that spiritual transformation, a citizens' boycott of wasteful and destructive consumerism could, over time, have a profound effect in reshaping the marketplace and altering the very values of the culture. The thing Madison Avenue most fears is that people will stop listening to its mindless and manipulative advertising. Why don't we try it? Just turn it off. Let them ramble on in their trivialities and falsehoods; we won't be paying attention.

We simply cannot go on living as we do, consuming as we please, profiting as much as we can, and running the economy as we are, while using the money that is left over to "help the poor." There won't be "enough" left over and the poor will lose the political debate.

It is we who have to change, and it is our patterns and institutions that must be transformed. There is much work to be done and many jobs to be created in bringing us the things we all need—education, health, energy efficiency, a safe and restored environment, healthy food, good roads, strong bridges, easier and cleaner transportation, affordable housing, stable families, and vital communities.

Such things will be achieved only through a combination of solid values and sound social policy. And it will require a number of fundamental shifts—from unlimited growth to a sustainable society, from endlessly consuming goods to re-valuing social goods, from the ethic of competition to an ethic of community. Such shifts will not be easy, nor will they be without cost. But the cost of not making the changes will be even greater.

Part Three

Toward an
Alternative Vision

Chapter Eight

Signs of Transformation
The Marks of an Emerging Prophetic Vision

I was in the midst of a long argument with a group of economists in Canberra, the capital city of Australia. After more than two hours of discussion, these public-and private-sector policy makers admitted that both of the world's economic systems had failed, especially in regard to social justice, environmental stewardship, and spiritual values. Regarding the fundamental human issues of meaning, quality of life, and ethical integrity, we agreed that our dominant ideological options had exhausted themselves.

The immediate response of these analysts was to plunge into an academic discussion in search of a blueprint for a new economic system. I interrupted the conversation to suggest that those old ways won't work anymore. Even if these experts (all white and male) were to barricade themselves in a room for six months and not emerge until they had constructed a new system, they would never find the answer. In fact, their process would ensure that they found the wrong answer.

We don't have any blueprints for a new system, and we shouldn't look for any. At best, what we have are some spiritual guideposts and road maps. The process of change will feel more like a journey than a policy conference or board meeting. And the sojourn itself is part of the solution to our many problems. We don't have ideological manifestos and position papers to answer all the contingencies, but we do have core values that could cut a path to a different future, and we have some marks along the trail to show us the way.

What are the evidences of transformation in a society, the indicators of new visions for public life? Such visions must be both spiritual and political and must have concrete social, economic, and cultural consequences. New visions are usually best expressed in movements rather than political parties or bureaucracies. Even in our media-controlled society, they more often originate from the margins and the bottom than from the center and the top. Even in a day when economic, political, media, and entertainment elites seem to dominate, a new moral sensibility will arise from ordinary people. Indeed, it is the moral failure of our powerful institutions and the ethical poverty of our successful elites that will create the need for new visions and possibilities.

Social movements that can change history must eventually affect our leading institutions. But new visions cannot arise from those old structures, new values will not be created from old assumptions, new leadership does not often emerge from the ranks of old elites, who are the most imprisoned by the old systems and options. A new vision must come from new places—new places in all of us.

Vision comes more by renewal than by reaction. The deepest changes come from a revolution of the spirit rather than a revolution of the gun. Hope has always been a more powerful force for change than despair. The renewal of our best values and moral sensibilities has the best chance of forging a new covenant. People and societies are lifted to new and higher ground by engaging the best that is within them and their traditions.

Underneath failed social values, corrupted institutions, and destructive personal behavior is a reservoir of moral conscience. Our religious traditions call that "the image of God" stamped upon our hearts. At the same time, the twentieth century has shown us the depths to which humanly conceived evil and brutality can go. The Bible calls that our "fallenness."

It is the appeal to the image of God within us that is the most persuasive weapon against human fallenness. New social visions are forged by such an appeal.

Political realism requires us never to underestimate the human capacity for evil. Yet political hope calls us never to discount the possibilities of human transformation. Both realism and hope have deep theological roots. And a dynamic relationship between politics and spirituality causes us to take both very seriously.

New visions are marked by distinguishable signs. These signs are the expressed commitments that demonstrate both old moral values and new social possibilities. They are, indeed, rooted in the human image of God, and they are a powerful counterpoint to our worst social and cultural instincts and behavior. The signs of a new vision are indicators of new directions and evidence of spiritual transformation. Together they point us to a different political future.

The stories that follow indicate the change of heart, transformation of thinking, and liberation of spirit that must undergird any serious endeavor toward real social change. These stories do not answer all the questions we will face, but they can help to shift our conceptual frameworks and spiritual sensibilities in order to provide the foundation for genuinely new social experimentation. They don't offer systematic solutions, but they do point in practical directions. Together, they are signs of an emerging prophetic vision.

CONVERSION

The Priority of the Poor

Many years ago, I was part of a group of seminary students in Chicago. We decided to do a study to find every biblical reference to one particular subject—the poor and oppressed. We searched the Scriptures for each mention of the subject and found, to our astonishment, that there are thousands of verses about the poor in the Bible. Those who are marginalized and forgotten by everyone else, those who are mistreated and abandoned on the bottom of society keep appearing in the Bible as a central concern. The Bible, we discovered, was full of poor people. And even more startling to discover, God is portrayed throughout the Bible as the deliverer of the oppressed.

In the Old Testament, the subject of the poor is the second most prominent theme. Idolatry is the first, and the two are often connected. In the New Testament, one out of every sixteen verses is about the poor! In the Gospels, the number is one out of every ten verses; in Luke's Gospel one of every seven, and in the book of James one of every five.

One zealous seminarian in our group decided to try an experiment. He found an old Bible, took a pair of scissors, and then proceeded to cut out every single reference to the poor. It took him a very long time.

He came to the prophet Amos and read, "Take away from me the noise of your songs; I will not listen to the melody of your harps. But let justice roll down like waters, and righteousness like an ever-flowing stream." Then he cut it out. He got to Isaiah and found the prophet thundering, "Is not this the fast that I choose: to loose the bonds of wickedness, to undo the thongs of the yoke, to let the oppressed go free, and to break every yoke? Is it not to share your bread with the hungry, and bring the homeless into your house; when you see the naked, to cover them, and not hide yourself from your own kin?"[1] He cut that out, too.

The books of the prophets were all decimated. So were the Psalms, where God is revealed as the comforter of the afflicted. The Exodus story of God's deliverance of an enslaved people out of the hands of their oppressors, likewise, disappeared. So did the record of the Jubilee, a Hebrew tradition for the periodic forgiving of debts, redistribution of land, and sharing of wealth.[2]

In the New Testament, the young seminarian put his scissors to work again when he came to the Song of Mary, the Magnificat that prophesied the mission of the child she carried in her womb: "He has scattered the proud in the thoughts of their hearts. He has brought down the powerful from their thrones, and lifted up the lowly; he has filled the hungry with good things, and sent the rich away empty."[3] After a few snips it was gone. You can imagine what happened to Jesus' teaching in Matthew 25 about caring for "the least of these."

He also cut out Jesus' first sermon at Nazareth where he announced the manifesto of his ministry, "The Spirit of the Lord is upon me, because he has anointed me to bring good news to the poor. He has sent me to proclaim release to the captives and recovery of sight to the blind, to let the oppressed go free, to proclaim the year of the Lord's favor."[4] A few quick cuts, and the prophetic vision of Jesus' ministry had disappeared.

The beatitudes from the Sermon on the Mount, "Blessed are you who are poor," and "Blessed are the poor in spirit," had to go, too. All those teachings had to be removed, since they announce a whole new way of living that turns all our cultural assumptions and established status quos on their heads. The clear injunctions in the epistle of James not to treat the rich differently than the poor didn't survive the scissors, nor did the exhortation in John's letters that if we do not love our neighbor in need, we simply do not love God. Of course, the testimony of the early church where goods and property were shared freely and "There was not a needy person among them" quickly disappeared.[5]

All of that and more was snipped right out of the Bible. When the seminarian was finished, that old Bible hung in threads. It wouldn't hold together; it fell apart in our hands. It was a Bible full of holes. I used to take that holey old Bible out with me to preach. I would hold it high above American congregations and say, "My friends, this *is* the American Bible—full of holes from all that we have cut out." Protestants, Catholics, evangelicals, Jews, liberals, and conservatives—we all hold Bibles that are full of holes. Any one of us might have taken that pair of scissors ourselves and cut out all that we have ignored.

At the time, I wondered how I could have heard nothing about such a great biblical theme while I was growing up in the churches. How could such a central biblical teaching be so disregarded, especially among those whose religion is supposedly rooted in the Bible?

In America and throughout the Western world, we have responded to all that the Scriptures say about the poor by pretending it just isn't there. We have cut the poor out of the Bible.

The God of the Bible is the deliverer of the poor. This God has a special love for the disenfranchised and marginalized—those who are on the bottom of everybody else's priority list. If that isn't clear from the Bible, then nothing is. It is evident from start to finish.

Therefore, from a biblical point of view, questions concerning the poor and oppressed cannot simply be regarded as matters of politics, or safely delegated to the social concerns committee of a religious congregation. Instead, what is at stake is nothing less than restoring our biblical integrity. It is a matter of conversion.

To place the reality of the poor at the center of our attention will require a fundamental change in priorities and direction. Our task is much deeper than social charity; it is to put our decimated Bibles back together again, to recover the meaning of the sacred text in our personal lives, our congregations and communities, and in our world.

Fidelity to Scripture is finally tested not by dogma and doctrine but by how one's life demonstrates that he or she believes the Bible. Belief results in obedience. In wealthy nations, that fidelity will best be tested by our relationship to the poor.

Jesus is not a blue-eyed right-winger, as some have implied; nor is he a guilt-ridden liberal or compromising centrist. Jesus is the one who entered the world among the dispossessed and the outcasts to announce an entirely new way of thinking and living. The way of Jesus and the prophets isn't just a welfare program; it calls for a change of heart, a revolution of the spirit, a transformation of our consciousness. It moves us beyond the familiar options of abandoning the poor, controlling the poor, or even "helping" the poor from places of isolation and comfort. Instead, it leads us to a new relationship with one another, a deep reconnection, a restoration of the shattered covenant.

An Aboriginal woman from Australia says it well: "If you're coming to help me, you are wasting your time. But if you have come because your liberation is bound up with mine, then let us work together." [6] The good news is that the Bible is already being put back together. Biblical integrity is being restored in our time, if you know where to look.

The priority of the poor in the Bible has been one of the best-kept secrets in the churches. The passion of God for the oppressed of the earth is a secret long hidden from the religious and nonreligious alike. But now the secret is getting out.

It is the poor themselves who are learning the secret. They are now the majority in the world, comprising the largest numbers in the church across the globe. To know that God is with them in their struggles for life, justice, and a decent future for their children has become a tremendous source of hope, comfort, and power.

To witness that hope is to be evangelized by it. In the most forgotten places of the world, something is happening that will profoundly change the rest of the earth.

To reach my destination in the Philippines, I had flown across the Pacific by jet, and my friend Karl Gaspar met me at the airport in Manila. A Redemptorist brother who helps establish base communities among the poorest rural people, Karl was to be my guide on this trip. I had learned to trust his perspective. I was greatly looking forward to these two weeks in the Philippines, both to get a clear view of the situation there and to have a reunion with Karl.

Karl and I had been close for many years, having become fast friends at a conference between first- and third-world theologians and activists. Our backgrounds in the student movements of our two countries are very similar, as are our perceptions of the meaning of faith for our present circumstances. Shortly after our first meeting, Karl had been put in prison under the repressive regime of the famed Filipino dictator Ferdinand Marcos. Persistent efforts to keep Karl alive and, eventually, to get him released formed a strong bond between us, as did our extensive personal correspondence.

Karl's letters were like modern prison epistles, making a profound impression on people all over the world. In the introduction to the volume in which they were later published, I wrote:

> They have locked up your body, but they have not imprisoned your spirit. They have taken away your liberty, but you are still free. They have controlled your movements, but they haven't controlled your conscience. They have accused you with lies, but they have not been able to suppress the truth. They have tried to silence you, but your voice is stronger than ever. They have taken you from your community, but you have formed another one behind the bars. They have tried to quench your faith, but the fires of persecution have only made it stronger.[7]

A prop plane took us to Davao City, on the island of Mindanao. Days later we rode a very crowded bus, which bumped and swayed over rough and dusty roads for several hours, heading for the Bukidnon province in central Mindanao. Here Karl was working with a team of young people in the mountainous rural barrios among some of the poorest peasants in the Philippines. We continued our journey in a taxilike truck called a "jeepney" and eventually in an even smaller motorized tricycle.

As we approached the town of San Fernando, I could see the effects of the deforestation that Karl had told me so much about. Logging companies had come in and removed the trees from the hills and mountains, causing great ecological damage. Once-beautiful hillsides were now scarred with countless tree stumps on barren slopes.

We finally arrived at the small convent that served as the base for the mission team. This was as far as any vehicle could go. The rest of the way to the barrio would be on foot. "You ready for a walk?" Karl asked with a twinkle in his eye.

"Sure," I replied with great enthusiasm.

"We'll have to cross a river to get to the barrio," said Karl.

"Fine," I replied. "How deep?"

Karl smiled. "Well, it could be up to our ankles. It could be up to our waists. It might even be up to our necks! In fact, maybe we'll have to swim. You can swim?" he queried. I told him I used to be a lifeguard. "Let's go," said Karl.

After about an hour, we reached the place where we would cross the river. We had walked five kilometers, mostly through mud. The river looked wide and deep. The water would be at least chest high. Carrying our packs over our heads, we waded out into the fast current. The rocks underfoot were slippery, and I noticed that the caribou crossing alongside us were having a much easier time of it.

Once we reached the other side, we rewarded ourselves by

resting on the bank and letting the sun dry us off. After a while, the sun began to set over this very beautiful and relaxed riverbank. Karl told me this was one of his favorite places on earth, and I could see why.

We talked a long time about our lives and loves, about our communities and families, about my neighborhood back home in Washington, D.C., and his barrio called Candelaria, which we were about to enter. Mostly, we both talked about the life choices we had made.

While we sat and talked, many others crossed the river. All were friends of Karl and they stopped to greet us. Both young and old cross this river as a matter of course many days of their lives. It is the only way to go to the market, to school, to work beyond the barrio, or to a doctor. Eventually, we put our packs on our backs and began to walk the last half-hour stretch to the barrio—through more mud. I had never seen so much mud.

It was almost dark when we arrived at the little hut where we would be spending the night. I met the host family—mother, father, and eight children—with whom Karl and I would share this simple one-room home.

Inside the small thatched-roof house was a simple grill over a wood fire, where the evening meal was being prepared. Normally, dinner consisted of rice and perhaps some dried fish. Tonight, because they had company, a special meal was in the making with rice and dried fish, green beans and noodles, and a few small sardines. The woman had made a special trip across the river to the market for the green beans, which we helped shuck. Karl said the dinner was a rare treat.

The house was full of children, and they were full of smiles. Ging-Ging was just four years old, with deep searching eyes. Her ten-year-old sister was only in the first grade. When I asked Karl why, he said the older daughter was weak and missed school because she often couldn't cross the river. But all were full of life and questions about their new visitor.

After a wonderful meal, other families from surrounding homes came in to join us. Together, they were to prepare the sermon for the next Sunday, a responsibility that is rotated in their base Christian community. But first, a guitar was brought out and everyone began to sing. The happy smiles on their faces told me that this was the children's favorite part.

Then the biblical sharing began. The young mother of my guest house was the leader and, according to Karl, the catechist of the group. The scene was riveting—a vivid experience of poor rice farmers squinting to read their Bibles by the light of kerosene lanterns after a hard day's work. Karl quietly translated as these humble children of God wrestled with the meaning of the gospel for their lives and circumstances.

This is the true meaning of liberation theology: biblical reflection arising not from intellectual academies, but from among the poor of the earth. Basic questions are asked. What does this Scripture mean for us and our families? What does the good news say about our future? What does God require of us? How will justice come to our land?

Karl said the people often spoke of the relationship of gospel teaching to the practical issues they were facing, like the ecological destruction of the logging companies. These base Christian communities had already launched a campaign to stop the deforestation and protect their community. That campaign eventually succeeded. But what was most evident was how powerful a force faith is in the lives of these people. Indeed, it is the center of their lives.

This was a weeknight, and it was getting late. Rice farmers arise early in the morning. Nevertheless, the sharing and singing went on for two hours. Afterward, everyone stayed to enjoy "sticky rice," rice sweetened with coconut milk. More stories were told, with plenty of time to laugh and hear the children sing some more songs. The group wanted to hear stories from the United States as well and were startled to hear that there were poor people in America, too.

These peasant farmers were especially taken with the fact that I had never seen rice growing before. They were eager to show me the process of rice growing and seemed proud that I was learning it from them. When all but our hosts had left, grass mats were brought out for everyone who would share the floor of the one-room house. Mosquito nets appeared from the walls, and before long we were all fast asleep.

Before I drifted off, I thought of the nine-year-old boy named Andreas who had curled up in my lap an hour or so before. He was Karl's favorite. His parents often worried about him when he disappeared at night without a trace. After searching high and low, they would find him sitting on a log somewhere, looking up at the stars. I wondered what kind of future he imagined for himself.

We were up at 5:30 the next morning for a breakfast of—that's right, more rice. Soon we were saying good-byes and were on our way. As I trudged through the mud, our young catechist and mother seemed to glide past us on her way to the market. She smiled at my slippery steps, and I marveled at how she kept life together for so many with such grace and joy. A real spiritual power existed among these people that seemed to hold great promise for community development and social transformation. But surely change would not come without struggle.

More than two thousand miles from Candelaria, I saw the courage that such struggle takes. We were in a black township called Duncan Village in the Eastern Cape of South Africa. A young community leader named Jam Jam was showing us around when we were surrounded by dozens of South African security police, who had been surveilling us. With their automatic weapons menacingly pointed at us, the officers ordered me, my companion, and Jam Jam to the police compound in the township, known as "the strong point." We were forced to wait an hour for a security officer, who then interrogated us for another hour. The elite police commander was a huge man, and he was backed up by several other officers who kept their weapons trained on us. The purpose was to intimidate, threaten, and seek information.

After asking us many questions without getting the answers he desired, the military man began to threaten the young man. Jam Jam had just been released from prison where he had served eighteen months and, like most young black South African prisoners, had been tortured. This giant hulk leaned down into the face of the young man and said, "We know who you are and what you are doing. And if you don't watch out, we'll throw you right back into prison; and you know what that means." Surrounded by such hostile threats and drawn weapons, Jam Jam reached into his pocket and pulled out a New Testament. Looking his accuser right back in the eye, the twenty-four-year-old dissident said, "I am a Christian." He was not to be intimidated.

When we were finally released, we took Jam Jam out of the township with us. He would stay away for a while until things cooled down a bit. I asked him why he would take such a risk to show two white strangers around his community. Jam Jam talked about the nonracialism at the core of the new South Africa he and his friends are building and about how important it is that people in the townships see whites who are with them in the struggle. "We are not fighting against whites; we are fighting against injustice. We are just going forward. It's not the time to be afraid." [8] I knew that kind of courage would ultimately be stronger than the apartheid system. [9]

I heard another story while in South Africa about a young widow whose husband had died and left her alone with eight children. She was poor, black, a woman and a South African, and that was very close to the bottom in her world.

The widow and her children lived in an old, dilapidated house that she wanted to fix up, but as a seamstress making only two dollars a week, she had to work long, hard, and extra hours to save enough money to buy bricks. When she had finally saved enough, she ordered 400 bricks to fix the house. But when the truck came to deliver them, she counted and found only 250.

The woman asked the man who brought the bricks where the rest of them were. He was a wealthy and powerful man; he told her not to bother him and that she had all the bricks she was going to get. So she said to him, "I will never forget this. But that's okay, you don't have to worry about the bricks. The God I believe in is the protector of the widow and the fatherless. And somehow you're going to know that." [10]

One of her children, a twelve-year-old boy, was listening, and the words of his mother made a great impression on him. Two weeks later, the same man pulled up to the house again in the truck and, with his hired men, unloaded the rest of the bricks. "Why are you here?" the woman asked.

He told the widow that two of the houses he had been building had mysteriously burned to the ground and he thought her God had something to do with it! He was embarrassed and afraid, so the men completed their work as quickly as possible and were gone. The woman's young son was again looking on.

That young boy was Allan Boesak, who later became a leader in his people's fight against apartheid. He told me,

I saw all this at age twelve, and it made a tremendous impression on me. I saw that in a very tangible way, God does take care of the poor and the meek and the lowly and the oppressed. That is something I have never forgotten. So today I am very impassioned about these things. I keep on telling people that this is the biblical message and that it doesn't matter what the situation looks like; God will make true the promises that have been made. And there is no doubt in my mind that God will. [11]

Belief in the truthfulness and faithfulness of God's promises runs deep in the church of the poor. I see it all the time in our neighborhood center in inner-city Washington, D.C. In late 1992, I invited some potential financial donors in for a meeting at the center. I hoped to share a glimpse of the vision of our community with them. I arrived at 8:00 A.M. to set up chairs and make coffee, but I discovered that Doris Knight had been there since 7:00, heard that visitors were coming, and already had the coffee on.

Doris was there to send off the van for an early morning food run and to prepare for the next day's food line. The smell of fresh coffee and sausage filled the place, as did the sounds of laughter and singing among the volunteers who were already hard at work to get the food ready for the hundreds of people who would be coming. When my guests arrived, Doris was there to greet them, wearing her Sojourners Food Program apron that displays the verse from Matthew 25, "I was hungry, and you gave me food." Like most of the volunteers, Doris came from the food line herself and proudly announced to our guests that she had been involved with Sojourners for ten years.

Ray Ford was already busy out back, planting the seeds that would grow into the trees and bushes he would place around the neighborhood to make it more beautiful. Arthur Harrington was in the kitchen frying up some catfish he had caught so everyone could have lunch. "If we all give what we have to offer, there will be enough to go around," he told me. I realized that the vision I hoped the visitors would experience was already there for all to see. The people at the center are a parable of what the gospel is trying to teach us.

At this critical historical moment in the world, something new is happening, and it's coming from a very unexpected place. Its impact is being felt throughout the global church so profoundly that it is becoming a new reformation.

The Reformation of the sixteenth century had as its central theme "salvation by faith alone." The simple and powerful insight of this new reformation is: "The gospel is good news to the poor." Like the first, the new reformation promises to transform the church and the society around it. This is not just the miracle of personal conversion, but the conversion of the church itself, with the poor as its evangelists.

We could be at a turning point. Our society has forgotten something very important, something we lack that must be recovered. It is the dignity that all people deserve and that no one must be denied. Our social attitudes and economic structures have allowed us to deny that dignity to whole populations of God's children. Most middle-class Americans, if they are really honest, don't believe that the vulnerable children in the horn of Africa, on the streets of Calcutta, or in their own city's homeless shelters are as important as theirs.

Yet the gospel tells us that we have turned away from Jesus as we have turned away from the poor. Mother Teresa of Calcutta and Dorothy Day of the Catholic Worker have spoken of Jesus coming to us "in the distressing disguise of the poor." Some who have been raised in the affluent religious world call this the second conversion—to see the face of God in the face of the poor.

I had the privilege of meeting Dorothy Day several times, and I found in her a clarity about the meaning of that conversion that I had rarely seen before. Converted to the Catholic faith from the American left, Dorothy gave her life to the poor and led a movement that profoundly influenced the lives of thousands of people. In her presence, everything became simple and clear. I'm told that is a common quality of the lives of saints. In the Catholic Worker's houses of hospitality around the country, the gospel is rediscovered among the poor, and faith becomes credible again. At the end of her autobiography, *The Long Loneliness,* Dorothy describes how the Catholic Worker came to be and always continued.

We were just sitting there talking when lines of people began to form, saying, "We need bread." We could not say, "Go, be thou filled." If there were six small loaves and a few fishes, we had to divide them. There was always bread.

We were just sitting there talking and people moved in on us. Let those who can take it, take it. Some moved out and that made room for more. And somehow the walls expanded.[12]

Dorothy understood that in our relationship to the poor we are mysteriously converted to Christ. She said:

How can I help but think of these things every time I sit down at Chrystie Street or Peter Maurin Farm and look around at the tables filled with the unutterably poor who are going through their long-continuing crucifixion. It is most surely an exercise of faith for us to see Christ in each other. But it is through such exercise that we grow and the joy of our vocation assures us we are on the right path.

The mystery of the poor is this: That they are Jesus, and what you do for them you do for Him. It is the only way we have of knowing and believing in our love. The mystery of poverty is that by sharing in it, making ourselves poor in giving to others, we increase our knowledge of and belief in love.[13]

Dorothy Day was an American forerunner of the second conversion and the new reformation.

Every project, idea, and system must be evaluated by whether it moves us toward greater connection with one another. A good example is what the Catholic diocese of Saginaw, Michigan, has done. They have decided that before making any decision as a diocese regarding programs, buildings, or events, they will ask one simple question: How will this affect the poor? What a revolution would occur if public policy decisions were subjected to the same process!

Conversion is a sign of transformation.

COMPASSION

No More Us and Them

Evangelists for this new reformation are ordinary people. One such story of ordinary people comes to us from Brazil. A number of poor farmers were about to lose their land to a government project, and they knew that to lose their land was to lose everything. For campesinos, land is life, and without it poverty and death soon follow.

The people met to decide what to do. Most were despairing; past protests against big government projects had failed, often with protesters being shot and killed. The vote on this project would come up soon in the Senate, and the outcome seemed certain. No one could think how to save their land.

But then some of the women had an idea. They decided to go with their children to the neighborhoods of the rich where the senators lived, and they decided to go on the day of the critical Senate vote. When they arrived, they were awestruck by the size of the houses and especially the beautiful green lawns with so many lovely trees providing shade from the hot sun. The poor women sat down with their children on these lawns, making quite a sight in the neighborhood. After a while, the senators' wives sent their servants out to ask if the visitors wanted some food. "No, thank you," replied the women. "We did not come for food."

The senators' wives were perplexed and eventually came out themselves to ask the poor women if they needed some money. "No, thank you, we are not here for your money," they said. The senators' wives became even more confused. Finally, the women in the big houses asked in bewilderment, "What is it that you people want? Why have you come here?"

The poor campesino women looked into the eyes of the wealthy senators' wives and said, "We are going to die. This seems like such a lovely place, so we thought we and our children would just come here to die." The wealthy women were shocked and asked why these people thought they were going to die. The campesino women told their story—of why land was so important to them, of how they were about to lose it, and of what that would ultimately mean for them and their families.

Soon, the women and children were invited into the big houses, and their storytelling continued. The senators' wives listened that day, and some also told their own stories. Before long, the phones began to ring at the Senate, and busy legislators were pulled away from their duties to answer urgent calls from home. They were told what had happened that day and what their wives believed they should do.

The government project was defeated, and the campesinos kept their land. It happened because some people had begun to listen to each other. Compassion always begins with listening. The word *compassion* literally means "to suffer with," to put yourself in someone else's position, to walk for a little while in her or his shoes. The listening that leads to compassion is the beginning of understanding.

We have not been listening very well. Instead, we've been content with easy answers, quick justifications, and rhetorical slogans that make it possible to dismiss the suffering of other people. We satisfy ourselves by arguing that we know about "them," what they are like, why they have problems, how most of it is their own fault, or how dangerous they are. We tell ourselves and others not to exaggerate the problem, that it's all being taken care of, that nothing effective can be done, or that it is somebody else's responsibility.

In America, a phrase is often used to keep problems at a

safe distance: "Not in my backyard." The "NIMBY syndrome," as some have named it, is pervasive among us and symbolizes the walls we desperately hope will keep people away from us. But these same walls are ultimately unable to prevent us from experiencing the consequences of abandoning our neighbor. The walls divide us, but they don't protect us.

Those illusory but oppressive walls must be broken down. And nothing does that better than the experience of listening directly to the people on the other side of the wall. Getting close enough to see, hear, touch, smell, and taste the reality of others is what always makes the difference. In listening to the stories of those so seemingly different from us, we find similar but unexpressed voices inside of ourselves. Hearing one another's stories is the beginning of new understanding and the foundation of compassionate action.

I remember a day in Cleveland, Ohio, in the mid-eighties. I was visiting a team of people who had just come back from Nicaragua as a part of the Witness for Peace program. We were discussing changing events in that country when I got an urgent call from home with some very bad news. Our office had just heard from the Maryknoll sisters in Ocotal, Nicaragua, that their little town near the border between Nicaragua and Honduras was under attack. Six hundred contras had invaded early in the morning, and many civilians were already wounded and killed.

As I shared the sad news with the Ohio group, I could see tears in many eyes around the circle. I didn't fully understand the depth of their response until I was told that these people had stayed in Ocotal during their visit to Nicaragua. They had experienced the hospitality of the people, played with the children, prayed with the parents, shared in these families' hopes, fears, and faith. Now their new friends were under attack and perhaps some had already died. I shared their feelings; I'd been to Ocotal, too. We bowed our heads to offer intercessions for our sisters and brothers in danger.

Suddenly, I realized the extraordinary thing that was happening. I was listening to Midwestern Americans pray, by name, for ordinary people in a faraway Central American town, strengthening the bonds between Americans and Nicaraguans that would eventually obstruct the U.S. war against that country.

Thousands of people traveled to the war zones of Nicaragua, then came home to testify to what they had seen and heard. Those who went would never be the same again. They had been changed, and their actions reflected the transformation.

The day after the last contra aid vote failed in the U.S. Congress, the State Department blamed the churches. They were right, and I wasn't surprised. Touching the lives of others creates compassion; compassion leads to action for justice and peace.

On another evening in Northern Ireland, I was addressing an audience of 2,000 Catholics and Protestants during a week-long conference on the beatitudes. I was startled by the response of a group of women sitting in the front row of the church. They were crying, and their faces showed that pain as well as a radiance that was undeniable as they quietly grasped each other's hands.

I met the women afterward and learned that they were all Catholic and Protestant mothers whose husbands or children had been killed by the other side. Now they stood together in their grief and in their stubborn determination to resist the violence. Their common experience of suffering had given them a compassion for one another and for their embattled country. It had led them to action.

I've met with mothers like that in many places. Sometimes they are called the "Mothers of the Disappeared" or the "Mothers of the Martyrs," and they have become one of the most potent forces in the world for reconciliation and justice. At times I think the truest image of God today is a black inner-city grandmother in the United States or a mother of the disappeared in Argentina or the women who wake up early to make tortillas in refugee camps. They all weep for their children, and in their compassionate tears arises the political action that changes the world.

The mothers show us that it is the experience of touching the pain of others that is the key to change. It is not the book or the class or the idea that changes us, as important as those things are; it is the experience. Invariably, it's an experience of crossing over boundaries, touching someone else's reality, and hearing others' stories that change people. For middle-class Americans, it's often the pilgrimage into the inner city or to places like Central America, India, or South Africa that becomes the converting moment. Our reality looks forever different after we have experienced somebody else's, especially if it required that we cross over the lines that divide us.

If that is true, such experiences should be built into our lives. Religious congregations, community organizations and schools could make such crossover experiences a regular part of their spiritual formation and educational programs. A number of American churches and synagogues have become "sister congregations" with churches in El Salvador, South Africa, or the former Soviet Union. Those linkages have grown to have a significant impact on both communities.

Crossover experiences could also take place right here at home between suburban and inner-city people and communities. The exchange of resources and the establishing of bonds between the middle class and the underclass could significantly impede the implicit policy of abandoning poor communities that is resulting from the changing domestic and global economy. Such an interaction could also create the essential human dialogue and relationship that lead to creative new initiatives. Most of all, it could change our perspective and generate the compassion that breaks down the walls between us and them and provides a spiritual foundation for social change. Compassion is a sign of transformation.

COMMUNITY

A Moral Foundation for Economics

In Mexico an organization called Habitat for Humanity was building houses for poor families. The families who would live in these fifty houses helped to build them all. On the day the houses were completed, each family came forward to claim its new home. A single bowl contained the keys to every house, and a member of each family reached in to pull out a key. Then, keys in hand, all went to find their houses. Through the experience, everyone learned a lesson in community.

For decades now, we have been enmeshed in endless arguments between the two options of the "command economy" of state-directed socialist systems, and the "market economy" of world capitalism. The failures of both systems, which we discussed earlier, cry out for something new. What could it be? Perhaps the new concept we are searching for is best described as a "community economy."

I will not try here to specify the details of what a community economy would look like. Rather, I want to ask what shifts in our economic ethics, assumptions, and ways of thinking are now required. Asking some fundamental questions can help to suggest some new directions. Instead of merely asking what will make a profit or what a central bureaucracy could do, we might begin to ask ourselves what would best serve the needs of a human and ecological community.

For example, goods and services need to be produced, but the wealth from such production could certainly be shared more equitably than it is now. The enormous income disparities between the top echelons of corporate America and the bottom rungs of the economy—for example, the head of a major airline making hundreds of times the starting salary of a flight attendant[14]—simply cannot be justified by differences in class background, education, opportunity, or even ability. How can we assign people quality of life in such vastly disproportionate ways? How do we square the enormous polarities with the ultimate moral worth our ethical and religious traditions would ascribe to each individual? Is the labor of one person really hundreds of times more valuable than the labor of someone else?

To decrease the distance between the top and the bottom and thereby more highly value the contribution of each person to the productive process cannot easily be specified in legalistic detail. However, we could move toward some new shared social values regarding both the minimally acceptable levels of decent human existence and the upper limits of financial remuneration. What legal coercion cannot accomplish, new standards of social affirmation and social shame might be able to do.

Instead of flaunting excessive wealth, which seems such an accepted cultural practice today, it could become a matter of social embarrassment to live so extravagantly while others suffer so grievously. Instead of television shows that celebrate "the lifestyles of the rich and famous," we should document the consequences of such living upon the ecosystem and "the life struggles of the poor and powerless." Rather than creating envy through media fascination with the salaries of sports stars, talk show hosts, and big corporate executives, we should generate a sense of emulation by profiling those who forgo lucrative rewards for social responsibility.

Already some small and midsize businesses are making decisions to compensate their leading executives with less money, reducing the gap between the top and the bottom. Meanwhile, they make substantial contributions to saving the environment or assisting economic development among the poor. The profits to the community are thus greatly increased. The truth is that many more human incentives exist than financial ones, and there are greater enhancements to personal and community well-being than endless economic accumulation. The fact that noneconomic incentives seem so foreign in the contemporary marketplace indicates how far we have strayed from a balanced definition of quality of life.

Other new and creative efforts encourage and enable wealthier people to contribute to a leveling process through various forms of voluntary "tithing"—a tradition familiar in religious congregations (though almost forgotten in many). The sources of property value and individual wealth are also social and not merely personal, and therefore commitments can be made to allocate portions of earned income to projects that generate economic development where it is most needed. Such a process of redistribution is based on notions of accountability, a deeper response than charity.

Why is real estate speculation that displaces the poor regarded as shrewd investment rather than as unacceptable antisocial behavior? Since the actual value of land comes from social factors and community investment, as well as individual enterprise, why does the increased worth of property in prosperous areas only accrue to its individual owners? Meanwhile, the diminished worth of property in declining economic environments impoverishes those who happen to live on the wrong end of a lucrative real estate market. Isn't the religious notion of stewardship a better way to approach the enormous problems of land and resources, rather than the idea of exclusive private ownership that is accountable to no one?

New patterns of individual, family, and cooperative ownership of property—all shaped by community standards of land use—could provide a greater measure of equity and environmental responsibility. Various experiments in community land trusts and cooperative housing corporations are already demonstrating some alternative directions. Again, the willingness of people and institutions to tithe some of the "social value" of their property or income toward employment, land, or housing for the poor would result in a creative redistribution of resources.

Ultimately, we must move toward land reform—the democratic redistribution of usable land—in the so-called developed countries, just as surely as it is needed in the so-called developing countries. The destruction of our forests, farmlands, water resources, and wildlife can be reversed only when community-based commitments to stewardship replace the selfish and shortsighted practices of acquisitiveness that are ruining the earth and our fragile ecosystem.

Neglected biblical instructions and traditions could guide us today, such as the practice of leaving the edges of the fields unharvested so the poor can glean from them, leaving land fallow occasionally to replenish its fertility, observing the Sabbath both to rest and avoid overproduction, and periodically forgiving debts and redistributing land in the Hebrew idea of the Jubilee Year. Modern equivalents of such biblical practices are urgently needed. For example, there is no reason not to apply such basic principles to the enormous problem of international debt, which cripples developing nations and prevents their ascent from poverty.

In the area of capital investment, why should a narrow profit motivation predominate over all other considerations? Why couldn't there be social and economic incentives for investing in critical areas of development such as business enterprises for low-income people, affordable and energy-efficient housing, family farm-based agriculture, rebuilding the country's infrastructure, safe and ecological transportation, preventative health care and wellness programs, education and job training for a changing society, and environmental conservation? If these are identifiable community needs, why couldn't we invest in such social goals instead of producing an endless and mostly useless array of luxury consumer items?

Social investment can also create economic activity, jobs, and wealth, while at the same time generating more natural equity and protecting the earth. Indeed, more jobs could be created in the aforementioned areas of economic and environmental activity than in the high-tech, corporate global economy now envisioned by the world's economic elites. As it is now, some of the most creative projects in all of the above areas are languishing for lack of resources because they fail to meet the narrow and rigid profit criteria for financial investment. Pioneering a different direction are new nonprofit loan funds that defy the conventional financial wisdom yet show great success in funding a wide variety of socially constructive projects. In fact, a whole field of alternative social investment is emerging that in most cases demonstrates an equal if not better record of repayment than many of the more traditional investment options.[15]

The religious community, which has enormous financial resources itself, should be particularly challenged. The Inter-Faith Center for Corporate Responsibility's (ICCR) 250 Roman Catholic orders, dioceses, health care institutions, and Protestant denominations and agencies have in their various stock portfolios investments worth 35 billion dollars.[16] According to ICCR's Clearinghouse on Alternative Investments, by 1993, 250 million dollars of that huge sum was earmarked for investment in some form of community economic development. That's less than 1 percent. The rest was invested in traditional ways and places.

At the end of an all-day hearing of the National Council of Churches Urban Strategy Committee following the Los Angeles riots, I raised a question. We had talked all day, in Los Angeles, about a new commitment to the cities. But when I suggested that the churches' money should support that new commitment, you could have heard a pin drop in the room.

Afterward, several church executives told me I was treading on holy ground.

Well, that's true; money is a profoundly spiritual issue. Why did Jesus and the prophets spend so much time talking about money? "For where your treasure is, there your heart will be also," says the Gospel.[17] Notice it doesn't say, Where your heart is, there will your treasure be. No, where our hearts are will be demonstrated by where we have placed our money.

Countless projects and ideas for economic development and ecological renewal are waiting for the critical resources to make them possible. In many cases, what is needed is some initial investment capital just to get them going. Often, other money would be made available if the initial commitment were present from an investor ready to take the lead. Who better to take such a leadership role in alternative investment than the religious community and other socially motivated organizations? A whole new arena of community-based economic development is waiting to flourish. It just depends upon someone leading the way.

Decision making is still the crux of economic policy. The decisions made in the executive suites and corporate boardrooms of monopolistic capitalism have proven to be as insulated from democratic accountability as the endless five-year plans carried out by the rigidly bureaucratic commissars of state socialism. Both Wall Street and the Kremlin have functioned as elite centers of top-down control, oblivious to the real needs of ordinary people. Giant conglomerates and centralized bureaucracies both seem to be enemies of genuine citizen participation in economic decision making.

Why should the manipulators of the so-called free market or the managers of closed societies make most of the decisions that affect the quality of life for millions of people? Economics now controls politics, and some social critics rightly ask if political democracy is even possible without more economic democracy. When some participants in the political process have an enormously greater influence than other participants because of their economic power, any notion of political equality among citizens becomes cruelly theoretical.

Most of the really important choices about the way our society is run never come up for a vote. There simply are no political referenda on the economic decisions that most directly affect our way of life. Electoral politics usually concerns the details, after the big decisions already have been made in places carefully shrouded from political debate.

Why shouldn't citizens have some say beyond their consumer "vote" among very limited options? How do consumers vote for higher mileage from safer cars, healthier food, affordable health care, better public transportation, or living environments free of toxicity?

Why shouldn't workers participate in managing the companies that shape so much of their existence? And shouldn't local communities have some influence over what is done in and to their own environments?

Planning is taking place in every economy; the question is: who is doing the planning? Workers, consumers, and local communities—along with businesses—need to become primary actors in the economic planning and decision making process if democracy is to have real meaning.

Movement toward decentralization, community-based economies, ecological planning, appropriate technology, sustainable organic farming, and reasonable regional self-sufficiency is key to the future. Many projects for economic democracy, workers' control, consumer rights, community accountability, and ecological sustainability are already under way and hold great promise.

The key question is one of values. Important questions of scale, forms of technology, and patterns of ownership and decision making will need creative thought and experimentation. But the critical issue is a change in our ethics and assumptions regarding economic activity. And the key shift is the movement toward community—the idea of the common good—as the criterion by which we evaluate our economic structures and practices. Community is a sign of transformation.

A DREAM

Let's take a few moments to dream about this future. It began in the mid-1990s. And it started in a most unexpected way. . . .

The violence in the cities has escalated enormously. Politically motivated crime bills are helpless in stopping the growing carnage. The political, business, and media elites don't have a clue what to do. For that matter, church leaders are just as out of touch with and confused by the realities of life on the bottom of the society as their secular counterparts. Without a vision, the people are perishing . . . literally.

Quite unexpectedly, a new voice emerges. Members of urban street gangs in a number of cities begin truces among themselves. "We just woke up," they say. Their language sounds remarkably like biblical conversion talk. Their efforts, first quite unconnected, begin to weave a pattern of gang truces across the country. Even more surprising, these urban youths invite some church people, whose record in the streets they trust, to become partners in trying to turn things around. An antiviolence movement begins to grow.

The diagnosis of the problem goes deeper than it had before. Both the young people and their church companions know they are facing a fundamental "spiritual crisis." The violence goes deeper than the random, chaotic, and senseless destruction that paralyzes the nation with fear. The invisible violence of unjust structures, destructive social policies, and perverse values is at the heart of the problem.

These new companions go to work and others begin to join

them. The violence, they say, results from a vacuum in their inner-city communities, a vacuum both spiritual and economic. An alternative vision is necessary beyond the familiar appeals to stop the killing. The young people and the churches begin to explore how the human, moral, and economic infrastructure that is ripped out of vast urban territories can be put back together. They decide to begin at the grassroots—in the neighborhoods.

Many of their efforts are built on the foundation of local churches that are willing to take the risk and become involved. Churches open as safe spaces and sanctuaries from the violence. Pastors and "urban missionaries" hit the streets and do everything from one-on-one evangelism with drug dealers to advocating for youth in the criminal justice system.

Then the churches begin to think about the economic problem as well. Isn't that a spiritual issue too? In the vacuum left by corporations that abandoned the inner cities and shipped jobs to places like Asia and Mexico, can the churches help to rebuild the devastated urban landscape left behind?

In many places, the drug traffic is the only functioning market economy left. As in the source countries in Latin America, the drug trade supports many people. What can they all do if people stop dealing drugs? Good jobs for wages that can support families simply aren't available to most urban youth. Part-time work without benefits at fast food restaurants isn't going to solve the problem.

But other questions arise. A growing materialism is also devastating suburban congregations and communities. Shallowness, loneliness, anxiety, isolation, individualism, and a lack of community are not just the alarming characteristics of middle-class life; they are also the chief impediments to the formation of vital churches.

People dust off their Bibles. To their great amazement, they find the Bible full of such subjects as money, wealth, poverty, land, work, and economic lifestyle. Especially, they discover an overwhelming number of Scriptures about poor people and how they are to be treated. Long ignored in the churches, these economic questions are central spiritual matters in the Bible. The Scriptures offer a vision of justice, and not just for poor urban populations. They open up an ethic of transformation for everyone and in all of their communities. Small groups begin to form for Bible study, prayer, and self-examination. Before long, such reflection leads to action.

New strategies begin to emerge. In the spirit of the prophet Nehemiah, religious communities and former gang members form an unusual partnership to rebuild the broken walls of their cities. Some begin to have visions for a myriad of small-scale economic enterprises that can repopulate urban communities with new life.

At first the ideas and energy are plentiful. What is missing are the capital and the technical training to get the new projects off the ground. Big banks aren't about to lend to former gang members and poor families with no credit rating. Many young people are brimming with entrepreneurial potential, but who will take a chance on them?

Again, the churches begin to look at themselves. Some people point out that their churches have tremendous resources that are doing absolutely nothing—except keeping the churches heavily invested in the economic status quo. Much of their investment portfolios is from church pension funds, endowments, and other assets. While some efforts to raise the issues of socially responsible investment are being made, most of the churches' money is going to support companies and institutions whose purposes don't reflect the biblical values of economic and environmental justice.

Those who are studying these matters in the small groups begin to ask, Doesn't Jesus require that we just give all this money away? Others reply that at least they ought to move it around where it can do some good. Still others suggest, why not invest in the visions and directions that our churches say they support? These are quite controversial questions. For years, the churches' money has been handled almost solely on the basis of presumed sound principles of fiduciary responsibility. Applying the church's theology and spirituality to its money isn't often seriously considered. But that's just what people begin to do.

Economic practitioners who work in the area of community-based economic development begin to work with the churches. They point out, to most everyone's surprise, that the loan repayment record of many low-income people's projects is often actually better than that of more traditional loan recipients. Their experience with nonprofit loan funds and other alternative economic institutions shows that a combination of social commitment and focused technical assistance can prove to be very successful. They point to examples, like the Grameen Bank of Bangladesh, where thousands of poor families are being enabled by this poor people's bank to start economic enterprises that dramatically change the quality of their lives and their communities. National denominations, religious orders, and local churches begin a serious and fundamental reexamination of their financial life and priorities.

Soon financial and human resources from the churches become available for a whole variety of community-based projects and initiatives. Land and housing cooperatives, low-income banks and credit unions, worker and consumer cooperatives, democratically run community development corporations, and a myriad of micro-enterprise projects begin to spring up. In violence-torn urban centers a strong call for community-based economic development is included with evangelism, pastoral work, moral sex education, racial reconciliation, empowerment of women, and conflict resolution.

The social action committees and finance committees in local churches begin to meet together, some for the first time. Old polarities between "sound investment principles" and "helping poor people" begin to break down as everyone comes to understand the power and potential of community economic empowerment. Slowly at first, but then in ever more significant amounts, the churches begin a mighty transfer of their resources—from self-interested financial decisions to "the things that make for peace." Jesus wept over the city of Jerusalem and lamented how people had forgotten those things. Well, now the churches are remembering.

Catholic religious orders of women lead the way. Courageous bishops and other church leaders bring their own church bodies along. Eventually, many denominations and Christian organizations are involved. When new capital resources suddenly become available "out of nowhere," as some said, new possibilities begin to emerge.

Capital has sometimes been likened to birds on a wire. After one bird flies over to perch, others usually follow. Before long, all the birds have made the trip to the new resting place. In financial investment, what is often needed is for someone to take the initial "risk." Others can then more safely follow.

The churches provide venture capital for a whole array of new and creative economic initiatives. But for the church people being converted at the point of their money, it isn't venture capital; it is simply applying faith to finance.

With the example of the churches before them, and the substantial resources they supply, more traditional financial institutions decide it is now safe for them to become involved as well. Banks that are looking for ways to reinvest in their communities and companies that feel they ought to give something back find new opportunities to make positive contributions.

In a society that had become so dominated from the top by a small number of large corporations, a new grassroots economy is beginning to emerge. With the Cold War over, fresh discussions about the need for new economic ideas, values, and options going beyond those of either corporate capitalism or state socialism are becoming commonplace. The emergence of concrete community-based economic initiatives is making a whole new conversation possible. People are no longer leaving economics to the experts but are participating themselves in asking what kind of political economy they want for themselves, their children, and the earth.

That is how it all began. It's been growing ever since and is in full swing now. Despair is replaced with hope, drug dealing with economic rejuvenation, and violence with a new spirit of community responsibility. For the first time, many of the former gang youth think they have a future and believe they have literally been saved. And in the process, the churches realize that they are being saved too. In fighting for the young people, religious communities rediscovered the meaning and power of their own faith. In recovering the biblical call to justice, their own lives and congregations are put back in order.

There are young people in the churches again, and many say it is a dream come true.

REVERENCE

Honoring the Whole Creation

The colors burst across the horizon like a gigantic canvas of exquisite beauty. Reds, oranges, yellows, and hints of blue seem to rise out of the ocean to fill the early morning sky. Back home in the city, I seldom notice the sunrise. But here at the edge of the sea, it is a show that simply must not be missed. With the sunrise beckoning each day, I find myself going to bed a little earlier at night than usual. The late-night diet of news and political discussion has become less appealing than the feast for my senses that awaits me in the morning.

An afternoon excursion into the intercoastal waterway

yields more delights. At central Florida's Ponce Inlet, the changing tides cause sandbar islands to appear and disappear throughout the days and nights. The possibilities of wading on the tops of sandbars from island to island can give the appearance of walking on water. But the funny looking pelicans are not impressed. Along with the soaring gulls and scampering sandpipers, they have their own Sunday afternoon activities. The water feels cool and refreshing, and the horizon seems to shimmer in the warm March sun.

On the journey home we discover we are not alone, as silvery porpoises swim alongside the boat, performing effortless and graceful dives in and out of the blue-green Atlantic. Manatees hug the shoreline just out of sight, while stories of recent whale sightings out beyond the ocean channel are excitedly shared. Children romp, splash, laugh, and seem quite at home in the natural wonder.

This is a time for writing for me, but it has also become a season of rest and reflection. In walks along the beach, my urban mind and heart seem to respond differently with the waves at my side. Somehow, in the midst of our technological and media-filled times, we have lost touch with the creation that heals and renews. Religious wisdom suggests that is so because we are connected to the creation, indeed an integral part of it. We human beings are a strand in the web of life, yet we have become distant from that circle of creation, and the capacity to feel really alive often eludes us. That's what my brief sojourn at the ocean is beginning to restore. I can feel it in my body, just like the old Aboriginal grandfather told me in Australia.

Centuries-old ideas from the Enlightenment and the industrial revolution have allowed us to ravage the earth in the name of development and progress. Religious distortions of the notion of dominion provided a theological justification for exploitation. A poisoned environment now poses real threats to us all from ozone depletion, acid rain, the destruction of rain forests, the desertification of vast areas, contaminated water and food, polluted air, toxic and nuclear wastes, endangered wildlife and loss of species, global warming trends, and more.

Because we've been no kinder to the earth than to the poor, we are all paying the price; the environmentalists tell us we have fewer than forty years to turn things around before massive irreparable damage is done. Enormous threats to our natural order grow each day while the earth weeps and mourns, cries out to us for mercy, begs us to stop before it is too late, and pleads with us to restore the fragile and damaged relationships upon which all of life depends.

We are in need of a profound change in our attitudes toward the natural order. Our children may lead the way here. They seem to have a special sensitivity to the preservation of the environment. The change occurs as more people make the fundamental shift from the ethic of exploitation to the ethic of conservation, from the ethic of profit and progress to the ethic of balance and sustainability.

But huge battles still define the issue. In a declining economy, endangered species are easily pitted against endangered jobs. In circumstances of utter poverty, the survival of small farmers in the Third World competes with the survival of the rain forests. And the places where our society dumps its most toxic wastes are, disproportionately, in communities of the poor and people of color.

The major institutions of our society are being challenged to catch up to an emerging change in public consciousness. But so far, most of the biggest corporations still see real change in environmental policy as a threat to their profits. Their response is to alter advertising rhetoric and product labeling more than basic business practices. Some corporations have even decided that environmental consciousness can be exploited for profitability. Nevertheless, the pressure upon social and economic structures to make real change is bound to grow. Whether it will be in time is the crucial question.

Ultimately, an ethic of protecting the environment is not enough. Instead, we need an ethic of relationship with the environment. The movement from protection to relationship is key. Here is where the insight and spirituality of native peoples can be most instructive. From the Aboriginal people of Australia to the Indian populations of North and South America, native peoples still possess a knowledge and experience of living in harmony with the earth that are critically needed by the societies that have committed genocidal crimes against them. It is a remarkable and divine irony that the very people the dominant civilizations tried to destroy are the ones who have great lessons to teach us in this time of environmental crisis.

In 1991, the People of Color Environmental Summit was convened in Washington, D.C. The significance of the event lay in the way it began to change the perception of the environmental movement. Until then, especially in the United States and Europe, the environmental cause was perceived as a concern of affluent white people. Indeed, all of the major environmental organizations were almost entirely white in their leadership and agendas. It was thought that poor people were not very concerned about the ecological crisis.

But that wasn't true. In fact, the United Church of Christ's Racial Justice Commission had produced their groundbreaking study showing that toxic waste was being dumped and stored within communities where low-income people and racial minorities were the majority population. They displayed two now-famous maps of the United States, one with all the toxic waste sites shown in one color, and the other with areas where poor and people of color live in another color. The two maps were then superimposed, and the colors overlapped almost entirely.[18]

The fact that people on the bottom of society are the most affected by ecological destruction was seldom mentioned by the mainstream environmentalists. Environmental destruction is directly linked to issues of health, infant mortality, economic survival, and quality of life; and people of color had been working on these questions for years. The summit brought many of these activists together, and it was at that gathering that the term *environmental racism* was coined.

Also arising out of the People of Color Summit was the central concept of *environmental justice*. It is a broad term with deep and far-reaching meaning. Environmental justice means the establishing of right relationships in the whole of creation. It removes the wall between the concern for human rights on the one hand, and the natural order on the other. Environmental justice is much more inclusive and, as such, has the potential to bring together previously unconnected constituencies and concerns.

The notion of environmental justice is also rooted in the concept of shalom, an ethic of right relationship and wholeness for all of God's creatures and their natural habitat. The prophetic vision of Isaiah says it well: "They will not hurt or destroy on all my holy mountain; for the earth will be full of the knowledge of the Lord as the waters cover the sea." [19]

From now on, all of our visions must be tested by their relationship to the earth. Reverence for the whole of creation is a sign of transformation.

DIVERSITY

Beyond Integration

In response to the crying child, a volunteer at the Sojourners Neighborhood Center asked the girl what was wrong.

"I'm ugly," she responded through her tears.

"That's not true," said her friend. "You're a beautiful little child."

"No, I'm ugly," came the reply.

"Why do you say that?" asked the young woman.

"I'm ugly because I'm black," said the girl.

That's why issues of self-worth and esteem are so central in our center's children's program. In a poor and black neighborhood, we take an Afrocentric approach—one that teaches young men and women the richness and power of their heritage. The children study the great freedom fighters and learn how they can become fighters for freedom, too. On an image of Africa, a red, green, and black T-shirt proudly displays the theme of the children's summer program, "Remember your past, create your future."

These are the children of integration, having been born long after the historic civil rights legislation of the 1960s. And yet integration has not created in them a sense of freedom, dignity, or security. The concept of integration has failed these children; the theory has not lived up to expectations.

What's wrong with integration? Plenty, says a rising tide of voices, especially in the black community. Integration, the ruling national concept of race relations in the decades since the civil rights movement, has not produced what was promised. Instead of equality, integration has meant selective assimilation for middle-class blacks while the urban underclass and rural poor are simply left behind.

In the critical areas of income and employment, education, housing, and health, life for most black Americans is still separate and very unequal. Despite increased visibility in the media and popular culture, black America has not yet entered the social and economic mainstream and, most significant, does not yet genuinely share power in what is still a white society.

Not only is justice yet to be achieved through integration, but the black sense of self and community has been greatly diminished, say many critics. Indeed, what is most wrong with integration is simply this: It always has taken place and now proceeds on white terms.

Rapidly changing demographics in the United States will only serve to heighten the failures and contradictions of integration as growing populations of Latinos, Asians, and other people of color combine with African Americans to transform America's racial minorities into the new national majority. The 1990 census revealed dramatic changes in the ratio of white citizens to Americans of color.[20] In 1990 *Time* magazine ran a cover story on "America's Changing Colors" and asked, "What will the U.S. be like when whites are no longer the majority?"—a reality it predicted by the year 2056.[21]

This is a cultural and psychic shift of enormous proportion as a country established by and for white Europeans becomes a nation where most people will trace their descent from Africa, Latin America, or Asia. White America, which has yet to come to terms with its minorities, is totally unprepared for its own minority status. Yet that fundamental identity shift is inevitable and, in many parts of the country, is already occurring. In light of this seismic disruption in American history, the present concept of integration will soon be even more outmoded.

Perhaps the first question to be asked is whether integration was ever really the goal of the black freedom movement of the 1950s and '60s. Perhaps the concept of integration, as it developed in the years following the civil rights movement, can be better understood as the white society's attempt to contain, control, and reduce the potential impact of the movement.

Certainly, the motivations and aspirations of social movements and their participants are many, varied, and even often contradictory. And surely many involved in the civil rights movement were simply interested in ending legal segregation and winning the opportunity for black people to assimilate individually into the mainstream of white American society. However, as some other movement participants point out, at the heart of the black freedom struggle was a call for social transformation.

If the freedom movement was not simply aiming for integration into the dominant values and structures of the white society but rather envisioning a fundamental transformation of that social order, the revisiting of these questions is indeed a dangerous discussion. The answers to the questions depend greatly on which streams and leaders of the movement we are referring to, both then and now.

It is clear that Martin Luther King Jr., especially in his later years, and Malcolm X were both calling for radical social transformation rather than assimilation. But with the assassinations of the movement's two greatest leaders, assimilation gradually took precedence over transformation. The result has been the selective and still partial integration of the black middle class, the social and economic abandonment of the black majority, the widespread white attitude that the "racial problem" has been solved, and a country whose basic structural realities remain unchanged.

In other words, integration has proceeded under mostly white terms and control. Integration has never been a two-way street and, indeed, was never meant to be. It has always been, in every way, white directed.

One example is my own high school, which was all white when I attended it more than two decades ago. It is now more than one-third black. In a recent conversation with a teacher there, I asked how much the curriculum had changed over the years. None at all. African-American history, culture, and perspectives were still absent, and when some students formed a black student union, the white perception was that integration wasn't working.

In a March 13, 1989, *Time*[22] cover story on the black middle class, the magazine reported that "the passions and sufferings of the civil rights struggle have culminated, as they were meant to, in the mundane pleasures and pangs of middle class life." That is what *Time* magazine wants to be true. But the problem isn't just that *Time* missed the spiritual center of the freedom movement. Rather, like all the governing institutions of American life, *Time* has a powerful vested interest in defining the movement's goal as assimilation instead of transformation. The threatening possibilities of the black freedom struggle can thus be checked, domesticated, and even coopted while making Martin Luther King Jr.'s birthday a national holiday sponsored by Coca-Cola.

It must also be said that integration has allowed white liberals to feel good about "racial progress" and what they have done to "help" blacks. By not challenging the structure of white power and privilege, integration has, in different ways, served the self-interests of both white conservatives and liberals.

Vincent Harding, an active participant in the civil rights movement and now one of its best historians, believes the freedom movement is not yet over. As he shared with me once in a personal conversation:

> We didn't see the depth of what we had to do. To root out things that are centuries deep takes tremendous imagination and experimentation. We have been thinking much too superficially about what integration means. If we look seriously at our country today, we will discover that the changes we need cannot come about without great energy and sacrifice.
>
> We thought we had done our sacrificing in the sixties and wonder why it hasn't worked. But early in the process, we said we were trying "to redeem the soul of America," and you don't do that in a decade. We must not settle for elitist solutions but open our eyes and our hearts to the hurt and pain of the masses of the people.[23]

Integration begs the question—integration into what? What kind of a society prefers selective assimilation over transformation? The answer is, one that still seeks to cover over the fundamental questions of justice and compassion. Integration has served that cover-up.

The reign of insatiable materialism over human dignity in American society destroys the souls of rich and poor alike. And the acceptance of an economic system based on theft from the poor at home and around the world will continue to keep masses of people at the bottom. In a white-controlled society, a disproportionate number of those will be people of color.

When Sojourners Community moved to the inner city of Washington, D.C., in 1975, we quickly discovered that the black residents of our southern Columbia Heights neighborhood were not particularly interested in forming an integrated church. What they were interested in was working together on the issues of housing, food, education, and the crises their children face. Out of a common agenda came the sharing of faith and struggle in Bible study and prayer groups, retreats, and celebrations of thanksgiving for the work we've been given to do together. Slowly, we are learning that equality will come from partnership in a shared struggle more than through integration for its own sake.

The movement we must make is from integration to transformation. Integration of white and black elites in an unjust society leaves too many people out and the fundamental questions of justice unanswered. The spiritual heritage of the freedom movement is one of personal and social transformation, and that spirit must be reclaimed now.

White society has preferred integration to equality. The integration of paternalism and dependence must come to an end. In its place will be a multicultural partnership of equals—a partnership for the democratic transformation of the United States. Diversity is a sign of transformation.

EQUALITY

Beyond Inclusion

For gender justice to be possible, men must change.

One of the most poignant moments of the Gang Summit came in the final worship service. A young African-American man from Washington D.C., walked to the pulpit and asked all the men to sit down. Then, on behalf of black men like himself, he apologized to black women in a prayer.

"I pray that you forgive the brothers. We seek your mercy and your forgiveness for allowing our women to raise their children on welfare cheese. For having them stand in [public assistance] lines for themselves and miss doctors' appointments because we were not there.

"I ask the sisters to soften their hearts now that we have returned, and to open your door of mercy and let us in. We have returned. I ask you to forgive us for allowing you to bear our children and we were not there. I ask you to forgive us for allowing our sons to lie in the streets with that yellow tape draped around them and we were not there. We so humbly beseech you sisters to forgive us. This is your day as much as it is ours.

"We only ask you to welcome us back into your arms and your hearts and your minds. We are home, sisters. No longer will they have to say, Where is their African-American man? We are home!"

The integration of racial minorities into a white society does not change enough. Similarly, the mere inclusion of women into male-dominated structures will not suffice. Social transformation is the promise that genuine racial and cultural diversity brings to America. And likewise, the promise of gender equality and partnership is the vision we must seek in order to really change the relationship between men and women.

When women simply adopt the patterns of a male-driven society we all become further impoverished. Let me be clear here. Just as there is nothing wrong with being white, there is nothing wrong with being male. It is the patterns of domination which are the problem. Those patterns not only oppress people of color and women, but they trap whites and men in structures and behaviors that diminish their own humanity and block their fullest self-expression.

Women's movements have succeeded in opening up more space for the inclusion of women in almost every area of society. That inclusion offers a profound opportunity for change, *if* we refuse to settle for mere inclusion. Inclusion must become the opportunity for transformation. Genuine equality between men and women will only be made possible by making fundamental changes in the ways we think about gender, in the ways we evoke the gifts and participation of all people in our social institutions, in the ways we make decisions in which more people can take part, in the ways we structure family life and the raising of children, in the ways we connect the personal and the public spheres.

Probably the greatest difference between a new generation of men and their fathers is the extent of their participation in the raising of their children. At places like *Sojourners* magazine, men on the staff have given fundamental priority to their roles as fathers. The institutional patterns of flex-time are built into the work schedules of both men and women to accommodate the commitment to shared parenting. Because of that, life will be very different for their children than it was for them. Both sons and daughters are presented with alternative models for the roles of mother and father which create, for the next generation, a whole new set of assumptions.

Work and vocation are still very important to the men and women of Sojourners, but a different balance is struck between the commitments to the workplace and the homefront. Indeed, the definition of vocation itself is expanded for men to include their roles as fathers—just as mothering has historically been central to most women's sense of vocation. Such a balance is not easy to achieve in the workplace or the home. Tensions, tradeoffs, and compromises become a regular part of life. But most of the young couples engaged in the experiment testify that the rewards and fulfillments are worth the price.

The changes are perhaps most challenging to the men, most of whom were raised with a very different and traditional set of expectations. The journey toward equality involves a process of male relinquishment of those former assumptions and expectations. To value the vocation of women as equal to that of men and to assume the shared responsibilities of nurturing and caring for children is a revolutionary change in a patriarchal society. And it does not come easily.

Equality in the workplace and the public arena will also require a revolution in our attitudes and assumptions. It means asking the question, *continually,* of whether the voice and perspective of women is being heard. And more than just being heard, are the experience and gifts of women helping to shape the decisions and outcomes of our work together? Being equal partners in social projects will inevitably alter the nature and results of those projects.

Many have pointed out that language is power. To change exclusively male language to more inclusive language is not a peripheral and merely "symbolic" matter, as some critics have suggested. Language is central to any culture and to the ways we define ourselves. When "generic male" language is allowed to speak for all of us it defines a society by male definitions. The implications of that definition are far-reaching. Little girls learn at an early age that they are not really included. As they "adjust" to a generically male society, their sense of self is successively diminished.

Inclusive language is freeing for everyone. It opens up new possibilities and self-definitions for both men and women.

When it is "women, mothers, daughters, sisters, she, her" *and* "men, fathers, sons, brothers, he, and him" everyone is re-enfranchised and no one suffers the burden of either being left out or carrying the "generic burden" of the entire society.

At the Gang Summit, a young man stood up to say, "We've got to stop saying 'brothers' all the time; we've got to start saying 'brothers and sisters.' " And an older gang leader replied, "Strong men are not afraid of strong women."

These issues are especially controversial in the religious community. Here male definitions of God, faith, and patriarchal authority have long kept women in a subordinate role. At the same time, the essential cores of those same religious traditions have provided liberating affirmation and energy for women's movements toward equality and justice. At many places like Sojourners Community, the use of inclusive language in worship, the pastoral and liturgical leadership of women, and the efforts to re-imagine God in more inclusive and biblical ways are helping to create the space where women can feel affirmed and safe in the religious community.

Gender equality is essential to political transformation. Women bring the voice and perspective from the outside, which is so necessary to change. That's why when women simply join men as "insiders," their creative potential is lost. Women also tend to bring a heightened sensitivity to the priority of children, which many men often ignore and which is so critical to the political process. The deeper connection many women feel to creation often results in a keener awareness of environmental survival. In many arenas, women have often been the ones to take the leadership in conflict resolution and to look for alternatives to violence and war. As those who have learned the lessons of giving birth in so many ways, women are often the political actors that become the midwives of new social possibilities.

Gender equality in the political arena will increase the influence of such qualities in the public square. This is not because such values are unique to women, but because they have been marginalized by a narrowly defined notion of male politics from which many men are also eager to be freed. A wider, deeper, broader, more human, and more inclusive style of politics is what we now need. And the presence of women in the public square will enable both women and men to practice that new kind of politics. Equality is a sign of transformation.

PEACEMAKING

The Path to Real Security

I'll never forget an experience one freezing night in the foothills of the Rocky Mountains that forever changed my understanding of peacemaking. It was the early spring of 1978, and I was part of a group of religious and other peace activists who sought to block the plutonium-laden trains entering the Rocky Flats Nuclear Weapons Facility outside Denver, Colorado. Rocky Flats was the place where all the triggers were made for every nuclear warhead produced in the United States. About 140 of us sat down on the railroad tracks on a Saturday afternoon, not knowing when the next train was scheduled to arrive.

But another worry was soon upon us. No more than ten minutes after we walked onto the tracks, a mountain storm began to set in. It started to rain hard; the temperature plummeted and the rain soon became freezing rain, sleet, and finally a driving snow. Soaked to the bone, we were quickly chilled through. Doctors arrived and warned all the protesters to go home because of the real danger of hypothermia.

Some of us decided to stay. I settled in under wet blankets for what would be the coldest night of my life. During that long and restless night, my mind was filled with images of soldiers who had for centuries braved the elements, endured hardship, risked injury and death, and, indeed, given up their lives in order to wage war. Then it dawned on me. Why should we expect the cost of peace to be less? What would happen if we were to "wage peace" with the discipline, sacrifice, and even willingness to suffer that so many have accepted to wage war? Peace, I realized that night, would not be achieved simply because it is a better idea than war, but only when a sufficient number of people pursue it with the same commitment and determination.

Jesuit priest and peacemaker Daniel Berrigan writes:

> Because we want peace with half a heart and half a life and will, the war, of course, continues because the waging of war, by its nature, is total—but the waging of peace, by our own cowardice, is partial. So a whole will and a whole heart and a whole national life bent toward war prevail over the [mere desire for] peace.[24]

War is not merely an activity; it is a system. It is a system supported by economic and political assumptions and by structures that drive us toward competition and conflict, which is then resolved by chosen methods of violence. It is those assumptions and institutions that we must begin to question. The methods of resolving our persistent conflicts must be replaced with practices that are more effective in providing real security and are less dangerous to ourselves and the earth.

Most of our religious traditions suggest the contradictory nature of the human condition, expressed in our propensities toward selfishness and great evil, as well as our potential for wonderfully creative good. Any serious idea of peacemaking must be based upon a realistic assessment of our human condition and not be predicated on illusive notions of human perfectibility. In other words, human beings will inevitably become engaged in conflicts—in their relationships and families, between groups, and among nations. Human conflict will not be ended; to assume that it can be is both morally naive and politically irresponsible. It is our ways of handling human conflict that must be reexamined.

While human conflict is inevitable, war is not. War is one system for resolving human conflict. With the sophistication and destructiveness of modern weaponry, that system is becoming increasingly obsolete. Its cost and consequence are simply too high—for its many victims, for its financial burden, for the planet, and for the dangerous escalation of violence that the scope and power of today's modern weapons make possible. The most decorated soldier in the Vietnam War, Marine Colonel David Hackworth, now says,

> War machines . . . have gotten so horrendous in terms of the destructive capability; weapons of war have become geometrically so horrendous and so destructive that there are no winners. Then you look at the cost of one cruise missile—and we used hundreds of them in the Gulf—a million bucks; the cost of one bomber, a B-2, a billion dollars. We can't afford the toys of war.[25]

Modern warfare has made us not more secure, but less.

Just as many people once believed that it was naive and impractical to think that we could live without slavery, most today cannot imagine how we could live without war. Creating that imagination is the essential job of peacemaking.

We must stop thinking of war in terms of victory and defeat; rather, war is always a sign of failure—failure of the warring parties to resolve their conflicts in some more peaceful, effective, less costly, and less violent way. War should be a cause, never for celebration, but rather for grief and repentance. All the wars fought to "end all wars" have just led to new ones. Gandhi said, "I object to violence, because, when it appears to do good, the good is only temporary; the evil it does is permanent."[26] The only thing that has changed about war is the weapons, which have become ever more lethal and destructive.

We must begin to believe that there is a better way. First of all, nonviolent resolution of conflict has worked in a great variety of situations. Gandhi and King are but the best-known practitioners of nonviolent movements that have obtained freedom, secured justice, defended others, and made peace without recourse to violence. Similarly, whole groups of people and even nations have lived their lives and sustained their security for long periods of time by neither making war nor seeking war's protection.

The truth is that most nations, most of the time, resolve their conflicts with other nations by means of diplomacy, negotiation, the imposition of various forms of economic and political sanctions, mutual security agreements, and the mediation of international bodies. These methods usually work. Peacemaking is a strategy to expand the scope and number of conflicts that can be resolved without war.

War is the decision to reject these peaceful means in favor of violent means to achieve a desired victory; it is the imposition of the concepts of victory and defeat in a situation of conflict. War is the decision to go for victory instead of resolution. Peacemaking is an attempt to resolve the sources of the conflict and restore a situation to justice or balance, thereby eliminating the need for victory and defeat.

In 1992, a cease-fire was implemented in El Salvador after ten years of bloody civil war. What finally changed to make a peaceful resolution possible was not the circumstances that led to conflict; they remained the same. What changed was the realization of both sides that war would never lead to victory. A peaceful agreement was made to seek to resolve the issues at stake through a new political process in the country. The former U.S. ambassador to El Salvador, Robert White, observed that the same political agreement could have been entered into at any time during the previous ten years.[27] But all the parties involved (including the United States) were unwilling to give up the prospect of total victory. In the meantime an estimated 75,000 lives were lost.

While the grievances of the two sides in a conflict may not be balanced, they will most often have some basis, either real or perceived, in the shared history of the parties. Even if those grievances are being used and manipulated to justify selfish violence (as in the case of Iraq's Saddam Hussein), they still must be dealt with if the violent behavior is to be exposed and resolved. The wisdom of Jesus' saying is relevant here: "Why do you see the speck in your neighbor's eye, but do not notice the log in your own? First take the log out of your own eye." [28] Some recognition of the perceived grievances of your adversary and an admission of your own part in the conflict are generally necessary for resolving personal and family relationships. Why should it be any different in confrontations between nations?

Another Gospel saying is pertinent: "Love your enemies, do good to those who hate you, bless those who curse you, and pray for those who abuse you." [29] This statement may be the most admired and most ignored teaching of Jesus. But rather than being naive and impractical advice, this is the insight at the heart of effective peacemaking.

What is being suggested here is not idealistic sentiment but practical wisdom. Jesus says we should love our neighbors, including our enemies, "as yourself." [30] In other words, our enemy's security and well-being must become as important as our own. Here lies the key to peacemaking. If we seek our security and peace at the expense of someone else's, it can only fuel the cycle of retribution. By investing our security in more weapons to protect ourselves, we merely further the cycle and generate endless arms races, knowing our adversary will do the same. And then our security will be further threatened. This was the insanity of the nuclear arms race and the superpowers' deterrence policy of massive retaliation, which was officially named mutually assured destruction (MAD).

Only by guaranteeing the security of our enemies can we guarantee our own security. By making their prosperity and peace a priority, we make ours a possibility. Caring for the well-being of our enemies—loving our enemies—is the only thing that can break the cycle of violence and ultimately protect our own well-being. Ironically, our security ultimately depends less on our superior weaponry than it does upon the security of our potential adversaries.

Peacemaking can resolve conflicts. However, it cannot establish empires, maintain political hegemony, gain unfair control of land and resources, seek advantage over others, and sustain unjust systems of economic production and distribution. War does those things best. Indeed, they require war, and that's why it has been so popular with the world's superpowers. To overcome war, therefore, we must attack the unjust systems that are dependent on military force and lead inexorably to aggression. Peacemaking is much more than resolving conflicts; it is the commitment to overcome the injustice that creates conflicts.

Therefore, peacemaking certainly is not passive. It requires action, courage, commitment, and sacrifice. It asks us to persevere in energy and creativity until we can resolve our conflicts. It invites us to search ourselves as well as our enemies for the sources of our confrontations. It means regarding our enemy's well-being as highly as we regard our own. It demands the pursuit of justice as the prerequisite to peace. Only such a definition of peacemaking could demonstrate a "moral equivalent" to war and have some hope of overcoming it.

In confronting the kind of naked aggression and inhuman brutality we face in Bosnia, for example, any nonviolent response must find that moral equivalent to war, with commensurate courage, risk taking, and sacrifice. Most pacifists aren't ready for that; pacifists are still mostly known for what they won't do rather than for what they will do for the sake of justice, freedom, and peace.

Perhaps it is time to explore the meaning of a nonviolent army, of which Gandhi dreamed. Trained and disciplined but unarmed people could be deployed in sufficient numbers to make a strategic difference in many situations of both domestic and international conflict—but only if they were prepared to make sacrifices and suffer casualties just as soldiers are. It is a profound challenge, but only the strength of such an alternative has any hope of replacing the system of war. In a world of dangerously escalating violence, peacemaking is a sign of transformation.

JUSTICE
The Hunger That Heals

It was Sunday night and the Sojourners Community had gathered together for our weekly worship. Our preacher was Nathan Jernigan, a young African-American man who codirects the Sojourners Neighborhood Center. His text was from the beatitudes, "Blessed are those who hunger and thirst for righteousness, for they will be filled." [31] We had been doing a series on these foundational sayings of Jesus, taking one each week and asking someone who had a particular interest or experience with that beatitude to help us all understand what it might mean for us today. When I asked Nathan which one he was drawn to, he immediately leaped on this beatitude.

In the Bible, *righteousness* is often synonymous with *justice*, and the two words are sometimes used interchangeably. Over the years, Sojourners Community has heard many sermons on justice and righteousness, but, nevertheless, I could feel the hunger growing again within me as Nathan began. As I listened to this young man preach, I realized that he was making his listeners hungrier and thirstier as he spoke. Why?

Because he was so passionate, so hungry and thirsty himself.

The prophetic tradition insists that religion that does not manifest itself in action for justice is false religion. The Hebrew prophets boldly proclaimed that God rejected the worship and prayers that ignored social injustice. Jesus asked, "Why do you call me Lord, Lord, and do not what I say?" And the New Testament epistles claimed that "So faith by itself, if it has no works, is dead." [32]

Nathan Jernigan directs the children's program at the neighborhood center. What this Howard Divinity School graduate student sees every day in our neighborhood and center makes him hunger and thirst for justice and righteousness. It is a holy demand for action. And that action is rooted in the hunger for justice.

Trying to oversee a children's learning center in a neighborhood in which a majority of the young people never finish high school makes him hungry for change. When that program consistently turns things around for neighborhood kids and enables every one of them (so far) to progress to their next grade—but then struggles to find the funds to continue, Nathan gets very thirsty for that river of resources that would make righteousness more possible.

When Nathan, Elaine McLean, and other center staff and volunteers reach out to young mothers in a neighborhood with a higher infant mortality rate than that of Jamaica,[33] they get hungry to see healthy babies. When they run a summer program on conflict resolution for sixty children, all of whom have lost brothers, sisters, other relatives, or friends to street violence, they become thirsty for an end to the senseless carnage.

Nathan hungrily searches for words to convince kids to stay off drugs and out of their lucrative and lethal traffic, while black youth unemployment is higher than 60 percent, the only jobs available are part-time positions at McDonald's, and the ever-present, all-consuming message of their society is that material things are the measure of life. When he sees the obvious hunger of hundreds of families who wait in line at the center for food, just blocks from the White House, Nathan feels starved for economic justice and social righteousness. When he sees his young black brothers wasting away in prison or on the streets and his peers become an endangered human species, the hunger makes his heart ache.

Perhaps that's why this particular beatitude spoke to Nathan. He is hungry and thirsty and longs to be satisfied. Are we? I don't mean are we *for* righteousness and justice. We know we're for it. But are we really *hungry* and *thirsty* for it? And does our hunger lead us to action?

When we are hungry, we become increasingly concentrated on relieving our hunger. When we are thirsty, we become more and more diligent to quench the thirst. When we are hungry and thirsty, the desire to satisfy our need seems to grow and grow. We are not easily distracted or drawn away by other things. We get single-minded, focused, and persistent. Are we hungry and thirsty enough to act for righteousness and justice? Or are we continually pulled away by other cares and concerns?

The movement from social concern to a hunger for justice has both spiritual and political significance. Our concern for the poor does little to bridge the enormous distance between us. Indeed, it creates the patronizing dynamics of some people "doing for" others, a pattern that can become destructive to everyone. But to become genuinely hungry for justice makes it more possible to join with the poor and oppressed in a common struggle. It is our own hunger, not somebody else's problem, that begins to drive us to action. Together we long for the day when we shall all find satisfaction. When hungry people learn to share the bread of hope together, a new kind of community becomes possible and the first fruits of justice can begin to be enjoyed.

The day when a substantial number of middle-class Americans have moved from social concern to a hunger for what is right will be the day when justice becomes more possible in this country. As long as the poor are marginalized in their isolation and the concerned people are paralyzed in their guilt, no real action is possible. It is the hunger and thirst for justice, of which the beatitude speaks, that could bring us together and transform the political landscape. In the process, we might all find the healing and wholeness that have eluded us, the equality and mutuality that real human cooperation requires, and the dependence on God that could set our hearts free. Maybe that's what Jesus was talking about. Justice is a sign of transformation.

CONTEMPLATION
The Inward Journey

During the Gulf War, I undertook a Lenten fast, from Ash Wednesday to Easter Sunday morning. It was, for me, the interior battlefield of the war. I undertook the fast after I had done everything in my power to prevent the outbreak of war. Courageous voices for peace had done everything they could think of to do, and the efforts were not enough. We watched war fever overtake the country, and there was nothing we could do or say, no sacrifice we could make, no strategy we could create that would stop it. I knew it could plunge the nation and the peace movement into a spiritual crisis.

I had never fasted extensively before, never more than a few days at a time. But something compelled me to go deeper than I had ever gone, to find, through fasting and prayer, the places within me that still fueled the momentum of war. Contemplation may be the most difficult thing for activists, yet it may be the most important thing. Action without reflection can easily become barren and even bitter. Without the space for self-examination and the capacity for rejuvenation, the danger of exhaustion and despair is too great. At an even deeper level, contemplation confronts us with the questions of our identity and power. Who are we? To whom do we belong? Is there a power that is greater than ours? How can we know it? Contemplation can be a frightening thing.

Forty-seven days on just water and juice brought on many changes in me. When the ground war began and ended so quickly and national euphoria ensued, I witnessed the public vindication of everything I had long and deeply opposed. Yet I experienced, inexplicably, a strange peacefulness in my spirit. Many friends around me were in the throes of despair, to which I too am easily susceptible. But this time I felt a calm centeredness, and as the weeks went by I began to understand why. Gradually it became clear to me that the fast had begun to bring about a kind of rest and belief and even trust in the power beyond myself in the midst of my own powerlessness. That is certainly not characteristic for me; I organize and speak and act and sometimes despair over how little difference is made.

Where my hope really lies became the question. Is it in the power of the world to save itself, to reform itself, and even to transform itself? Is it in our power to affect, influence, and change the world? Or is it in the spiritual power to bring healing and justice to our lives and to this earth? To just hope in the results of our work and strategies is to hope in ourselves and finally to hope in the power of this world. How do we find hope in the power beyond ourselves that empowers us to be and do far more than we can ever be or do on our own? That's a question for contemplation.

I recall often what my friends in the street gangs call "spiritual power." These young people have learned that they can't turn their lives and communities around by themselves. They're also learning to stop in the middle of hard struggles or discussions to be quiet, to sing, to pause, and to pray. In my own tradition, it's called trusting in the power of God. Whether one is religious or not, the time and space taken to reflect on the real spiritual power beyond us or within us, or both, is critically important. It's a way of finding our centers and regaining our bearings. And when we are facing the sometimes overwhelming odds against the social change we seek, such spiritual discipline is absolutely essential.

Walter Brueggemann says about the prophet Isaiah's time and ours, "The key question is whether the promissory possibilities of God have a chance in the face of the entrenched geo-political realities."[34] The book of Isaiah expresses profound confidence that God's promises will prevail—against, within, despite, and through geopolitical realities. I believe that only such a conviction can energize and sustain the long journey toward justice and peace. For without such a passion and confidence, we will sooner or later succumb either to realpolitik or to despair.

Contemplation helps us to find that knowledge, to know that truth, and to experience that trust. Time apart for silence and whatever forms of prayer or meditation are meaningful to us helps to root our political hope in spiritual realities more than in socioeconomic realities.

The mystics often say that contemplation is putting ourselves in the presence of God and resting there. Quiet reflection, they say, brings a heightened mindfulness of love and grace in our dailiness and a renewed perspective on the purposes and promises of God in the world. And, as history has often shown, the most dangerous threats to any unjust social order are those who believe in the promises of God.

For more than a decade, Sojourners Community has made an annual retreat together. It is always a long-anticipated event. The children especially enjoy it, and there is no other occasion during the year when we have so much uninterrupted leisure time just to spend with one another.

Several times we have been led by Gordon Cosby, pastor of the Church of the Saviour in Washington, D.C., and a sort of spiritual director to our community. The spiritual trademark of the Church of the Saviour is the combining of the inward journey and the outward journey.

With wisdom and grace, Gordon has helped us to navigate through the many pressures and temptations of community and has led us into silence to search, each of us, for the still point where God breaks through. For most of us, the silence is as unaccustomed as the quiet but arresting beauty of the Maryland fields and hills where we retreat. The deprivations of natural beauty, space, silence, and solitude that come as a consequence of a call to the inner city take more of a toll on us than we realize. Long periods of silent wandering over the pastoral landscape are as refreshing as the cool fall air itself.

We have come back to this particular place for several years—a former plantation turned into a school and eventually converted to an Episcopal retreat center. When I start walking in the morning through the fields and out toward the old barn, I'm headed to a place I know well.

It's a slave cemetery from the old plantation days. There are no markers or memorials here, nor are there any gravestones. This was a common burial ground, bordered all around by a waist-high stone wall, which is now crumbling in many places. A grove of trees surrounds the sacred resting place. Inside the rectangular wall sits an old bench, and it is there that I usually come to rest. I often just sit for a while with these children of God who knew so much sorrow and pain and yet were brought closer to their Creator than most of us ever get.

They waited all their lives for deliverance and it never came. But in their waiting and hoping, they discovered a presence and a power never understood by their oppressors. How is it that out of the experience of such violent suffering came the most powerful spirituality this country has ever produced? The spirituals, preaching, gospel music, prayer, and social transformation that have flowed from that mighty river of human pain have shown the redemptive truth of the gospel more clearly than almost five hundred years of white Christianity in North America. I need to rest here among the slaves—to listen with them, talk with them, and pray with them. Theirs is the only faith that touches the depths of my own heart and soul. Nothing else reaches down quite far enough.

The slaves knew powerlessness, and out of it they found the power beyond themselves. For me, that is the deepest struggle. It's far easier for me to embrace the suffering than to accept the powerlessness—the great scandal of faith. This is what's called the paschal mystery of the Christian faith; death leads to life, dying to rising. It's the complete giving that unlocks the power. Never achievement or success—certainly not for Jesus—but rather the giving of ourselves in faith leads to life. In that powerlessness lies the real spiritual power.

Contemplation calls us to such a fundamental change. Nothing less than a shift of our whole modus operandi is required. Our very foundations are uprooted so that we might be planted in deeper ground.

Through contemplation, we realize that our own power proves inadequate, and we learn to trust a power that is beyond ourselves. We are shaken from our natural talents to accept our spiritual gifts. Our slow movement is from achievement to self-giving, from filling up to emptying out, from being the center to becoming a channel. Only then will we finally relax and act out of gratitude more than obligation, grace instead of law, hope rather than expectation.

But contemplation is more than relaxing; it's letting go. Our drivenness must give way to peacefulness and our anxiety to joy. So concerned with effectiveness, we learn instead to be content with faithfulness. Strategy grows into trust, success into obedience, planning into prayer. Our lives become measured more by our fidelity and integrity than by our accomplishments. The consequence of our former path is dissipation, the end of our new course is re-creation.

What the slaves have left us is the fruit of redemptive suffering and the ultimate power of powerlessness. Their legacy has outlasted every other memory and achievement. Through their faith, ours may still be saved. On a quiet fall day in the Maryland farmlands, their voices can still be heard, their courage still felt; their wisdom still teaches, their lives still heal ours. Contemplation is a sign of transformation.

COURAGE

Taking the First Step

There is a wonderful story in the third and fourth chapters of Exodus, from the Hebrew Scriptures, about how Moses gets his calling. It's an extraordinary dialogue, an argument really, between Moses and God.

The story begins with God announcing to Moses, "The cry of the Israelites has now come to me; I have also seen how the Egyptians oppress them. So come, I will send you to Pharaoh to bring my people, the Israelites, out of Egypt."

But Moses says, "Who am I that I should go to Pharaoh?" At the moment of his great call, Moses responds with, "Who, me? Not me, Lord. There must be some mistake. You must mean someone else. I can't do it. I'm not ready." That's the gist of Moses' protest and the beginning of the reluctance that follows.

God says to Moses, "But I will be with you." Yet Moses continues to argue, "But they won't believe me. They won't believe you sent me. I won't know what to say." So God tells Moses what he should say. Then God shows Moses great signs and promises to perform the same wonders before Pharaoh if need be. And they are impressive signs indeed. God promises to "smite the Egyptians" if they refuse Moses' demand for the freedom of the slaves.

Moses still isn't convinced: "O my Lord, I have never been eloquent. . . . I am slow of speech and slow of tongue." He claims not to be a good speaker. I've always suspected that Moses was a stutterer and therefore was nervous about such an important public speaking assignment (an issue with which I am familiar). God is getting exasperated and says, "Who has made a person's mouth. . . . Is it not I? I will be your mouth and teach you what you shall speak." But even though God has promised to be with him and show him what to say, Moses finally replies, "Oh, my Lord, send, I pray, some other person."

The text then reads, "The anger of the Lord was kindled against Moses." By now, God is quite frustrated. Finally, God tells Moses that his brother Aaron will be sent along to help ("I will be with your mouth and with his mouth"). God is clear about Moses going to Egypt. This is not a very auspicious beginning for, arguably, the greatest liberation story in history.

Though Moses never did quite agree to go, he went, albeit reluctantly. He went to Pharaoh and spoke the word of God, "Let my people go!" We know the rest of the story—a story taken by oppressed people down through history as their story. Generations of people have taken courage, found strength, and discovered hope for their own liberation through the exodus of the Hebrews from their captivity. The cry of Moses to "let my people go" has become the battle cry for those of every age in bondage.[35]

But this is Moses' story, too. And it is our own story. It is the story of all who didn't feel ready to do what they were called to do, who felt reluctant about the task before them— all those who have been afraid to do what they knew was right. Moses' excuses are so much like our own. Moses didn't feel ready. Moses didn't feel like Moses, the great liberator.

And it's certain that Moses didn't feel like Charlton Heston, who played his role in the famous Cecil B. De Mille movie *The Ten Commandments!* Heston always seems to be ready.

In December of 1955, a black seamstress named Rosa Parks refused to give up her seat to a white man on a bus in Montgomery, Alabama. She sparked a bus boycott that led to a social revolution, but she didn't feel ready. The young twenty-six-year-old minister named Martin Luther King Jr. became the leader of the boycott, partly because he was the newest minister in town and hadn't made many enemies yet. He led a movement that shook the nation and the world, but he didn't feel ready either. At his kitchen table in the middle of the night he cried out to God for fear of the death threats against his family.

Young college students sat in at lunch counters in North Carolina and made freedom rides across angry state lines, mothers registered voters in Mississippi, and young children marched to turn the tide in Birmingham. None of them felt ready either, and they all felt afraid. Inspired by their example, Desmond Tutu marched in Cape Town many years later with other church leaders to the citadel of white South African power and kneeled to pray for freedom. He was arrested in front of the eyes of the world. Later he told me, "If you were close, you could have heard my knees knocking together. I had butterflies in my tummy."

They were all afraid, as were all the others who have stood up for justice, witnessed for peace, or given their lives for freedom. But each one had heard a call, a voice that said, "There's a job for you to do." Let the Pharaohs of our day be warned: New calls are being heard in our day, and they are calls to a new vision for this world. New visions are made possible when people in all circumstances respond to the call.

Most of us probably already know what it is we need to do, but we feel inadequate and overwhelmed by our weakness and fear. We don't feel ready. It's all right, we don't have to be. God is calling out afresh, crying out to those who know they are her children, saying, "I've got a job for you to do." All we are ever asked to do is take the first step.

A song that many of those who haven't felt ready have often sung together is the great freedom anthem "We Shall Overcome." Originally an old hymn in the church, it later became a labor song and, finally, the theme of the American civil rights movement. Now it is sung all over the world. The lyrics to the version we sing today were put together at the famous Highlander Center in the hills of Tennessee, where many a labor organizer and civil rights worker got her or his training.

One story about those lyrics says that a black youth choir was on retreat one weekend at Highlander. They were just finishing an evening in the chapel, where they had all been singing together. Suddenly, the chapel was surrounded by members of the White Citizens' Council, carrying torches and brandishing shotguns. They ordered the young people to come outside, but the youths wouldn't move. The intruders became louder and more insistent. Someone turned off the lights and plunged the chapel into darkness as tension and the threat of violence filled the night air.

Then from a corner of the chapel, a quiet voice began to sing. The tune was familiar, but the words were new. The words sung out were, "We are not afraid, we are not afraid, we are not afraid today. Oh deep in my heart, I do believe that we shall overcome someday." Before long, the one voice became many voices, all singing together "We are not afraid" over and over again. The angry voices of the white vigilantes were drowned out; they left in frustration and defeat. A new verse to an old song had just been written.

We sing because we are afraid, and our singing makes us strong. We are not asked never to be afraid, but we are invited to keep on singing. Courage is a sign of transformation.

———

RESPONSIBILITY
How Change Begins

I met young Alan Storey in Australia. As a white South African, Alan had been called up for the military draft. All white South African men were drafted to serve in the black townships to exercise the minority regime's violent control over the majority population. The South African military was the enforcer of the brutal system of apartheid, and at the same time it became an invaluable tool for socializing the country's young white males. Alan and his family opposed apartheid, and he did not want to enter the military. Knowing he would be drafted if he stayed, Alan left South Africa to travel for a while and figure out his options. The penalty for refusing military service in South Africa was six years in prison.

When we met, Alan was full of questions. Was civil disobedience the moral response? What does the Christian faith say about this? What is nonviolence? How does one deal with the personal consequences? How can we change the system? What should he read? We talked for many hours, and I suggested some resources for further study and reflection.

A year later I returned to Australia for a national youth conference. Alan was the first to greet me. He had read everything and was ready to resist the draft. But after the first evening session, the young man became gripped with fear over his momentous decision. Six years in a South African prison is a very long time. And after his release, it was likely he would be called up again.

Throughout the week, we had many more conversations. Sometimes no words would suffice, and I held this young man in my arms through his tears and fears, as he wrestled with the demands of conscience at a tender age. On the last night, I called for the young men and women to make a commitment to the gospel path we had been visioning together. Alan Storey was the first to come down the stadium aisle to stand in front of the stage. With quiet but strong conviction, he decided to return to South Africa and tell his government that he would not serve in their military.

Alan went home. Every day his resolve deepened, and when his time came he made his decision clear. That act of moral obedience and civil disobedience made an impact around the country and linked Alan with so many other black and white young people who had decided to risk their lives for the sake of a new South African future. Eventually, with mounting pressures for political change, the government decided not to prosecute Alan or any other young men who refused to serve. Alan had been ready to go to jail, but now he could pursue his calling to be a Methodist pastor. It's a good way to begin a vocation in the church. The decision had been agonizing but it was an act of personal responsibility that influenced politics.

The room was bathed in soft light as spirituals quietly played in the background. More than a hundred people came to see the one many called a good friend and to say their last good-byes. It was the first wake we'd ever had at the Sojourners Neighborhood Center. The next morning, the funeral was held here too. It was the appropriate place—the place where James Starks had come almost every day for many years. It was where he had become part of a family and found a home.

About ten years ago, James was sitting out on the stoop one Sunday morning when someone invited him to come to church at Sojourners Community. After a few more weeks of invitations, he came—and he stayed. Before long, James became involved in the food program and soon was one of its most tireless workers.

Many stories were told at James's funeral. We cried and we laughed and decided that James would have been glad that we did both. Mostly we were very grateful, even in our sadness, for the life of one who had touched each of ours.

On most days, James would go out to pick up food wherever we could get it. Someone said, "Whenever you saw the van, you saw James." Another co-worker told of a pickup at the food bank one winter day in an absolute blizzard that dissuaded everyone but James. He made it all the way there and back and didn't stop until the van came to an abrupt halt in a snowbank in the center's driveway. The next day three hundred families had food to take home.

But James's favorite thing was to take the food back out to people who needed it most. He was known to make up to thirteen deliveries in a single day, mostly to senior citizens who could no longer get out. He brought food, but also his famous smile and the comfort of good company. He so loved to visit people and stay to talk that one co-worker testified at his funeral, "I had to go with him just to make sure he didn't stay all day!" When there wasn't food to pick up or deliver, James would do whatever else needed to be done around the center. He was the ultimate volunteer.

Once when I came home from a trip, I was surprised to see that the front porch of my house had been painted. Puzzled by the sparkling porch, I asked around to see what had happened. The next day, a smiling James Starks came by to ask if I liked the color. "Why did you do that?" I asked. "Well," replied James, trying not to embarrass me, "it needed it."

James had become an alcoholic when he was only eight years old. At fifty-three, his body was much older than his years, and finally it just gave out on him. Coming to church and finding the center had given him a new start, though the up-and-down battle with alcohol would continue through the years. When getting straight and receiving successful surgery saved his one good eye, James decided to celebrate by taking all his friends out to dinner at a Mongolian barbecue. It must have cost a small fortune for someone on a meager disability income, but he insisted on treating "my friends who helped get me through." He was like a kid again and claimed he could see so well now that he was going to go out to his boyhood Virginia and "shoot me a squirrel." What we could see was the generosity that was so characteristic and abundant in this man who had become such an important part of our little community.

Week after week, James would never miss church. I think his favorite part was the passing of the peace. James loved to hug. I think the image of James that will remain for me is the picture of him coming toward me with his arms outstretched, ready for a hug. Sometimes he would hold on so tight I thought he might never let go.

It was hard for us to let him go as we together shared the memory of his life among us. The funeral brought together James's family and friends. More than one person from James's much earlier days commented that they didn't know he had this "other life" with Sojourners. They were all moved by how much James was loved and how many lives he had touched. One relative said, "His life had a purpose," and reflected that she would like to begin doing similar work to give her own life more meaning. Even in death, James was bringing people together.

We buried James at the cemetery, and at the end of the morning someone said, "I'm sure this day made James very happy—he's probably smiling now." We'll always remember that smile and be forever thankful for the blessing of James's life. I will miss James; he was my friend. I know that James is happy now and finally at rest in the hug of the arms of his loving God.

It's never too late to take responsibility for your life and turn things around. That's what James Starks learned and taught. Our little food program and thousands of projects just like it around the country depend on people like James Starks. They make all the difference. From the top to the bottom of the society, things begin to change only when people take responsibility.

To be the Catholic bishop in Amarillo, Texas, is not a very prestigious thing. After all, the First Baptist Church, Amarillo, has more members than the whole Catholic diocese. A good and decent man, Leroy Matthiesen had been a high school football coach before being a bishop.

One day Bishop Matthiesen got a phone call requesting a pastoral visit. A young priest from outside the diocese had done an unusual thing. In the middle of the night, the young man had climbed over the fence at the Department of Energy's Pantex plant and walked into the high security facility carrying only a lighted candle. He said it represented the "light of Christ." His solitary candlelight vigil to halt the nuclear arms race abruptly ended when he was discovered by startled security officers, who arrested him and put him in jail. The caller thought the priest-intruder was probably a little crazy, but he was a priest, and a visit from the local bishop seemed appropriate.

The Pantex plant was the final assembly point for all nuclear weapons in the United States. Leroy Matthiesen realized he had driven past the nuclear bomb factory many times and had never thought anything about it. After some procrastination, the bishop visited the priest. The young man wasn't crazy. In fact, as the priest spoke to his visitor about the danger and immorality of the nuclear arms race, the bishop thought he sounded more sane than the rest of us.

Matthiesen was troubled; the young priest had said things that had both moved and shaken him. He began to think, in different and deeper ways than he ever had before. After several months of reflection, further visits, and much prayer, Bishop Leroy Matthiesen wrote a pastoral letter to Catholics in the diocese of Amarillo, asking them to consider no longer working at Pantex on the basis of moral conscience. His pastoral letter made national headlines.[36]

About the same time, an archbishop named Raymond Hunthausen announced he would no longer pay the portion of his taxes that is used to build nuclear weapons.[37] Again, a bishop had been moved by the witness of others—this time a handful of courageous Catholics in his diocese who repeatedly climbed over the fence at the Trident Nuclear Submarine Base at Bangor, Washington. Later, both bishops would recall how the martyred Salvadoran Archbishop Oscar Romero was first moved to act for the poor because of the witness of a few brave priests who were killed by the military. All these demonstrated the power of personal responsibility.

A student, a neighborhood volunteer, a bishop. Through these acts of personal responsibility and many like them, alternatives are being born, visions created, hope rekindled, and concrete solutions found to the many crises we face. But they all begin with actions of faith and courage, actions that have a prophetic quality.

When men take responsibility for being parents and not just fathers, they help restore family life. When marriage covenants are honored in a culture of infidelity and family strength is preferred to career advancement and material accumulation, the power of the personal relationships is regained. When young women and men refuse the pressure of their peers for casual sexual relationships, they begin to reestablish the boundaries of responsible sexuality.

We need businesspeople who create good jobs, healthy workplaces, and useful products; who don't cut corners, abuse their workers, or pollute the environment. We need unions that are honest and courageous in representing their workers. We need teachers who don't just put in their time but invest in the lives of their students. We need religious leaders known for their service instead of their fundraising. We need journalists to investigate for the truth, not to create sensational stories. And we need political leaders who refuse to separate their personal behavior from their public life.

Taking personal responsibility is important in a society

where blame always belongs to the next person and where people consider themselves smart when they take all they can get. Leadership is still best done by example. And examples of personal responsibility are what could make the greatest difference in charting new social directions. Responsibility is a sign of transformation.

INTEGRITY

The Quality of Leadership

The glare of the camera lights showed the anguish on Joseph Bernardin's face as he arrived at the annual meeting of U.S. Catholic bishops in November of 1993 in Washington, D.C. The highly respected sixty-five-year-old cardinal of Chicago, the largest archdiocese in America, had just been accused of sexual abuse by a former seminarian. After forty-three years as an ordained priest, Cardinal Bernardin would later describe the months that followed as "the worst experience of my life."

Under treatment with an unregistered Philadelphia hypnotist, Steven Cook thought he remembered Bernardin molesting him when he was in seminary in Cincinnati, where the prelate had been the archbishop. There was no other evidence.

Cardinal Bernardin has earned a reputation as a man above reproach. Known as good, decent, honest, and humble, Bernardin rose through the ranks of the Catholic church. In every position he has held, as priest, bishop, archbishop, cardinal, and then general secretary and eventually president of the U.S. Conference of Catholic Bishops, he has performed well with no hint of scandal around him.

Bernardin probably became best known for pioneering the vision of "the seamless garment," a consistent ethic of life that applies to every social issue, including nuclear weapons, abortion, poverty, euthanasia, and capital punishment. In doing so, Bernardin helped many Catholics and other Christians transcend the predictable political categories of Left and Right on a variety of controversial questions. Bernardin also chaired the crucial committee that developed the groundbreaking pastoral letter on nuclear weapons issued by the U.S. Catholic bishops in 1983.

On the matter of sexual abuse by clergy, Bernardin has taken a strong stand and has helped lead the way on the issue in the Catholic church by forcefully dealing with offending priests and advocating for their victims. The Chicago archdiocese has set up clear and tough procedures for dealing with this very real problem in the church's life and has taken action in many cases.

In February of 1994, the young man who made the damaging charges voluntarily admitted that his memory had been "unreliable" and apologized for the accusations. Cook dropped the charges with no pressure, no deal, and no settlement involved. Cook's charges against another priest in Cincinnati still stand, and a court procedure is pending.

The way Bernardin handled the painful situation demonstrates his character. When accused of sexual misconduct, he denied the allegations emphatically but then turned the matter over to the established processes the diocese had set up for handling such charges. Most important, Bernardin instructed his lawyers not to pressure, harass, or try to discredit Cook in any way. Bernardin was concerned that he not do anything that might deter other victims of sexual abuse from coming forward.

Barbara Blaine, a survivor of sexual abuse, a lawyer, and the head of the Survivors Network of Those Abused by Priests, told the *Chicago Sun-Times,* "Our hearts go out to Cardinal Bernardin. Steven Cook did the right thing by withdrawing the suit, and we hope that other accused church leaders follow the cardinal's example of defending himself without attacking his accusers." [38]

Bernardin did not want to condemn Cook, who is dying with AIDS and resurrecting painful memories. The powerful Bernardin did not let this confrontation become a personal matter.

We have seen too many cases where leaders of religious and other organizations act swiftly and brutally in attempting to dismiss, discredit, buy off, or even crush those who dare accuse them of sexual misconduct. Unfortunately, leaders known for their prudence, probity, compassion, and integrity are rare these days. But Bernardin is such a spiritual leader. He acted differently, and the church is better for it.

Despite his own difficult experience, Cardinal Bernardin told a recent Chicago news conference that his commitment to eradicate sexual abuse in the churches has only deepened.

> The ordeal of the past several months has been painful, very painful. I was totally humiliated by the public attack on my character. I have tremendous sympathy for anyone who has been falsely accused. I hasten to add that this experience has also strengthened my resolve to reach out to victims of sexual abuse and to do all in my power to eradicate the causes of abuse wherever it exists. [39]

While Bernardin says he harbors "no ill feelings" toward Cook, the cardinal does seem still troubled and even angry at "the instantaneous judgment" made by some of the media before he had a chance to respond or the legal system had deliberated. [40]

The case raises many questions for the future. The continuing legacy of church sexual abuse, the victims' agony, the need for clear, courageous church policy and procedures, the vulnerability of all church leaders to such charges, and the media frenzy such cases invariably create: we are a long way from adequately dealing with these issues. But Cardinal Bernardin has offered us great help and exemplary leadership, once again.

Penny Lernoux was just forty-nine years old when she succumbed to cancer. The prophetic free-lance journalist who reported to us for more than two decades from Latin America fell silent. Whether in *Newsweek* or the *National Catholic Reporter,* her writing had a prophetic quality.

During her national book tour for *People of God,* I introduced her at a book-signing party in Washington, D.C., as "a journalist who tells the truth and keeps the faith." It was that combination that made Penny Lernoux so rare and extraordinary in our time or in any time.

For other journalists, she provided a bright light. She practiced her vocation with great integrity and courage and in so doing demonstrated how a Christian should be a journalist and how a journalist can be a Christian.

The memorable time we shared together over dinner shortly before she died became an even more precious event in the light of her passing. That evening, Penny expressed great concern for her own Catholic church. The future of the church is with the poor, she believed, and Rome's fear of the base communities and liberation theology might cause the hierarchy to miss such a critical historical moment.

In all our conversations, Penny wrestled with the questions of integrity. How do we find the strength of our convictions to say and do what is true? Especially, how do we persevere in vigorous and honest truth telling in the face of opposition, intimidation, and threats? Penny loved the church enough to challenge it to be all the world needs the church to be. She once wrote, "Guts—the courage to be different for Jesus' sake—was what the early Christian church was about."[41]

Bastions of entrenched political, economic, and ecclesial power were dealt serious blows by her writing. Penny Lernoux was a most profound and persuasive critic of the United States government's policies toward its neighbors in Central and South America. But she also upset some ideologues of the left by not toeing the party line. She was too independent for them as well and also too consistent.

Penny Lernoux could be counted on for finding the people whose rights were being trampled and destroyed. The perspective of a peasant was always more important to her than the perspective of a president. As a journalist, Penny Lernoux practiced the biblical bias for the poor.

Poor people were really the only ones who could take comfort from her words. In all of her writing, Penny Lernoux articulated the "cry of the people," which was appropriately the title of her best-known book. She once said, "At stake are two different visions of faith: the church of Caesar, powerful and rich, and the church of Christ, loving, poor, and spiritually rich."

As a journalist, she displayed a breadth and a depth of courage that were truly remarkable. In whatever subject she took on, she became an expert. For sheer hard work, exacting standards, and quality of writing, she had no match in her field. Most journalists treat foreign assignments as career stepping stones. Penny Lernoux stayed at her assignment. In covering Latin America she became a Latin American.

As a woman, she showed the strength of compassion. In a church where women struggle to find their voice, her voice was one of the clearest and most compelling. To Latin America's most prophetic church leaders, she was an adviser and friend. Of church leadership she wrote, "The power of . . . great church leaders comes from the people, and it grows in proportion to its use for the common good." [42]

The vocation that she took most seriously was her vocation as a Christian. Her faith was truly at the center of her work and her life. Though she was a great success in the journalistic and literary world, she measured her own success in terms of the gospel. She believed that "faith is lived out through service to the community, such service being an expression of deep spirituality." [43]

In the closing words of her last book, Penny left us a call to faith:

> The People of God will continue their march, despite the power plays and intrigue in Rome. And the Third World will continue to beckon to the West, reminding it of the Galilean vision of Christian solidarity. As a young Guatemalan said, a few months before she was killed by the military, "What good is life unless you give it away—unless you can give it for a better wor... 'n if you never see that world but have only carried your grain of sand to the building site. Then you're fulfilled as a person." [44]

Penny Lernoux surely left her grain of sand at the building site of a better church and a newer world. Indeed, she left us much to build upon. Although it was cut short, Penny's life was fulfilled. Most important, her life fulfilled the words of Jesus in his first sermon at Nazareth: "The Spirit of the Lord is upon me because he has anointed me to preach good news to the poor." Penny took those words as her own commission and carried it out with great faithfulness, courage, and love.

Representative Tony Hall had just been informed that the House of Representatives' Select Committee on Hunger, which he chaired, was being terminated for budgetary reasons. Hunger had captured the heart, time, and energy of the young legislator from Ohio from his earliest days in Congress.

But over the years hunger had become more than an "issue" to him. Hall had seen the human face of hunger in famine-plagued countries around the world as well as in the poverty-stricken inner cities and forgotten rural areas of his own nation. Those faces stayed with him. They motivated him to try to move the U.S. government to action.

The Select Committee on Hunger spent just 652,000 dollars per year, and James Grant of UNICEF credited the committee with saving millions of lives. By contrast, the powerful House Appropriations Committee spends 19 million dollars a year—just for overhead. Nonetheless, the hunger committee didn't have clout and was cut without debate, process, or even bothering to tell its chair until after the decision was made.

"Why don't you fast? Why don't you go on a hunger fast?" When Janet Hall raised the question of fasting to her husband, Tony Hall was amazed. He told her he had thought about fasting a couple of weeks before but had worried about the pressure it might put on their family. "Some things are worth standing up for," she replied. Together they read Isaiah 58, "Is this not the fast I choose . . . to share your bread with the hungry. . . ."[45]

After much prayer and seeking counsel from friends, a respected eight-term member of Congress began an open-ended water fast to bring attention to the urgent question of hunger. By his own admission, this was not typical.

On the twelfth day of his fast, Hall told me, "Sometimes I feel alone because I've done something that is politically incorrect in my environment. I stepped out of my comfort zone and challenged [my colleagues]. I said, 'What do you stand for here? If you cannot stand for the poor and the hungry, if you cannot stand for the 35,000 people that are dying every day, if you're not going to focus on this problem, then something is really wrong with this institution.' When I did that, I separated myself from my colleagues; I feel like I'm standing alone." But he added, "I am at peace."

A fast has a way of bringing focus to an issue, which was Hall's goal. "I'm trying to get Congress and the country to focus on the issue of hunger. Congress is for everything and for nothing. We fund everything but never solve anything because we never focus. We never decide what is important."

Both before and during the fast, I spoke with Hall about the power of fasting and its spiritual consequences. "One of the things I am learning is that this is a very humbling experience," he said. "I'm also learning that I want the fast to be successful. But God's not calling me to be successful. He's calling me to be faithful. He's saying let the results be up to him. There are times when I can be very lonely, and therefore have to draw very close to God. I'm trying to learn how to completely give in to God in this fast, and I haven't gotten there yet. But that's how I got this far. I don't know what else is going to come."

The limits of his political world were very apparent to Hall. "We need a politics of conscience. We politicians suffer from a disease called 'everybody has to love us.' We don't take giant steps, we take little ones. We're always worried about reelection, thinking about raising money. So we never move the agenda. We fill potholes, but we never take a stand. After a while you wonder, What do we stand for?"

Two weeks into the fast, Hall had no hopes that his committee would be restored, but the fast was developing a broader and deeper purpose. At first, Hall's congressional colleagues didn't quite know how to respond. But in Ohio and around the country, many others were responding.

High school and college students, community groups, and just ordinary people were so deeply touched by a member of Congress taking such a personal stand that they began fasting themselves in support. Amazingly, 205 universities got involved as well as countless high schools. People from forty-six states became active, with thousands fasting or donating time and money to the cause of hunger. Hall's office on Capitol Hill was soon overwhelmed with a resounding public response to a very different kind of political leadership.

No one was more surprised than Hall when, in the third week of the fast, Agriculture Secretary Mike Espy called the thinning congressman to offer national and regional summits on the issue of hunger in America. "We're moved by your fast; we want to do something," said the new Clinton administration cabinet member. Then the World Bank phoned to suggest a series of similar summits on world hunger.

When Hall was called to appear before the Democratic Caucus of the House of Representatives, he didn't know what to expect. He certainly wasn't prepared for the standing ovation he received. After Hall spoke, Majority Leader Richard Gephardt rose to say, "I feel ashamed. You've embarrassed us in the right way." Gephardt said the speech Hall had just given was one of the best he had ever heard on Capitol Hill, and he promised to appoint a new task force on hunger to be followed by his own recommendation for a permanent committee on hunger.

After ending his fast, Hall was "feeling really good." In just twenty-one days, he had seen the winds of Washington shift. A relatively obscure politician had demonstrated again that one person's stand can make a difference and that principled direct action can make the most difference of all. Perhaps most important, Tony Hall showed even the cynical Washington establishment that politics can, indeed, be moral.[46]

Cardinal Joseph Bernardin's demonstration of integrity, even under fire, reminds us of leadership qualities we've lost and urgently need to recover. Journalist Penny Lernoux showed the integrity of putting vocation and faith ahead of career. And Representative Tony Hall offered the unusual political integrity of preferring conscience to success.

Celebrity status can no longer be confused with leadership, and America's preference for celebrities instead of leaders is a deadly flaw. Charisma, sex appeal, excitement, flair, and flash all have their appeal. But they are no substitute for integrity when it comes to leadership. Consistency, honesty, humility, decency, self-discipline, dedication, and faith are the leadership qualities we must now rediscover. Integrity is a sign of transformation.

IMAGINATION
Dreaming New Possibilities

The prophet Habakkuk lived in a time much like our own. Public corruption, social injustice, and chaotic violence were the orders of the day. In frustration, he pleaded to God for some clarity and direction. He climbed up a tower to wait and listen, until he finally heard a clear word. The prophet wrote,

And the Lord answered me:

> "Write the vision; make it plain upon tablets,
>   so he [or she] may run who reads it.
> For still the vision awaits its time;
>   it hastens to the end—it will not lie.
> If it seem slow, wait for it, it will surely come,
>   it will not delay." [47]

"For still the vision awaits its time. . . ." Today the visions we most need have hardly yet appeared. But they are on the way. That's the message of hope in this text. People who know the new visions are coming can begin to live, even now, in anticipation of them. History has always depended on visionaries to do that very thing. And dreamers depend upon the power of social imagination.

Visionary people and communities can play a decisive role as we move into a new decade and new millennium. They can imagine the new ideas that must be tried, tested, and preserved until others are ready to embrace them. In the Middle Ages, monastic communities kept alive vital human resources and values as the wider society passed through difficult times.

Today, new prophetic political and economic experiments are being generated by groups and communities willing to take an alternative path. They become experimentation grounds for new democratic visions and dreams. When the time is right, it will be far better to offer new possibilities that people have already begun to put into practice than just ideas they think others should try.

When religious and socially concerned groups can avoid the great dangers of withdrawal or sectarian self-righteousness, they can make a decisive contribution. They can serve as crucibles where new ideas are refined, and they can collaborate with other voices who are singing a new song. Small groups and institutions committed to alternative visions could become centers of imagination for the sake of the future.

Our capacity to construct such communities of hope depends on the quality and vitality of our imagination. Creative and constructive imagination depends on deepening our connection to spiritual traditions that have nurtured us and can guide us to deeper perspectives than are available in a consumer culture.

Spiritual formation for ordinary citizens, therefore, becomes crucial. The practices of retreat, rest, and re-creation are being renewed in many places today. A vital network of religious and spiritual retreat centers has steadily grown across the country and provides a reflective anchor for new personal and social possibilities. We must learn to rest our souls in the spirituality that is the source of our lives and the seedbed for the imagination of new visions.

To evoke new imagination, we need the fresh energy and perspectives that come from our artists, poets, and musicians. Artists are called to nurture the imagination; they have always translated the visions for popular movements. Indeed, some of the most creative signs of new vision can already be found in the lyrical scripts of the popular culture.

Young people especially often pay more attention to the messages of the popular culture than to those of the newspapers or the religious congregations. It is the duty of the young to question and be the guardians of the future. To address the call for new dreams and imagination means looking to our youth who have not yet had their creativity pressed out of them.

Vincent Harding has often reminded me, "You can't start a movement, you can only prepare for one." The untold story of the freedom movement that shook this nation in the fifties and sixties and reverberated around the world lies in the years of getting ready that preceded it. African Americans in this country spent years preparing, training, and building a movement for civil rights as they sensed that history was about to change. When the opportunity presented itself and the fullness of time had arrived, people and communities were ready.

History is about to change again. The depth of the crises we face will demand it. What kind of changes will occur is the critical question. To respond to the opportunity for positive change, we need to be ready. This is the meaning of the word *kairos* that we used before. Jesus uses the word in Matthew's Gospel: "You know how to interpret the appearance of the sky, but you cannot interpret the signs of the times [kairos]."[48] Kairos means a time that is full of potential, on the edge of something different, exploding into newness, alive with possibilities. It is a moment whose time has come.

Our historical crisis, in all its varied manifestations, could bring us together. Indeed, a kairos moment is already creating a new spiritually based community of response. Though most apparent around works of service and justice, social activism is only its most public expression. Much biblical reflection, spiritual searching, theological conversation, and community building are also going on in many places. This shared activity and discernment hold the promise for both transcending the old categories that have divided us for so long and revitalizing the faith traditions from which we have come.

A dynamic partnership is possible between spiritual renewal movements and the institutions of society. Renewal movements generate the imagination for change, and the institutions provide a sense of historical continuity. That creative cooperation makes many things possible that were not possible before. For example, the close collaboration between movement groups in the churches and their institutional leadership was the real secret to the strength of church-based opposition to the war in the Persian Gulf.

Prophetic imagination requires the possibility of free, safe, creative, and holy space. From that space, new visions can surely come. Our critical need is to lift up alternative social options at this crucial juncture of history, and our task is to demonstrate concretely what those alternatives might be. Imaginative actions, great and small, can enable people to see the possibilities of justice, peace, truth, goodness, dignity, grace, and love.

Adam Minchik's phrase, "living as if there was political space,"[49] is again pertinent here, for it is a way of living that calls the future into being. To live imaginatively in the light of the hoped-for future is a prophetic choice.

What does it mean to live in our time as if we have an alternative vision? Churches and other religious congregations could become a "safe space" for prophetic imagination—for political questioning, social experimentation, and economic innovation. In East Germany, the churches became that kind of forum. Dissenters, religious and unreligious alike, came together to talk about their discontent and raise their hopes for a different kind of society. In South Africa during the last decade, the churches moved into a political vacuum when the traditional political leadership was banned, imprisoned, exiled, or killed. People like Desmond Tutu said they would do whatever was necessary to keep a voice alive. In El Salvador, the blood of Archbishop Romero and a martyred church became the seeds of new possibilities of social transformation.

Perhaps the time is coming for American churches and religious communities to do the same. Many are willing to accommodate themselves to self-proclaimed new world orders, even while they see them unraveling in their midst. But others dare to dream new dreams and act on new visions.

Despite misuse and abuse, the richness of our religious traditions can be recovered. To quote Tim McDonald, a good friend and a great black preacher in Atlanta, "It's all in the book." The vision of racial and economic justice that we so long for—it's in the book. An understanding of community as the moral foun-dation of economy—it's in the book. A celebration of diversity and, yes, even the basis for our reconciliation—it's in the book.

The wisdom that the most vulnerable among us are the best test of our worship and of our society's moral integrity—it's in the book. And the recovery of the sacred in our relationship to our neighbor and to the earth—that's what we most desperately need, and it's all in the book. The bedrock truth that spiritual transformation is necessary for social transformation—it's in the book. It's already within the Scriptures and traditions that are the foundation of our religious life. And it all has a profoundly radical personal and social meaning, particularly at a time like this.

Many of our churches and congregations are in rapid decline and pitifully out of touch with the realities that have broken our hearts and fragmented our society. But perhaps religious communities therefore have little left to lose.

Why not return to our "first love" at this critical moment in history? Why not risk everything for the vision that our hearts still believe in? Why not do what a farmer in rural Americus, Georgia, did in the 1940s? Clarence Jordan established a community for blacks and whites called Koinonia and he reminds us that "faith . . . is betting your life on the unseen realities [50] [and] living a life in scorn of the consequences." [51]

Our measures of success must not become immediate political success or cultural acceptability. That way lies disillusionment, burnout, and despair, as many can testify. The meaning of being faithful becomes the vocation to keep a vision alive, well, and growing until the time is right for its broader acceptance. To be bold in offering such vision is an evangelistic responsibility. But its reception is simply not in our hands.

Imagination means the ability to invent the future, guided by core values, and unrestrained by present ideological assumptions and structural status quos. In particular, imagination requires that we go beyond the frozen systems of thought, politics, and social organization that have governed us for so long.

We are at a crossroads. A new time is coming. And the question is, who will be ready? Imagination is a sign of transformation.

RECONSTRUCTION

From Protest to Rebuilding

The often overlooked prophet Nehemiah provides a timely vision for our own period of social transition. In the biblical story, the children of Israel are in exile in Babylon, defeated and demoralized. Their sages lament the anguished difficulty of "singing the Lord's song in a strange land." In the narrative, certain people come to Nehemiah to report on the state of Jerusalem and those who had escaped or survived the captivity. They say, "The survivors there in the province who escaped captivity are in great trouble and shame, the wall of Jerusalem is broken down and its gates have been destroyed by fire." Nehemiah says, "When I heard these words, I sat down and wept and mourned for days, fasting and praying before the God of heaven."

Nehemiah goes to King Artaxerxes of Babylon, the foreign king under whose rule the children of Israel have had to live. Nehemiah reports, ". . . So the king said to me, 'Why is your face sad, since you are not sick? This can only be sadness of the heart.' Then I was very much afraid. I said to the king, 'May the king live forever. Why should my face not be sad when the city, the place of my ancestors' graves, lies waste and its gates have been destroyed by fire?' Then the king said to me, 'what do you request?' "

Nehemiah asks permission to rebuild Jerusalem. Upon receiving it, he goes to Jerusalem and gathers the survivors still in and around the city. "You see the trouble we are in, how Jerusalem lies in ruins with its gates burned down. Come, let us rebuild the wall of Jerusalem, so that we may no longer suffer disgrace." "Let us start building!" the people exclaimed. The Scripture says, "So they committed themselves to the common good." [52]

This is the prophetic call after the exile. The Jewish people are dispersed. They have no land and no home, and this is the beginning of the rebuilding of their ancient city. What is the relationship to our situation? The biblical theme that perhaps best fits our present condition is the theme of exile. We do not live in the promised land, as some on the Religious Right seem to believe. Nor do those who have experienced the "sweltering heat of oppression," as Martin Luther King used to say, yet know a true exodus in America. Despite the invocation of other religious themes in our early American history, the theme of exile has been the experience for many in modern America. Malcolm X and radical Christians like Daniel Berrigan and William Stringfellow have even referred to America as Babylon.

For many young whites, discovering the reality and pervasiveness of white racism early in our youth was a revelatory event. The civil rights movement and the explosion of the cities exposed the core and endemic racial injustice of America. And then there was Vietnam. Many of us grew up with Vietnam. Whether we fought in or against the war, we are all its veterans. The brutality, the lies, the death and destruction showed us painful truths about our own country.

"The War," as it will always be called by many of us, was also a revelation. We lost our innocence in the ghettos of Detroit and the jungles of Southeast Asia. We became exiles in our own country.

For those who came to America as slaves and who were set free only to be despised and oppressed by the descendants of their former masters, America has always been a place of exile. Women coming to consciousness in patriarchal systems or abusive family environments know too well the vulnerability of exile status. We have experienced new Vietnams in Central America, nuclear arms races, cities still burning and now unraveling in chaotic violence. "You see the trouble we are in, how Jerusalem lies in ruins with its gates burned." We again feel like exiles.

When the mayor of Washington, D.C., requested authority to call up the National Guard to deal with the city's escalating violence, it became a powerful symbol. The move suggested the helplessness and desperation of the people and their political leaders. But another response could be, "Come, let us rebuild the wall of Jerusalem, so that we may no longer suffer disgrace. Let us start!" But who will build and on what foundations?

We may be about to see a fundamental shift, a shift in direction. That shift is from exile to reconstruction, from protest to rebuilding. The values and experience honed by years in exile might now be offered for a rebuilding task. It is a move from the first prophetic task of truth telling to the second prophetic task of offering an alternative vision. And Nehemiah speaks that language to us.

The shift in me comes from many sources. It partially comes from working with the gangs. Nane Alejandrez and the young men and women of Barrios Unidos in Santa Cruz explained three ideas for community economic development projects that would involve former gang members in the process of rebuilding the life of the barrio. When I asked Nane what it would take to start these three initiatives, he told me it would require an investment of about 30,000 dollars. "For each one?" I asked. "No," he said, "for all three."

Several weeks later in Chicago we met with Gaylord Thomas of the Evangelical Lutheran Church in America, and 50,000 Lutheran dollars were committed with technical assistance for these hopeful projects. Nane said, "I have never seen churches in the streets before. But now I'm going home with the possibility of rebuilding in Santa Cruz."

Just weeks later, in November of 1993, we held another meeting in Chicago to put together a church-based support network for young people around the country who want to end the violence and rebuild their neighborhoods. This support network was created from several denominations, national organizations, and local churches. Those participating are Protestant, Catholic, evangelical, black, and white. It is one of the broadest religious alliances ever built in this country.

The network's vision is *practical.* Local churches and congregations will be connected to youth organizations trying to stop the violence and create positive community development. The network will offer concrete resources in the area of conflict resolution. Local congregations will be encouraged to apply the ancient idea of sanctuary in creating open and safe spaces in the midst of urban war zones.

The network's plan focuses primary attention on the necessity of community-based economic development as an alternative to lethal drug trafficking and as a way to solidify inner-city neighborhoods. And the network's plan challenges religious structures to make money and investment portfolios available for that crucial task.

The plan calls upon local churches to act as advocates for young people in the criminal justice system. Religious communities will be enlisted in the controversial task of keeping both drugs and guns out of their communities. Pastoral resources will be applied specifically to the epidemic problems of sexual irresponsibility and abuse as well as to the central task of family reconstruction.

The vision emphasizes that strategies for spiritual transformation are as essential as action in the community. Concrete resources are being offered to help local churches biblically interpret the signs of the times in our present crisis and to find the most practical ways to respond. Helping local congregations make the vital connections to the street will be a primary activity.

Congregations must also become vitally involved in advocacy on behalf of policy issues that affect children, for example. At the same time, they must avoid the partisan and ego clashes that inevitably attend such political debates. They will be encouraged to take the moral high road that leads to grassroots action.

Many hopeful examples of such new activity are already occurring. In Kansas City, the Break and Build program grew out of the 1992 Gang Summit in that city and is turning young gang members toward peace and jobs. A powerful network of mostly black evangelical urban ministries, called the Christian Community Development Association, is offering new hope for both evangelism and economic development in cities across the country. And the Catholic Bishops' Campaign for Human Development is making possible a myriad of community organizing projects.

A coalition of urban churches in Boston is offering a "Ten Point Plan" for citywide church mobilization. Their plan provides one concrete example of what could be done around the nation. Already adopted by many black and white churches along with the Catholic Archdiocese of Boston, and endorsed by the *Boston Globe,* the plan is very simple, straightforward, and specific:

THE TEN POINT PLAN

The following 10 point proposal for citywide church mobilization is born of the realities of our day-to-day work with the youth on the streets, in the crackhouses, and in the courts and jails of this city. We seek to generate serious discussion regarding the specific ways the Christian community can bring the peace of God to the violent world of our youth.

We therefore call upon churches, church agencies, and the academic theological community throughout the city to consider, discuss, debate, and implement, singly or in collaboration, any one or more of the following proposals:

1. To establish four or five church cluster-collaborations that sponsor "Adopt a Gang" programs to organize and evangelize youth in gangs. Inner-city churches would serve as drop-in centers providing sanctuary for troubled youth.

2. To commission missionaries to serve as advocates for black and Latino juveniles in the courts. Such missionaries would work closely with probation officers, law enforcement officials, and youth street workers to assist at-risk youth and their families.

   To convene summit meetings between school superintendents, principals of public middle and high schools, and black and Latino pastors to develop partnerships that will focus on the youth most at risk. We propose to do pastoral work with the most violent and troubled young people and their families. In our judgment this is a rational alternative to ill-conceived proposals to suspend the principle of due process.

3. To commission youth evangelists to do street-level one-on-one evangelism with youth involved in drug trafficking. These evangelists would also work to prepare these youth for participation in the economic life of the nation. Such work might include preparation for college, the development of legal revenue-generating enterprises, and the acquisition of trade skills and union membership.

4. To establish accountable community-based economic development projects that go beyond "market and state" visions of revenue generation. Such economic development initiatives will include community land trusts, micro-enterprise projects, worker cooperatives, community finance institutions, consumer cooperatives, and democratically run community development corporations.

5. To establish links between suburban and downtown churches and front-line ministries to provide spiritual, human resource, and material support.

6. To initiate and support neighborhood crime-watch programs within local church neighborhoods. If, for example, 200 churches covered the four corners surrounding their sites, 800 blocks would be safer.

7. To establish working relationships between local churches and community-based health centers to provide pastoral counseling for families during times of crisis. We also propose the initiation of abstinence-oriented educational programs focusing on the prevention of AIDS and sexually transmitted diseases (STDs).

8. To convene a working summit meeting for Christian black and Latino men in order to discuss the

development of Christian brotherhoods that would provide rational alternatives to violent gang life. Such brotherhoods would also be charged with fostering responsibility to family and protecting houses of worship.

9. To establish rape crisis drop-in centers and services for battered women in churches. Counseling programs must be established for abusive men, particularly teenagers and young adults.

10. To develop an aggressive black and Latino history curriculum, with an additional focus on the struggles of women and poor people. Such a curriculum could be taught in churches as a means of helping our youth to understand that the God of history has been and remains active in the lives of all peoples.[53]

The key to all these efforts is the willingness to move faith into the streets. Neither big steeple churches nor storefront congregations can afford to wait on young people to come in their doors. Recently, members of a prominent black Baptist church in Washington, D.C., spoke to me of how they sorely wanted to reach out into their neighborhood but didn't know how.

"Almost none of us live here anymore. Maybe some of us should move back," offered one church elder. Another woman said, "The kids on the streets don't have the clothes to come to our church. They don't feel comfortable given the way we all dress." In response, the church decided on a December "come as you are" Sunday, when everyone would be encouraged to wear ordinary clothes and the youth who hang out on the streets outside would be invited in. "If it works, we might all have to change," noted a church member.

Jim Offult, a black Mennonite pastor in the Chicago area, wants to see local churches establish "peace houses" in violence-torn communities.

"It is a mini-M.A.D. (mutually assured destruction) world at the 'hood level that has so many of our youth armed and arming to the teeth," he observes. "More than a sign of strength, their armaments are rather a sign of their common fear of each other." Gangs really don't want to kill each other, he says. "They desperately want someone, somewhere, somehow to reach out to them and help them save themselves from themselves."

Jim reports that the meeting house facility of the congregation he used to serve in Illinois became "a liberated zone." Many times warring gang factions came together on this neutral ground to peacefully resolve their differences. "We were successful on not a few occasions in defusing potentially deadly, explosive situations."

Jim suggests that neutral, liberated zones for working on conflict resolution be set up across the country in our many gang-ridden communities. Such facilities, called peace houses, could work in crisis situations on an ongoing basis. Further, he suggests, the idea of a neutral zone could be expanded to define areas marked for economic and entrepreneurial development.

The Reverend Jerry McAfee of the New Salem Missionary Baptist Church in Minneapolis, Minnesota, comes from a long line of preachers but believes that churches are not buildings but people. As a participant in the Kansas City Gang Summit and the antiviolence support network, Jerry has found his calling in the streets. Like Jesus, he is convinced that the church must "go through Samaria." Samaria symbolizes the mean streets, violent turf, racial strife, and gang territory that proper religious people have always traveled around. When we go into Samaria, into the community, we will find that "the people who you are going around are your relatives."

"This is our time," says Jean Sindab, a longtime church activist and a cochair of the antiviolence support network. "It is a time for the church." The contribution of faith communities to a social crisis comes precisely at the point of perceived lost causes and hopeless circumstances. The writer of the letter to the Hebrews says that "Now faith is the substance of things hoped for, the evidence of things not seen." [54] At critical historical junctures, faith makes possible the political imagination that sees solutions to seemingly impossible social problems.

Therefore, in reconstructing our cities, we begin with the work of prayer and the fervent conviction that our children are worth fighting for. As hopeless as things may seem and as helpless as we may feel, we must claim the sight that comes by faith in believing that our kids are not a lost cause, that violence will not have the last word, and that, as the Bible asserts, death will have no dominion. Our best religious traditions say that there is a God of redemption, of salvation, of miracles, of second chances, and of social revolutions. In the black churches one hears about the God "who makes a way out of no way." And out of this crisis, a new way will emerge, if we have the eyes to see and the courage to bet our lives on unseen realities.

The shift from exile to reconstruction comes partly from feeling the limits of dissent and resistance. The moral and political limits of the philosophical movement called "deconstruction" are increasingly apparent. The work of dismantling oppressive structures is essential, but it can never be the final goal. When deconstruction becomes an end in itself, we are in trouble. Deconstructionists who exhibit no real accountability to moral values beyond their own personal or group experience can, inadvertently, contribute to further cultural breakdown and disintegration. The political left has now become as morally vacuous as the political right; a radical individualism pervades both and reigns across the political spectrum.

The affirmation of basic social values is critical to the

health of any society. Seeking new ground for consensus is now a necessary task in constructing a more progressive political vision. Deconstruction may have now run its course. To continue only in that direction may just produce a deconstructed wasteland. Can those who have helped dismantle the assumptions of oppressive structures now show a real commitment to the values and requirements of social transformation?

Who will articulate a vision of both spiritual and political conversion? Who will call and work for the common good? Who will begin to create what Catholic activist Marie Dennis calls "societies that represent values"? For many, the energy for rebuilding also comes from the desire to reconstruct their own personal and family lives after years where fragmentation and brokenness prevailed.

But mostly, the longing for reconstruction comes from the tears that arise from looking out over the city. Nehemiah's rebuilding came from his tears, from mourning over "the trouble we are in." We all know those tears. Perhaps it's time to turn our mourning into building.

New leadership will only come from those who begin to build something new, not just who criticize the old. It is said that the best critique of the bad is the practice of the good. Nehemiah and his people rebuilt a new city on ancient foundations.

Today, only those who are rooted in solid spiritual values will be good builders. You have to build on something. Critical social movements have been doing the necessary work of truth telling, demythologizing, delegitimizing, and deconstructing the old structures that have failed us. But while you can deconstruct without a clear sense of values, you can't reconstruct without them.

Perhaps what deconstruction has most to teach us now is *who* will be doing the rebuilding. Black, Latino, feminist, indigenous, and countercultural movements have shown the bankruptcy of systems that exclude the participation and leadership of anyone but white rich men in deciding how our society should be run. The most vital legacy of liberation movements may be their commitment to inclusive patterns of social and political involvement and that central insight must guide the entire process of reconstruction. Everyone's perspective and participation will be needed. And that's why the results can be different.

In chapters 5, 6, and 7 of Nehemiah, the writer lists, at great length, individual people and the tasks they completed in rebuilding the city. This person built up the part of the west wall, another put the cross beam on the south wall, and so forth.

At first I skimmed, thinking the lists unimportant. But then I read more carefully and discovered the wonderfully detailed description of all the builders' contributions. Everyone's part was necessary, each builder respected. It's an evocative image of the wide array of builders and perspectives needed today.

Sometimes it's easier to remain in exile than to rebuild the city. We may even get comfortable with our exiled status. Some would rather only protest or tear down than build up, and some are skeptics and perhaps even are angry about rebuilding. Nehemiah faced that. He says, "And when they heard that we were building the wall they were angry and greatly enraged and began to mock the Jews." They said, "What are these feeble Jews doing? Will they restore things? Will they really sacrifice? Will they finish it in a day? Will they revive the stones out of the heaps of rubbish, and burned ones at that. . . . That stone wall they are building—any fox going up on it would break it down," said the skeptics. To their mockery the prophet replies, "So we rebuilt the wall and all the wall was joined together to half its height; for the people had a mind to work." Reconstruction is a sign of transformation.

JOY

The Unmistakable Sign of Life

A good friend left for El Salvador to work with refugees. During her first week there, Yvonne Dilling found herself helping people cross the Lempe River into Honduras to escape the Salvadoran military. The scene was as dramatic as it was dangerous, for U.S.-made helicopter gunships swooped down from overhead, strafing the river to prevent the campesinos from fleeing. Yvonne, who had been a swimmer in college, carried children on her back, swimming them across the river to safety. It was quite an introduction to her new work.

Her mission continued with great intensity, and it seemed that there was no end to it. She worked day and night. One day an old refugee woman asked Yvonne why she worked all the time. "You never stop. You don't join with us for our fiestas and celebrations. Why don't you ever take time to sit down with us and watch our children laugh or just look up at the stars at night? Why is it that you never have time to play or to pray?"

A bit startled, Yvonne responded by saying that the work she was doing was a matter of life and death. The suffering was so great, there was no time to rest. It was a noble version of the popular slogan, "It's a tough job, but somebody has to do it."

The wise old woman just shook her head. "That's not why," she answered. "I think it's because you don't intend to be here very long. You must be planning to go home soon, to return to your comfortable American life. No one can continue the way you do, day in and day out. As for us, we know we will be in this struggle for the rest of our lives. We can't escape it. So we have learned to rest, to play and pray, to celebrate and have parties, to enjoy our friends and our children."

Yvonne told me what the refugee women did when they set up new camps. They established three committees: the committee on sanitation, the committee on education, and the committee on joy. Yvonne learned many valuable lessons from the refugees. Now she is one of the best partyers I know, even in the midst of her still-important work.

I have always marveled at the capacity of the poor to be thankful and joyful. And I'm convinced the two are connected. It is a profound irony to see those who have so little being so thankful for their small blessings, while those with the largest share of the world's goods often seem so ungrateful.

Generosity seems also to be connected to joy. I've learned that it's usually better to be in a poor neighborhood if you need help from others. To be needy in more affluent places is to be lonely indeed. Time after time, I've seen those with very little share what they had with each other. At the same time, the affluent can be the most protective and selfish with what they feel they've earned. The joy that comes from both gracious and generous spirits is profoundly evident.

Perhaps one has to be a little foolish to be joyful. There is always plenty to be discouraged about, and the cynical logic of the world can easily lead to despair. But the Scriptures say, "For the wisdom of this world is foolishness with God." [55] In Pat Conroy's *The Prince of Tides,* his character, Tom Wingo, speaks wistfully of his eccentric grandfather, whom many regarded as a religious fanatic:

> I did not know how to cherish his sanctity; I had no way of honoring, of giving small voice to the praise of such natural innocence, such generous simplicity. Now I know that a part of me would like to have traveled the world as he traveled it, a jester of burning faith, a fool and a forest prince brimming with the love of God. I would like to have walked his southern world, thanking God

for birdsong and sheet lightning, and seeing God reflected in the pools of creekwater and the eyes of stray cats. I would like to have talked to yard dogs and tanagers as if they were my friends and fellow travelers along the sun-tortured highways, intoxicated with a love of God, swollen with charity like a rainbow, in the thoughtless mingling of its hues, connecting two distant fields in its glorious arc. I would like to have seen the world with eyes incapable of anything but wonder, and with a tongue fluent only in praise.[56]

A good sense of humor is an important part of joy and helps us keep our perspective. I remember a battle for rent control in the District of Columbia. Our local tenants' organization had mobilized with other groups around town who were seeking to preserve affordable low-income housing. It was a difficult fight, culminating in a crucial vote in the city council. Our side lost that vote. On the way home from the city council meeting, members of the tenants' union reflected on the event. In the Sojourners van, someone asked one of our neighborhood leaders if she was greatly discouraged. "No," she quickly replied. "Remember," she said, "the Bible says it came to pass. It doesn't say it came to stay." Everybody laughed and learned something about keeping our perspective.

Several hundred miles away and a few years later, I found myself in the middle of the Nevada desert, at the U.S. government's nuclear test site. A few of us had trespassed onto the testing grounds to protest the escalating nuclear arms race. We were quickly arrested and put into police cars.

I sat handcuffed in the back seat of the deputy sheriff's car while my friend, Franciscan provincial Louie Vitale, sat in the front. Louie and the deputy began talking casually; they had become pretty good friends, since the deputy had arrested Louie so many times.

Suddenly, the police officer realized he'd made a mistake. He had neglected to read us our legal rights and was now discussing the case with the defendants. Quickly he began the familiar litany, "You have the right to remain silent. . . ."

In the midst of the recitation, Louie's digital watch went off. This was no ordinary watch, but a Mickey Mouse watch that played the Mickey Mouse Club theme song. Because Louie was handcuffed, he couldn't turn off the watch. The police deputy just shouted louder, "You have the right to a lawyer" and over the legal instruction came the beloved strains of "M-I-C-K-E-Y, M-O-U-S-E." Nearly hysterical on the floor of the back seat, I marveled at how much fun civil disobedience could be.

Several years ago, in the departure lounge at the Baghdad airport, a group of church leaders was feeling discouraged. We had come to Iraq in hopes of speaking to Iraqi leaders about averting a war in the Persian Gulf. Much had to be resolved, but we believed that war was not the answer to the conflict. We had been given the impression that Saddam Hussein would speak to us and that some Iraqi leaders were searching for a way out of the impasse. Instead we spent most of our days in Iraq touring the city and waiting around in our hotel rooms for a meeting that never happened. It turned out that Saddam Hussein was no more interested in discussing an alternative to war than George Bush was. Finally, we decided to go home for Christmas.

I was standing in the small departure lounge with the leader of our delegation, Edmond Browning, presiding bishop of the Episcopal Church U.S.A., the most courageous church leader in opposing the war. We were discussing our frustrated mission and the things he was hoping to say to the Iraqi president, when I noticed a portrait of Saddam Hussein on the wall. That pictured face stared at us in almost every room we entered in Iraq.

I suggested to Bishop Browning that this was his chance to

talk to Saddam Hussein. He smiled mischievously and looked around the room. Slowly, the bishop walked over to the dictator's picture and began to speak his mind, complete with dramatic gestures. Other conversations around the room gradually ceased and gave way to growing laughter as people saw what their leader was doing. Our Iraqi military escorts were not so amused, but the power of satire was not lost on them either. For the rest of us, the humor provided a genuine release, reminding us that as intense as our work is, it's always important not to take ourselves too seriously. G. K. Chesterton once said that angels can fly because they take themselves so lightly.

Celebration is essential to joy. I recall a time when a dear friend was fasting on only water for forty days. We had invited her and another good friend over for "dinner." After she arrived, we carried out several tray tables, exquisitely spread with white tablecloths and flowers. On each table were several bottles of the best mineral and spring waters, flavored with scents of lemon, lime, and raspberry. It was a veritable feast for a water-only faster (and for all of us) and turned out to be a joyous celebration. Celebration is always possible, no matter what the circumstances. Joy is a sign of transformation.

HOPE

The Doorway to Change

St. George's Cathedral in Cape Town, South Africa, was packed to overflowing. An anti-apartheid meeting had just been banned by the government, and a church service was hastily put together to take place at the same hour the mass meeting would have been held. Police roadblocks were set up to keep young people in the black townships from getting to the church service downtown, but many had made it anyway, surging into the sanctuary like a powerful river of energy, determination, and militant hope.

There was no more room to sit or stand in the church. People were everywhere—in the aisles, the choir lofts, and the spaces behind and in front of the pulpit. People of all human colors waited for the worship service to begin and the Bible to be preached. Outside the cathedral, the riot police were amassing.

It was March 13, 1988, our first day in South Africa. The cathedral service provided a dramatic introduction to a forty-day sojourn in a country that proved to be a land of both great sorrow and great hope. Virtually all political organizations and activity had been outlawed. Only days before, courageous church leaders had marched to the seat of power at the Parliament Building just steps away from this great cathedral, signaling to the white regime that the churches would not bow the knee; they would stand alone, if necessary, to help lead the struggle for freedom.

The conflict between church and state had never been greater. The South African churches had issued a worldwide plea for help. Our invitation had arrived a few months earlier. We were there to support and report the historic events.

Archbishop Desmond Tutu began his sermon: "In the enveloping darkness, as the lights of freedom are extinguished one by one—despite all the evidence to the contrary, we have come here to say that evil and injustice and oppression and exploitation embodied in the very nature of apartheid cannot prevail." He continued to say that when all looks hopeless, "we must assert, and assert confidently, that God is in charge." Bishop Tutu was fiery and strong as he told the white rulers who enforced the brutal system of apartheid, "You may be powerful, indeed very powerful, but you are not God. You are ordinary mortals. God, the God whom we worship, cannot be mocked. You have already lost. We are inviting you to come and join the winning side!" With that, the recessional for this service turned into a chanting stampede of young people boldly singing freedom songs.[57]

We encountered that same spirit of defiant hope throughout South Africa, despite the deep despair that marked the political situation. I remember asking a fourteen-year-old boy in the township of Mammelodi, outside Pretoria, if apartheid would be ended. "Without a doubt!" he replied, though he thought it might take until near the end of his life. "Will your children someday breathe free air in South Africa?" I asked him. "I will see to it!" was his emphatic answer.

In South Africa during times of protest, burning candles were placed in windows to show solidarity and hope. The police were known to come into people's homes to blow out the candles. The children joked about the South African government being afraid of candles.

In June of 1990, I remembered that fourteen-year-old as I sat in a room in New York with other religious leaders awaiting the arrival of Nelson Mandela, who had just been released from twenty-seven years in prison. On the first day of Mandela's visit to the United States, it is estimated that one million people came out to see him. Massive numbers, especially from New York City's poorest neighborhoods, gave the South African leader the warmest and most amazing welcome this cynical city could remember. Governor Mario Cuomo said it was the most emotional event he had ever seen in all his years in politics.[58]

After our meeting, we processed into the packed Riverside Church with Mandela leading the way. Gardner Taylor, one of the nation's foremost preachers, introduced Nelson Mandela, saying, "This day and this occasion, under these circumstances, would be utterly impossible except for the truth that there is a God who presides over the affairs of history, who vetoes the schemes of evil people, and who decrees that truth crushed to the ground shall rise again." [59] After an eruption of deafening applause, Nelson Mandela quoted the words from the prophet Isaiah, " 'We have risen up as on wings of eagles, we have run and not grown weary, we have walked and not fainted,' and finally, our destination is in sight." [60] The black man most hated and feared by his country's white minority now stood as the best hope to bring both blacks and whites together in a new South Africa.

In biblical language, these are "salvation events." They are happenings filled with the pregnant promise of freedom, justice, liberation, peace, and reconciliation. They break the yoke of oppression while offering a healing balm to deep wounds. They testify to God's purposes and will for the earth.

Such events turn the tables of history; they shake the world upside down. They are beyond predictability and control, especially by those who rule. Those we thought to be all-powerful are undone by them. The lock of historical inevitability and determinism is broken open, and a new world of possibilities is again revealed.

When history appears to be static, it is the oppressed who are shut out. History is not only closed, it is specifically closed against them. The past is forgotten, the future is foreclosed, and there is only the never-ending present to be endured. The poor are told this is the way things have always been and forever will be. What cannot be allowed to be believed or imagined is the possibility of hope for a new day.

Hope is the most feared reality of any oppressive system. More powerful than any other weapon, hope is the great enemy of those who would control history. Victor Jarra, a Chilean musician, had his hands crushed by the military rulers for playing songs of hope on his guitar. What salvation events bring to the world, most of all, is hope, and the world's oppressed peoples are always the ones who have the most at stake in them.

Real social change is not just about great leaders, it's about releasing the aspirations of millions of people. The truly great leaders know that they are servants of ordinary people and of the God of history. Nelson Mandela's first speech in Cape Town began with these words: "I stand before you not as a prophet, but as a humble servant of you, the people."[61] Addressing an overflowing stadium of people in his first Soweto rally, Mandela testified, "I am more convinced than ever before, it is not kings and generals that change history. It is the masses of the people."[62]

When salvation events occur, we are all surprised. We don't expect they could or will ever happen. Most of us, to one extent or another, accept the dominant thinking of the world and view real change as quite hopeless. When it happens, we are taken aback.

Even those of us in faith communities (where we should by this time know better) are astonished by these things. We seem to believe that the rulers and powers are in full control—that they, not God, govern history. Because we religious people tend to believe in the powers of the world more than we believe in the power of God, we have already accepted their ways of doing things. When the ways of the world come undone, often so do the religious. What salvation events offer us again is the possibility of faith. History is open once more, God is acting, we can respond, and there is hope.

Through salvation events, we can also be set free from the illusions that so often govern us. The most appropriate response to salvation events is thanksgiving. The jubilant crowds on the Berlin Wall and the dancing South African masses welcoming Nelson Mandela are both fitting signs of it. Both show us the way to respond to the salvation events of hope. In the words of C. S. Lewis, we are "surprised by joy."[63]

The word *hope* is often used to refer to something mystical or rhetorical. Hope somehow lies outside the reality in which we have to live. Hope becomes a feeling or a mood or an inspired moment that is lived somehow above the painful and dull agonies of history. We're down here living in it all, and someone says, "Well, you have to have hope." And right away we think, "I'm supposed to feel something I'm not feeling—to get into a mood that isn't natural to me. Somehow I need to rise above this daily reality and be hopeful." But the more I wrestle with this word *hope,* the more I am convinced that we must see hope in a different, and indeed a more biblical, way.

From the perspective of the Bible, hope is not simply a feeling or a mood or a rhetorical flourish. Hope is the very dynamic of history. Hope is the engine of change. Hope is the energy of transformation. Hope is the door from one reality to another.

Things that seem possible, reasonable, understandable, even logical in hindsight—things that we can deal with, things that are not extraordinary—often seemed quite impossible, unreasonable, nonsensical, and illogical when we were looking ahead to them. The changes, the possibilities, the opportunities, the surprises that no one or very few would even have imagined become history after they've occurred. What looked before as though it could never happen is now easy to understand. Once it is upon us, we accept the inevitability of the first multiracial election in South Africa, and we forget the defiant hope of a fourteen-year-old boy, which helped make it possible.

In hindsight we can see how everything fell into place and that it was quite natural, even reasonable, that it would happen. It was inevitable, at least it seems that way in hindsight. Inevitable in hindsight and impossible in foresight.

Between impossibility and possibility, there is a door, the door of hope. And the possibility of history's transformation lies through that door.

The good news from the women at the tomb of Jesus became for millions of people the greatest hope that the world has ever known. And yet what did the male disciples call it?

"Nonsense." On one side of the door, it is nonsense. On the other side of the door, it is the best news Jesus' disciples had ever heard. And the door in between is hope.

Hope unbelieved is always considered nonsense. But hope believed is history in the process of being changed. The nonsense of the resurrection became the hope that shook the Roman Empire and established the Christian movement. The nonsense of slave songs in Egypt and Mississippi became the hope that let the oppressed go free. The nonsense of a bus boycott in Montgomery, Alabama, became the hope that transformed a nation.

The nonsense of women's meetings became the hope that brought suffrage and a mighty movement that demands gender equality. The nonsense of the uneducated, the unsophisticated, "the rabble," became the hope that creates industrial unions, farmworker cooperatives, campesino collectives, and a myriad of popular organizations that challenge and sometimes defeat monopolies of wealth and power.

The nonsense of oppressed people was the prayers of hope that brought down Anastasio Somoza in Nicaragua and Ferdinand Marcos in the Philippines. And the nonsense talk of nonviolent people often becomes the hope that challenges and even halts the devastation of war.

In each case, the gains, victories, and transformations seemed impossible at first and became possible only by stepping through the door of hope. Spiritual visionaries have often been the first to walk through that door, because in order to walk through it, first you have to see it, and then you have to believe that something lies on the other side. Not everyone can see the door, and most people can imagine nothing on the other side.

Those who walk through the door must also be prepared to suffer and even to die, because the door of hope always leads from one reality to another. History tells us again and again that we can't move from one reality to another without cost. It's never easy, never without pain or suffering. And it's always hardest for the first few who take those steps.

But after a few have passed through the door of hope, others can follow more easily. And as more and more follow, historical transformation takes place. It becomes easier to walk through, until finally everyone forgets how hard those first steps were.

That's also how personal transformation takes place. We can't imagine ourselves different than we are today or healed of that which binds and afflicts us. We can't imagine ourselves forgiven or free or whole. We can't imagine our own salvation. But when we walk through that door of hope and we look back at where we have been and where we are now, we see evidence of grace.

We can stand on the faith of those who have been given the news of resurrections before us, as they have walked through the doors of hope time and time again. Because of that faith and because of their legacy, we can say that it is not nonsense to believe that we can be healed of our hurts and fears and pains.

It is not nonsense to believe that our families can be restored and reconciled. It is not nonsense to believe that peace will come to Haiti and Bosnia or that justice and freedom will come to China.

It is not nonsense to believe that decent and affordable housing will be available to the poor of our cities. It is not nonsense to believe that the drugs and alcohol and crime that destroy so many of our youth will not do so forever.

It is not nonsense to believe that the arms race is not necessary and that war is not inevitable. It is not nonsense to believe that a child's race and class and gender will not always determine that child's future share of happiness and well-being. It is not nonsense to believe that we who have been divided from each other can, and will, one day sit down together at the welcome table of love and justice.

These thoughts are not nonsense. With the eyes of hope, we can see the door through which we too can walk, through which we are all invited. Walking through that door, we also will be given the news of resurrection.

With this hope, we can know our lives made whole. We can look into the faces of our children and believe there is a future for them. With this hope, we can look into the eyes of the poor, the suffering, and the dispossessed and believe that God is able to establish justice for all. With this hope, we can together build a new community, even in our own neighborhoods, that will someday overcome the barriers of race and class and gender. And with this hope, we can even look forward to a day when our nation no longer measures its security by its weapons and its status by its wealth.

With this hope, we can envision an America finally able to live without racism and without oppression, but no longer able to live without justice and compassion. With this hope we can plan and sow and build and create visions and dreams. And with this hope we can find the faith and courage to bear the cost of such possibilities. Hope is believing in spite of the evidence and watching the evidence change. And hope is a sign of transformation.

Afterword
A Time to Heal, A Time to Build

Our personal response to the issues raised in this book is perhaps the most important. To be honest, the crisis we face is now so deep and the transformation required so fundamental that real change can sometimes feel almost impossible. How do we keep from getting intimidated or overwhelmed?

Yet while optimism falls short, hope remains a dynamic and often unexpected force that keeps open the possibility of transforming our lives and our society. Indeed, hope often springs from the most unlikely and least predictable places, thus suggesting the possibilities of hope in every other place.

My own hope has been dramatically renewed through the young men and women from the streets who are trying to end the destructive violence in our cities. What they have taught me, leading up to the 1993 national Gang Summit in Kansas City and since, demonstrates the power and persistence of hope. In fact, the Summit and the gang truce movement is virtually a case study in hope. It encompasses most of the issues contained in this book and offers the beginnings of the kind of alternative visions and dreams we have been discussing—in one of the places they are most needed.

And my hope has been literally made possible again by the miraculous events in South Africa. I was there for the transformation—the inauguration of a new South Africa—and will never be the same. Never again can I say that hope is not a very concrete reality. Never again can I say that anything is impossible. The people of South Africa have opened the way for the rest of us to believe.

Whenever we feel stuck, paralyzed, intimidated, or overwhelmed; whenever we feel helpless and hopeless, we need to understand that our situation is never as static as it may appear to be. Hope always involves the breaking open of new possibilities from seemingly hopeless circumstances. In fact, at the heart of our best spiritual traditions is the wisdom of believing that life will arise out of death.

Scenes from the Gang Summit and the inauguration of the new South Africa are offered here as case studies in the potency of hope in all of our circumstances.

No one I know predicted the fresh initiative from current and former gang members to forge an urban peace and begin the long process of reconstruction. We all knew too well the death and mayhem resulting from gang activity around the country, as well as the systematic ills that foster it. What we didn't include in our agonized deliberations over ways to overcome the urban devastation was the prospect of new leadership emerging from the young people of the streets.

As a strategy session, prayer meeting, and family reunion all in one, the Gang Summit planted seeds of change in many. The National Urban Peace and Justice Summit sessions were closed to the media, both because of a longstanding hostility felt by most participants over the media's coverage of urban issues and gang-related activities, but also out of a desire to conduct serious deliberations without the glare and distortion of camera lights. I was one of several people invited by the organizers to participate as observers/advisers.

"I have something to say that is really moving me to tears. I've been gang banging for 22 years. I come out of Compton, California. I moved out to Portland, Oregon, selling drugs, banging, and putting destruction into their community. I ran into a brother—Akili. The brother is standing here today.

The brother is a Blood. Today I take my rag, and I say from now on there's a counterrevolution in progress. When you hear Crips and you hear Bloods, don't let it scare you, because we have a counterrevolution. This is the brother I tried to kill. This day I love him."

It was an "altar call" unlike any I'd ever seen. Two young men from rival street gangs—one a Crip and one a Blood—came together at the pulpit in St. Stephen's Baptist Church. The two confessed they had been trying to kill each other for more than a year. And then the enemy gang members "dropped their colors" at the pulpit and embraced each other, tears in their eyes. From now on, they said, they would walk the same road together. Enough killing; it was time for a new beginning.

For a gang member to drop a kerchief or piece of clothing with their gang's colors is a momentous thing. One can be killed for such an act. But this dropping of colors was not the only momentous thing that occurred in Kansas City during the weekend of April 29 to May 2, 1993.

The initiative for the Gang Summit came from the young people themselves in the ghettos and barrios. Expressing disappointment in the established political, civil rights, and church leadership, they decided to act on their own. The date chosen was the one-year anniversary of the first verdict in the Rodney King case and the subsequent explosion in Los Angeles.

One hundred and sixty-four current and former gang leaders and members from 26 cities, along with 53 observers, gathered in Kansas City for an event that may someday be viewed as a historic turning point in the life of America's cities. Most of the nation's largest and most powerful urban gangs were represented—Crips, Bloods, Vice-Lords, Black Disciples, Gangster Disciples, Black Souls, El Rukhns, Cobras, Stones, and Latin Kings. While national leaders call for an end to the violence on our streets, this was a gathering of people who potentially have the power to stop it.

Gathered together were tough gang leaders and former fel-ons, young men who had already served years in penitentia-ries, those who had lost many family members and friends, people who had themselves committed terrible violence against others. These intense days were fraught with tension, ego, controversy, and conflict. What held the Gang Summit together and ultimately overcame many obstacles was a com-mon passion to end the killing.

"Our barrios are suffering. We come here for peace. We're tired of seeing our mothers come to the graveyard," Daniel "Nane" Alejandrez of Santa Cruz, California, told the as-sembled crowd. A teenage gang member summed up the senti-ments of many at the summit: "We would rather live than die; it's as simple as that."

"We are on a mission," proclaimed Fred Williams, a youth worker from Watts who has helped to forge and maintain the gang truce in Los Angeles. Having killed another boy when he was only fourteen and gone to jail for it, Williams is now a veteran street organizer who generates much respect among the young gang members and exhibits a tireless energy to end the killing and rebuild his community. As "Mr. Fred" says, "It's time to get down to business."

The Reverend Ben Chavis, the newly appointed executive director of the NAACP, supported the summit from the be-ginning and told the opening day's press conference, "What brings us together is blood, and lives. This is a sacred event: a spiritual bond has come between us." While summit partici-pants came from many cities, they came from the same place of deep pain. Mac Charles Jones, one of two local host pas-tors, offered the welcome and invocation at his inner-city St. Stephen's Baptist Church where the event was held: "We are here to make our pain mean something. We want our pain to be redemptive."

Of great significance was the coming together of African-American and Latino gangs and agendas. "Black and

Brown!" became a constant chant. "Racism has driven us apart," cried one speaker. Participants in large numbers came from both African-American and Latino communities and the real commitment to diversity was evident in speakers, issues, language, and cultural expression.

T-shirts created by United for Peace in Minneapolis announced, "Apart We Can't Do It, But Together We Can." Unity did not come easily in Kansas City, and it was evident to most participants that it will not be won on the streets back home without a great deal of work. Yet unity was stressed as the key to progress. "Let's Fly to a Better Place," proclaimed a rainbow-emblazoned banner. A new peace sign was adopted by Gang Summit participants. Instead of a V sign with fingers held apart, the same two fingers are uplifted and held together—"not separate, but together."

The passion to end the killing was accompanied by a substantial political sophistication. "Gang-related violence isn't the only violence," said many participants. One young man described his experience, "I have to go to school without books. That's violence. I watch TV programs that degrade my people. That's violence. I never see anyone in power who looks like me. That's violence."

Ben Chavis said, "Ending gang violence is only the first step and not the last step. If we just end gang violence, but let racism, poverty, drugs, unemployment, and exploitation stay in our communities, we have not done our job."

Some put the issue bluntly: this summit was not about just ending gang-related violence so white people in the suburbs could feel safer. It was about stopping the senseless killing, so people could get on with rebuilding their own communities.

Everyone spoke of the need to create alternatives to the lucrative and lethal drug traffic, the mainstay of gang economic activity. One former drug dealer said, "When you sell dope, you will eventually fall. When you're selling drugs, you can't control your own life." But others pointed out, when a young drug dealer supports an extended family of 30 people with his profits, "just saying no" can mean only a job at McDonald's. Many people were talking about the need to develop small projects, businesses, and cooperatives that would serve the community and be accountable to it. The idea of community-owned and operated enterprises created much more enthusiasm than obtaining franchises from corporate giants.

Bobby Lavender, a convener of the economic development task force and an organizer from South Central Los Angeles, said, "We have to lift the community, not just individuals, out of poverty. We have to be motivated by more than just making money and then the money will follow." Lavender, who is himself suffering from cancer, added, "If you don't look out for the whole, and just look out for yourself, you're eventually going to lose out."

"If you don't love yourself, you can't love anybody else," said several young people. Self-respect, self-esteem, and self-control were ideas so frequently mentioned, it sometimes felt like a self-help convention. In many ways it was.

There was as much strong talk during the weekend about improving the quality of human relationships as there was about economic development, as much concern for personal transformation and individual character as for political change. The weekend continually defied traditional categories.

No word was more often heard than *respect*. "Don't disrespect your brother or sister" was a continual refrain. Respect is what these young men and women have felt the least of from their society; it is what they most seek for themselves and their communities. Young men and women were speaking about getting their own lives together as well as of society's responsibility to them. Some barely beyond children themselves spoke passionately about the need for effective parenting and traditional family values. All talked about re-claiming their cultural heritage.

The weekend summit had moved participants beyond a "gang truce movement." Now people talked of transforma-tion and rebuilding. There are 110,000 young people in the Los Angeles gangs alone. The potential of large numbers of young people turning from self-destruction to community re-construction is a hope that speaks deeply to all of us who live and work in our war-torn inner cities.

Perhaps most important, can the resources be found to sup-port the grassroots organizations that are so crucial to a last-ing peace? Will the political commitment and economic capital be secured for the community-based development that is necessary?

The economics is perhaps the biggest question. Truces won't hold without a visible and substantial alternative to the drug traffic and violence. The young people must begin to see that something else is possible and hear something more than the endless appeals to halt the violence. Such development will take a real investment of time, energy, and resources, both private and public.

Perhaps it was the enormity of such questions that caused summit participants to speak so often of the need for spiritual power. I haven't been to a church conference in years where we prayed as much as we did at the Gang Summit. Every session opened and closed in prayer, and every time tensions rose, which was often, we would stop to pray. The prayers were Christian, Muslim, and Native American, reflecting the religious experience and loyalties of those present.

I won't soon forget a moment, early on, when things might have fallen apart. In the midst of the shouting and chaos, Baptist minister Jerry McAfee stepped to the microphone and sang Thomas Dorsey's gospel hymn "Precious Lord" with a voice like Luther Vandross. It quieted and settled the crowd, led to a prayer, and allowed us to begin again in a much better spirit.

Two sermons were given. The first was from Sam Mann, the pastor of St. Mark's Church, who cosponsored the summit, a white man from Alabama who is known for his jumping while preaching. Mann's text was the passage in the book of Revelation where John is surprised to look into heaven and see all kinds of people who don't belong to his tribe. Worse yet, there are more of them than his own group.

"That's how many people felt about this summit and the people who are here. And most of the concerned people look like me!" Mann said. "Well," he thundered, "the text says you get to be in heaven, not because of who recognizes you, but because of who you recognize!"

Then Mac Charles Jones rose to preach on the parable of the prodigal son. When the text said how the young man just "came to himself" in the hog pen, I thought of the gang members who have often told us how they "just woke up" and decided to stop killing each other. Tears and shouts of joy filled the whole sanctuary as young men came forward at the altar call. It felt like church that day—the way it's supposed to be, with people who hadn't been there in years.

A case study in conflict resolution between gangs was provided later in the day. Some local Kansas City gangs had not been adequately brought into the national summit and had been apparently manipulated by local media people to speak against it. The summit leadership responded by bringing representatives of these gangs into the process and helping them resolve their own differences.

The scene for the attempted resolution was the choir practice room at St. Stephen's on Sunday afternoon. Intense, profane shouting could be heard—not typical for a Baptist church. But after three hours, a truce was made. Would we rather have our young people shooting it out in the streets or shouting it out in our churches? What congregations, mosques, and community centers will open themselves up to these men and women who are looking for safe places to resolve their conflicts and begin the rebuilding process?

The hope of the Gang Summit is a spiritual hope and a hope that can spread—kid by kid, gang by gang, city by city. It will grow by patience, perseverance, exhausting work, and undeniable love. It will be effectively spread, not through the media, but through hundreds of grassroots efforts and organizations that now desperately need our support.

Departing Kansas City, I thought about the men and women from the street gangs who had reached out their hands to one another and to us. Most of the rest of us at the summit come from the churches, despite the fact that our churches have mostly abandoned these youth. Yet here we were, all together.

Who will now take the hands of these brothers and sisters who have extended their hands to us? Who will covenant with these hopeful new leaders in forming partnerships to transform the urban landscape? Together we talked about a new day and a new beginning. Now the work begins.

New visions will require new visionaries. And they will likely come from ordinary people who are willing to become a part of the changes they seek for the very ordinary circumstances of their lives and their society. And that will be the extraordinary thing.

I had to go to South Africa. The birth of hope in the place the world has regarded as most hopeless was an event of far-reaching significance. Having been through the hard times with the South African people, I wanted now to be there for the celebration. My soul needed it, friendship required it, and I knew my own vision of political and spiritual transformation would be rekindled and enlarged.

Still bleary-eyed after a fourteen-hour flight to Johannesburg, I arrived at the famous FNB stadium in Soweto for what was billed as a "National Service of Thanksgiving," just two days before the inauguration of Nelson Mandela as the first democratically elected president of South Africa. Brigalia Bam of the South African Council of Churches welcomed the joyous crowd on this sun-drenched afternoon by describing the recent events in her country as a "miracle." I would hear that word over and over again in the extraordinary days that followed.

The FNB stadium had been the site of recent memorial services for murdered African National Congress leader Chris Hani and the ANC's revered former president, Oliver Tambo, as well as countless other funerals over the years. At Hani's funeral, a speaker lamented, "We have become accustomed to coming here to share our grief. May this be the last time we come to express only our sorrow. When will we come to share our joy?"

This was that day. The black township pastor sitting next to me called it a day of "celebration and release." New hope was now bursting forth all around the stadium under the bright blue South African sky.

The enormous contrast between the old South Africa and the new nation being born was almost overwhelming. I was here previously for almost six weeks during 1988. All of the freedom movement's political leaders and organizations had been imprisoned, exiled, banned, silenced, or killed.

Courageous church leaders like Desmond Tutu, Frank Chikane, Alan Boesak, and Beyers Naude had risen up to fill the vacuum, and the white government was cracking down on those churches and church leaders who dared oppose apartheid. We had to sneak into the country after being invited to offer support and to bring out the story of the church's resistance.

That visit was at a time of both great fear and stubborn hope among the people of South Africa. The prospects for change then looked extremely dismal, the cost of resistance was very high, and the possibility of South Africa ever being free appeared painfully remote. The ominous presence of the police and military dominated everything. The simplest everyday activities were fraught with tensions. All of human life seemed to be under constant siege for the majority of South Africa's people. Yet, I was constantly amazed at the spirit of determination I found everywhere, despite the predictions of almost everyone else around the world that a free South Africa was a vain and very distant hope.

Most expected an eventual bloodbath in that tragic land. Even in the days leading up to the April 1994 elections, many feared massive violence and a plunge into civil war. The amazing sight of peaceful, patient voting lines of black and white South Africans together ending apartheid would have seemed utterly unrealistic just a short time ago. But as someone commented to me on this new journey to South Africa, "oppressed people cannot afford to be 'realistic.' "

Now, a stadium of people who had just voted for a political transformation rose to pray together and give thanks for their miracle:

O God our loving Eternal Parent, we praise you with a great shout of joy! Your ruling power has proved victorious! For centuries our land seemed too dark for sunrise, too bloody for healing, too sick for recovery, too hateful for reconciliation. But you have brought us into the daylight of liberation; you have healed us with new hope; you have stirred us to believe our nation can be reborn; we see the eyes of our sisters and brothers shining with resolve to build a new South Africa. Accept our prayers of thanksgiving.

Leaders of formerly divided races and churches formed a circle around a rough-hewn wooden cross for a liturgy of reconciliation. In turn, each read a portion of a new commitment to one another and to a new South Africa. The entire congregation then affirmed, "We are all Africans. We commit ourselves to discover an African solution, under God."

Anglican Archbishop Desmond Tutu concluded, with unrestrained joy, "We used to say, 'We will be free—black and white together.' Today we say, 'We are the rainbow people of God! We are free!'"

At that moment, the peace was shared—across the borders of more than three hundred years of enmity in South Africa. There were great smiles, joyous embraces, vigorous handshakes, long and tearful hugs, until the whole stadium finally erupted in singing and dancing. In his sermon, a Methodist bishop and former political prisoner on Robben Island said, "Our beloved country cries no longer."

President-Elect Mandela rose to speak. He asked us to remember "those who would have liked to have been here today but could not." The emotion in the stadium was easily felt as we recalled those who had died in the long struggle for freedom.

The people of South Africa have lived under the most brutal forms of racial oppression in the system of apartheid, Mandela told the crowd. "Nothing I can say can fully describe the misery of our people as a result of that oppression, but the day we have been fighting for and waiting for has come. We are saying, let us forget the past, let us hold hands, it is time now to begin anew. The time has come for men and women, African, coloured, Indian, white, Afrikaans and English-speaking, to say, we are one country, we are one people."

Over and over, during these historic days, the truth about the past was told—then the past was forgiven. The words of forgiveness and reconciliation were heard from Mandela and former president F. W. deKlerk, from the ANC to the National Party and even the Inkatha Freedom Party, from white suburbanites to black township youth.

But Mandela set the tone. He invited his former jailers to

be special guests at his inauguration and he invited his opponents into the new government. He called on militant young people from angry townships to learn the words to the Afrikaaner national anthem, "Die Stem" (The Call of South Africa), and challenged whites to learn the African national anthem, "Nkosi Sikelel' iAfrica" (God Bless Africa)—*both* of which are the new national anthems of South Africa. In voting for political transformation, South Africans of all races and cultures had participated in a sacrament of healing, and their new president was inviting them all to participate in building a new nation.

On Monday, May 9, in Capetown, former political prisoners were sworn in as new members of parliament. I spent the night before the ceremony in the violence-torn township of Guguletu with the family of Phumzile Ngcuka Mlambo, one of the ANC's new MPs. She and her husband Bulelani, still in their thirties, have been long-time community activists. Both have been imprisoned and tortured, but they embody the hopeful spirit of the new South Africa. The whole family was very excited that night, anticipating the next day's events.

"I've never been beyond the gate of Parliament before," Phumzile said. "And whenever I went, there were always dogs and I was always in trouble. Now everyone smiles at me; it's all very strange." Barney Pityana, an old friend and a former associate of Steve Biko, came by and we all excitedly talked together, into the night, about the elections and the new political possibilities. Hope pulsated around the room. "See," said Phumzile to her American friends, "Don't give up on humanity!"

The next morning, Phumzile and Bulelani invited another American, Jean Sindab, and me to go with them to Parliament. At the huge fortified gate of the South African Parliament—a dramatic symbol of the closed system of apartheid—police quickly came to our car. Bulelani rolled down his window and confidently announced, "Member of

Parliament!" Like a miracle, the gate of the old South Africa swung open and we drove right through into the new South Africa.

Inside, we stood together on the Parliament steps as South Africa's new leaders ascended into the building to take their places. Thabo Mbeki, in exile since he was a small boy, now one of two new deputy presidents, walked up the stairs, as did Joe Slovo, the ANC elder statesman whose wife, Ruth First, had been blown up several years ago by a letter bomb.

"Were you always hopeful?" the press asked Slovo. "Not always," replied the South African Communist Party member. "Sometimes you would ask, 'How long, O Lord?'"

Many of these former freedom fighters obviously could still hardly believe this was all happening. More than one person told me they were half expecting to wake up and tell everyone about the wonderful dream they had.

Desmond Tutu, the happiest archbishop in the world, arrived and told the press, "It's a transfiguration—this country has gone through an incredible transfiguration. Victory is ours—all of ours, black and white, all of ours . . . Ha ha!"

In a simple, solemn, and moving ceremony, the new president, his deputies, and the members of parliament from all South Africa's races and parties took their oaths of office and pledged their loyalty to the new South Africa. Albertina Sisulu, called by many the "mother of the movement," and now a new MP, was chosen for the honor of officially nominating Nelson Mandela for president. Eighty women in all were installed in a parliament of 400, including Frene Ginwala as Speaker.

Afterward, President Mandela, and the two deputy presidents, Mbeki and F.W. deKlerk, emerged from the Parliament Building to meet the press and stand together for a historic picture. Even the media stood quietly in respectful tribute as the band played both national anthems. No one said a word;

there were more than a few tears as we watched the emotion-filled faces of the three political leaders who will shape a new South African nation.

When the band finished playing "Nkosi Sikelel' iAfrica," a lone voice shouted the traditional response "Amandla!" (power), to which the crowd responded, "Awethu!" (to the people). Mandela smiled, and another person began to sing "We Have Overcome."

One hundred thousand people were gathered at the Grand Parade to hear Mandela speak. This was the first place he had spoken to the people of South Africa on February 11, 1990, after being released from twenty-seven years in prison. When Mandela now appeared on the balcony of the city hall, as president of a democratic South Africa, a mighty roar went up.

"The people of South Africa have spoken in this election," said Nelson Mandela. "They want change—and change they will get." The seventy-five-year-old leader of the nation continued a theme of reconciliation. "We speak not as conquerors, but as fellow citizens seeking to heal the wounds of the past." In a dramatic gesture, Mandela released a flock of beautiful white doves into the cloudless sky, to the delight of the masses below. In a land known for blood and death, peace had come to South Africa.

On the way back to Johannesburg that afternoon, I was on the same flight as Desmond Tutu and we had a chance to talk. After serving as Master of Ceremonies for the City Hall event, he was still more excited than tired. The next day, he would say a prayer for the nation at the inauguration. "Incredible" was the word he kept repeating.

I reminded him of what he said to the South African rulers just six years before, in a packed St. George's Cathedral, during the height of the confrontation between the white South African regime and the church. "You have already lost. . . . We are inviting you to come and join the winning side." Finally the ruling whites had decided to do so, and most of them seemed happy about it. Today was the vindication of faith and hope, the demonstration that both, in the end, are stronger than political power.

Archbishop Tutu expressed gratitude for the long support of the overseas friends of South African freedom and told me this was our day too. The South African miracle has the real potential to infuse hope into every other struggle for freedom, justice, and peace throughout the world. In an irony of history, the nation that was once the world's pariah now has the potential to provide the models the world most needs.

Tuesday, May 10, 1994, more heads of state than had been together at any time since the funeral of John F. Kennedy came to Pretoria for the inauguration of Mandela. But they were not the real story. Thousands upon thousands of South Africans of all races, classes, and ages of men, women, and children filled the great lawns of the historic Union Building, while the whole nation watched and a billion others joined them from around the world. That day the government of South Africa took on the many colors of the nation itself.

Never have I seen such a large crowd so incredibly orderly, dignified, disciplined, cooperative, graceful, and united. And never have I been with so many happy and joyous people. When the crowd wanted to stand up, we all stood up *together* to clap, sing, or dance. When people were ready to sit down, we *all* sat down. Despite the hot autumn sun, the huge audience never lost its enthusiasm. A thousand South African artists were on hand to lead the people in the most gala celebration this country had ever seen.

A giant television screen gave the assembled multitude a close-up view of all the proceedings. Mandela's face, projected on the huge screen, captured my attention. As the national anthems were played and the oath of office taken, I could see the emotions etched on the face of the man who now embodies the hope of South Africa and, indeed, of the entire world. His is a face carved by discipline and solitude. I could see the memories of the struggle in his eyes, the pain of fallen comrades not here for this moment. I thought I saw the beginnings of tears that this day had finally come. His expression showed quiet determination and dignity, vindication and humility, gladness and serious recognition of the vast leadership responsibilities that lie ahead. It was the strongest yet gentlest face I have ever seen, a face you would instinctively trust. And at that historic moment, most of the world did.

Mandela's inaugural address was a "rainbow covenant" of promises to his people. "We enter into a covenant that we shall build a society in which all South Africans, both black and white, will be able to walk tall, without any fear in their hearts, assured of their inalienable right to human dignity—a rainbow nation at peace with itself and the world." Mandela vowed that "never, never, and never again shall it be that this beautiful land will experience the oppression of one by another."

In a ringing appeal for reconciliation, the president said, "The time for healing of the wounds has come. The moment to bridge the chasms that divide us has come. The time to rebuild is upon us."

This book ends as I stand listening to those words with thousands of celebrating South African people. With tears in our eyes and joy in our faces we hear Mandela proclaim, "We have triumphed in the effort to implant hope in the breasts of millions of our people." It is indeed that hope that will transform the soul of our politics.

Notes

Introduction

[1] In searching for a source for this list, Arun Gandhi of the M. K. Gandhi Institute for the Study of Nonviolence replied: "The seven deadly sins . . . were part of my lessons when I lived with Grandfather in 1945–46 as a boy of 12. He made me, and other children in the ashram, memorize them. . . . I don't know if there is any source you can attribute this quote to."

[2] Proverbs 29:18 KJV.

[3] ABC News's *Nightline,* 19 October 1992 (American Broadcasting Companies, transcript produced by Journal Graphics, New York). The show followed the third presidential debate of the 1992 campaign.

[4] ABC News's *Nightline,* 19 October 1992.

[5] Cornel West, *Race Matters* (Boston: Beacon Press, 1993), 18.

[6] E. J. Dionne Jr. treats this in the Introduction, "Living in the Past: How Liberals and Conservatives Are Failing America," in *Why Americans Hate Politics* (New York: Simon & Schuster, 1991), 18–19; as well as in chapter 13, "The Politics of the Restive Majority," 329–55.

[7] M. L. King Jr., delivered his "I Have a Dream" speech before the Lincoln Memorial on August 28, 1963, as the keynote address of the march on Washington, D.C., for civil rights.

During the 1988 presidential election, the George Bush campaign used the story of Willie Horton—the convicted murderer who, on a weekend furlough from a Massachusetts prison, raped a woman in Maryland—to display that Democratic candidate Michael Dukakis was "soft on crime." The Willie Horton example was used in both television spots and speeches on the campaign trail.

[8] "A Nation in Transition: Census Reveals Striking Stratification of U.S. Society," *Washington Post*, 29 May 1992, A1.

[9] According to *Poverty in the United States, 1991: Current Population Reports* (Washington, D.C.: U.S. Department of Commerce), Series P–60, #181, 45.9 percent of black children under the age of 18 and 40.4 percent of Hispanic children under the age of 18 live below the poverty level.

[10] U.S. House of Representatives Ways and Means Committee Print 103–18. Based on Arthur Kennickell (Federal Reserve) and Louise Woodburn (IRS), "Estimate of Household Net Worth Using Model-based and Design-based Weights" (Government Printing Office, April 1992) GPO, 1993, 1553.

[11] R. K. Prabhu, *This Was Bapu* (1954), 48. Quoted in M. K. Gandhi, *My Religion* (Ahmedabad, India: Navajivan Publishing House, 1955), 52.

1. Signs of a Crisis

[1] Isaiah 2:7–9a NRSV.

[2] Isaiah 19:2b NRSV.

[3] Isaiah 19:3a NRSV.

[4] E. J. Dionne Jr., "Why Are We Talking about Haircuts?" *Washington Post*, 25 May 1993, A19.

[5] Frances Moore Lappé and Paul Martin DuBois, *The Quickening of America: Rebuilding Our Communities, Remaking Our Lives* (San Francisco: Jossey-Bass, 1994).

2. Can Politics Be Moral?

[1] In the New Revised Standard Version, Hebrews 11:1 reads as follows: "Now faith is the assurance of things hoped for, the conviction of things not seen."

[2] The "Bloods/Crips Proposal for L.A.'s Facelift" is not available in a formal, published form. It was created and printed by the groups and has been circulated at their discretion.

[3] Cornel West, *Race Matters* (Boston: Beacon Press, 1993), 19–20.

[4] See Richard Barnet and John Cavanagh, *Global Dreams: Imperial Corporations in the New World Order* (New York: Simon & Schuster, 1994).

[5] See Vaclav Havel, *Summer Meditations,* trans. Paul Wilson (New York: Alfred A. Knopf, 1992).

[6] Richard Morin, "Majority Says U.S. Is on 'Wrong Track': Growing Number of Americans Concerned about Economy, Poll Finds," *Washington Post,* 23 May 1990, A4; Dan Balz and Richard Morin, "A Tide of Pessimism and Political Powerlessness Rises," *Washington Post,* 3 November 1991, A1; David S. Broder and E. J. Dionne Jr., "Voters See Big Needs at Home," *Washington Post,* 4 November 1991, A1, A12; Robin Toner, "Welcome to 1992: A Survival Guide for Elected Officials," *New York Times,* 10 November 1991, E1–2; B. Drummond Ayres, "Shadow of Pessimism Eclipses a Dream," *New York Times,* 9 February 1992, 1, 32.

3. Politics and Religion

[1] Stephen Carter, *The Culture of Disbelief: How American Law and Politics Trivialize Religious Devotion* (New York: Basic Books, 1993).

[2] Garry Wills, *Under God: Religion and American Politics* (New York: Simon & Schuster, 1990), 25.

[3] Walter Brueggemann, "History on the Margins," *Sojourners* 20, no. 7 (August/September 1991): 19.

[4] Brueggemann, "History on the Margins," 19.

[5] Carter, *The Culture of Disbelief,* 80.

[6] Eugene D. Genovese, quoted by Jim Wallis, "Not in Polite Company," *Sojourners* 23, no. 3 (April, 1994): 4.

[7] Charley Earp, "The Potential of the Christian Left in the 1990s," *Z Magazine* 7, no. 1 (January 1994): 21–22.

[8] Earp, "Christian Left," 21–22.

[9] Archbishop Desmond Tutu introduced the idea of moving the church toward a "spirituality of transformation" in a statement issued after a midterm sabbatical. In it he talked of shifting emphasis to "that of seeking to strengthen the inner life of the church, of pouring oil and balm on wounds, of nurturing our people for the tasks of transformation" ("Setting New Priorities," *Bishopcourt Update,* 18 June 1992, 3). The statement is available from the Office of the Anglican Archbishop of Cape

Town, "Bishopcourt," 16 Bishopcourt Drive, Claremont, Cape 7700 South Africa.

[10] *Webster's Ninth New Collegiate Dictionary,* s.v. "vision" (Springfield: Merriam-Webster, Inc., 1987), 1318.

[11] *Webster's Ninth New Collegiate Dictionary,* s.v. "imagination" (Springfield: Merriam-Webster, Inc., 1987), 600.

[12] *Oxford English Dictionary,* Second Edition, Volume VII, s.v. "imagination" (Oxford: Clarendon Press, 1989), 669.

[13] Oxford English Dictionary , Second Edition, Volume XIX, s.v. "vision" (Oxford: Clarendon Press, 1989), 688–689.

[14] Walter Brueggemann introduced this phrase in *The Prophetic Imagination* (Minneapolis: Fortress Press, 1978).

[15] Jonathan Schell, "Reflections: A Better Today," *The New Yorker* 61, no. 50 (3 February 1986): 47.

[16] Deuteronomy 30:19b NRSV.

4. A Tale of Two Cities

[1] Office of Policy and Program Evaluation, *Indices: A Statistical Index to District of Columbia Services* (Washington, D.C., 1991), 2.

[2] *Statistical Index,* 2, 78. According to 1990 Census used therein, the District of Columbia's total population is over 606,900, of which 65.8 percent are black, 4.5 percent other, and 5.4 percent Latino; 29.6 percent of the population is white.

[3] Charles Krauthammer verifies that he has made this statement but he cannot pinpoint the exact time nor date.

[4] Cokie Roberts made this observation many times throughout the 1992 presidential campaign, among them on ABC News' *This Week with David Brinkley,* 3 May 1992 (transcript provided by Journal Graphics, Inc., copyright 1992, American Broadcasting Companies).

[5] Jason DeParle, "Number of People in Poverty Shows Sharp Rise in U.S.," *New York Times,* 27 September 1991, A1.

[6] *Statistical Index,* 99–100; *Washington Post,* 18 February 1989; Larry VanDyne, "Money Fever," *The Washingtonian* 25, no. 1 (October 1989): 141–256.

[7] According to *Healthy, Housed, and Safe? A Progress Report on the District's Children* (Washington, D.C.: The Children's Defense Fund, 1993), 2, the infant mortality rate for Washington, D.C., in 1991 was 20.5 per 1,000 live births. The infant mortality rate for black children was 26 per 1,000 live births.

In *Bright Futures or Broken Dreams: The Status of Children of the District of Columbia and an Investment Agenda for the 1990s* (Washington, D.C.: The Children's Defense Fund, 1991), 50, it is noted that "an infant born in the District [of Columbia] was less likely to survive one year than a baby born in Jamaica."

[8] *Statistical Index,* 180; Dorothy Gilliam, "Despairing for the Young," *Washington Post,* 26 November 1990, E3.

[9] *Statistical Index,* 287.

[10] Office of Policy and Program Evaluation, "Tourism in the Nation's Capital," in *Statistical Index,* 145.

[11] VanDyne, "Money Fever," 141–256.

[12] David Brown, "Death Rate Gap Widens: Black-White Mortality Trend Continues," *Washington Post,* 8 January 1992, A1; Malcolm Gladwell, "Life Expectancy Gap of Blacks, Whites Grows," *Washington Post,* 30 November 1990, A3; Felicity Barringer, "Rich-Poor Gulf Widens Among Blacks," *New York Times,* 15 September 1992, A12; Carlyle C. Douglas, "In Black America, Life Grows Shorter," *New York Times,* 2 December 1990, E7.

[13] Jason DeParle, "42% of Young Black Men in Capital's Justice System" (National Center on Institutions and Alternatives study), *New York Times,* 18 April 1992, 1; Dan Colburn, "The Risky Lives of Young Black Men," *Washington Post,* 18 December 1990, WH7; Walter Dean Myers, "Least Likely to Succeed: Poverty and Bad Social Conditions Keep Many Young Afro-Americans from Going to College," *Washington Post,* 4 August 1991, ER1; Dorothy Gilliam, "The Future of the Black Man," *Washington Post,* 1 January 1990, D3; William Raspberry, "The Making of Certified Criminals," *Washington Post,* 30 December 1992, A19; "[Center for Disease Control] Report Shows Alarming Increase in Homicides of Young Black Males," *Wall Street Journal,* 7 December 1990, A5; Seth Mydans, "Homicide Rate for Young Blacks Rose by Two-Thirds in Five Years," *New York Times,* 7 December 1990, A26; Lynne Duke, "From Shaw, Success Looks Like a Long Shot: Dreams Vie with Harsh Realities as Young Black Men Size Up Life," *Washington Post,* 26 July 1992, A1.

[14] Sarah Booth Conroy, "The Democrats, Optimistically: At the Party's Gala, A New York State of Mind," *Washington Post,* 27 September 1991, B1–2S.

[15] Mohandas K. Gandhi, in *Seeds of Peace: A Catalogue of Quotations,* comp. Jeanne Larson and Madge Micheels-Cyrus (Philadelphia: New Society Publishers, 1986), 127.

[16] The United Nations International Children's Emergency Fund (UNICEF), *The State of the World's Children* (New York: Oxford University Press, 1993), cites 35,000 deaths of children under the age of five each day in the developing world for 1990 (on the statistical note page in the Introduction).

[17] This analogy is used often by antipoverty advocates. The former director of Bread for the World, Arthur Simon, currently with the Christian Children's Fund, has used the example before and says its origin is unknown, though based on reliable computations.

[18] Jacques Attali, *Millennium: Winners and Losers in the Coming World Order* (New York: Times Books, 1991), 4.

[19] Jacques Attali, *Millennium,* 5.

[20] Robert D. Kaplan, "The Coming Anarchy," *Atlantic Monthly* 273, no. 2 (February, 1994): 44–76.

[21] Kaplan, "The Coming Anarchy," 44, 54.

[22] Thomas Fraser Homer-Dixon, "On the Threshold: Environmental Changes as Causes of Acute Conflict," *International Security* (Fall, 1991), quoted in Robert D. Kaplan, "The Coming Anarchy," 60.

[23] Kaplan, "The Coming Anarchy," 60.

[24] Alberta Piccolino, "Killing the Innocents: The War on Brazil's Street Children," *Sojourners* 21, no. 2 (February/March 1992): 28–29.

[25] Archbishop Dom Helder Camara, conversation with the author, July, 1977.

[26] Sabra Chartrand, "Capital Is Capital of Gunfire Deaths: Washington Rate Is Double the Average for U.S. Cities," *New York Times,* 11 June 1992, A9.

[27] John Maines, "A Tale of Two Districts," *American Demographics* 12 (February 1990): 45; Donald Doane and Warner Ragsdale Jr., "The 'Other Washington' That Tourists Don't See," *U.S.*

News and World Report 92, no. 17 (3 May 1982); Richard La-
cayo, "A Capital Offense: Barry's Travails Are Just One Woe for
the 'Other Washington,'" *Time* 133 (14 January 1989): 27;
Marianne Szegedy-Meszak, "D.C., the Other Washington: One
City With Two Cultures and Many Tensions," *New York Times
Magazine* 138 (20 November 1988): 44.

28 In "700 Slayings Analyzed in D.C. Study," *Washington Post*, 18
February 1989, B2, Linda Wheeler writes, "The census block
showing the highest number of homicides—21—is in the Columbia Heights neighborhood of Northwest Washington."

29 *Boyz N the Hood,* directed by John Singleton, Columbia/Tristar
pictures, 1991.

30 This trip is described in *Mobilizing the Forces of Hope: Reflections on Martin Luther King, Jr. and the U.S. Military,* by Vincent
and Rosemarie Harding (Akron, PA: Mennonite Central Committee Military Counseling Network, 1989).

31 Jon Sobrino, "The Greatest Love," interview by Jim Wallis, *Sojourners* 19, no. 3 (April 1990): 16–18.

32 Sobrino, "Greatest Love," 16–18.

33 Advertisement in *Bobbin* Magazine 5 (August 1991): 16.

34 Matthew 25:43 NRSV.

35 Matthew 25:44 NRSV.

36 Matthew 25:45 NRSV.

5. Fire in the Sky

1 *Blade Runner,* directed by Ridley Scott, 118 min., Warner, 1982,
videocassette.

2 *U.S. Riot Commission Report of the National Advisory Commission on Civil Disorders* (New York: Bantam Books, 1968).

3 ABC News, *This Week with David Brinkley,* 3 May 1992 (American Broadcasting Companies, 1992, transcript produced by Journal Graphics).

4 Andrew Hacker, *Two Nations: Black and White, Separate, Hostile, Unequal* (New York: Charles Scribner's Sons, 1992).

5 National Public Radio, *Morning Edition,* 18 May 1992.

6 National Public Radio, 18 May 1992.

[7] Jason DeParle, "42% of Young Black Men in Capital's Justice System," *New York Times,* 18 April 1992.

[8] Jerome Miller, head of the National Center on Institutions and Alternatives, on WAMU's *Fred Fisk Show,* 3 October 1992.

[9] Dan Rather, quoted by Jim Wallis, "Time to Listen and Act," *Sojourners* 21, no. 6 (July 1992): 12.

[10] Suzan Shown Harjo, quoting from *New York Times* in "Goodbye Columbus?", *Sojourners* 19, no. 10 (December 1990): 35.

[11] Oliver Dunn and James E. Kelley Jr., trans., *The Diary of Christopher Columbus's First Voyage to America: 1492–1493,* abstracted by Fray Bartolome de las Casas (Norman and London: University of Oklahoma Press, 1989).

[12] According to *Poverty in the United States, 1991: Current Population Reports* (Washington, D.C.: U.S. Department of Commerce), Series P–60, #181, 45.9 percent of black children under the age of 18 and 40.4 percent of Hispanic children under the age of 18 live below the poverty level.

[13] Winona LaDuke, "We Are Still Here," *Sojourners* 20, no. 8 (October 1991): 14.

6. Pattern of Inequality

[1] Brenda Stoltzfus, with coauthor Saundra Pollock Sturdevant, provides a detailed and extensive treatment of this situation in *Let the Good Times Roll: Prostitution and the U.S. Military in Asia* (New York: New Press, 1993).

[2] Catharine A. MacKinnon, "Turning Rape into Pornography: Postmodern Genocide," *Ms.* 4, no. 1 (July/August 1993): 24–30.

[3] Elizabeth Holler Hunter, "Grief upon the Earth," *Sojourners* 22, no. 3 (April 1993): 25.

[4] Holler Hunter, "Grief," 25.

[5] Elisabeth Schüssler Fiorenza, "Introduction," *Violence Against Women,* Concilium 1 (London: SCM Press; Maryknoll, NY: Orbis Books, 1994), vii.

[6] Schüssler Fiorenza, "Introduction," vii.

[7] Schüssler Fiorenza, "Introduction," viii.

[8] Schüssler Fiorenza, "Introduction," ix.

[9] Schüssler Fiorenza, "Introduction," ix.

[10] Schüssler Fiorenza, "Introduction, x.

[11] Joyce Hollyday, "Selling Sex and Beer," *Sojourners* 21, no. 2 (February/March 1992): 4.

[12] Joyce Hollyday, "Trials and Triumphs for Feminism," *Sojourners* 21, no. 5 (June 1992): 4.

[13] Susan Faludi, *Backlash: The Undeclared War Against Women* (Crown Publishers, Inc., 1991).

[14] Wendy Kaminer, "Feminism's Identity Crisis," *Atlantic* 272, no. 4 (October 1993): 59.

[15] Joyce Hollyday, "Frontrunners and Backlashers: 1992 as the Year of the Woman," *Sojourners* 21, no. 9 (November 1992): 19–20.

[16] Shelley Douglass, "The Abortion Battle: Silencing the Middle," *Sojourners* 21, no. 6 (July 1992): 4–5.

[17] Joyce Hollyday, "Abortion and the Law," *Sojourners* 18, no. 10 (November 1989): 16.

[18] Jim Rice, "When Dignity Is Assaulted," *Sojourners* 23, no. 2 (February/March 1994): 6.

[19] Rice, "Dignity," 7.

[20] Rice, "Dignity, 7.

[21] Elizabeth Cady Stanton (speech delivered at the International Council on Women, 1888), quoted by Ginny Earnest, "On a Firm Foundation," *Sojourners* 17, no. 9 (October 1988): 30.

[22] Maria Riley, *Transforming Feminism* (Kansas City: Sheed & Ward, 1989), 46.

[23] Gloria Steinem, "Let's Get Real about Feminism: The Backlash, the Myths, the Movement," panel discussion with Naomi Wolf, Urvashi Vaid, Gloria Steinem, and bell hooks in *Ms.* 4, no. 2 (September/October 1993): 35, 43.

[24] Alice Walker, *In Search of Our Mothers' Gardens: Womanist Prose* (New York: Harcourt Brace Jovanovich, 1983).

[25] Emilie M. Townes, ed., introduction to *A Troubling in My Soul: Womanist Perspectives on Evil & Suffering* (Maryknoll, NY: Orbis Books, 1993): 1, 2.

[26] Delores S. Williams, *Sisters in the Wilderness: The Challenge of Womanist God-Talk* (Maryknoll, NY: Orbis Books, 1993), 185.

[27] Williams, *Sisters,* 185.

[28] Williams, *Sisters,* 186.

[29] Williams, *Sisters,* x, xi.

[30] The Sisters' Statement, quoted in Jim Wallis, "A Time to Heal, A Time to Build," *Sojourners* 22, no. 3 (April 1993): 16.

[31] Blanca Martinez, "I Should Have Been a Statistic," interview by Jim Wallis, *Sojourners* 22, no. 3 (April 1993): 27.

[32] Najma Nazy'at, "Fighting for All," *Sojourners* 22, no. 7 (August 1993): 25.

[33] Marion Stamps, "There's No Them Without Us," interview by Jim Wallis, *Sojourners* 22, no. 3 (April 1993): 23, 24.

[34] Stamps, "There's No Them," 23, 24.

[35] Rosemary Radford Ruether, *Gaia and God: Ecofeminist Theology and Earth Healing* (San Francisco: HarperSanFrancisco, 1992), 266.

[36] Ginny Earnest, "On a Firm Foundation: Building on the History and Achievements of Feminism," *Sojourners* 17, no. 9 (October 1988): 29–32.

7. I Shop, Therefore I Am

[1] *Chariots of Fire,* directed by Hugh Hudson, Columbia Pictures, 1981.

[2] *Gandhi,* directed by Richard Attenborough, Columbia Pictures, 1982.

[3] According to the National Criminal Justice reference service, in 1992 there were 883,593 persons in prison in the United States, a rate of 329 per 100,000 residents. This is the highest rate in the world, according to Mark Mauer, *Americans Behind Bars: A Comparison of International Rates of Incarceration* (Washington, D.C.: The Sentencing Project, 1991), and Mark Mauer, *Americans Behind Bars: One Year Later* (Washington, D.C.: The Sentencing Project, 1992). These studies are available from The Sentencing Project, 918 F St., NW, Ste. 501, Washington, D.C. 20004.

[4] Leon Dash, "A Dealer's Creed: Be Willing to Die," *Washington Post,* 3 April 1989, A1, A8.

[5] "Reaction to Bush's Anti-Drug Speech," ABC's *Nightline,* 5 September 1989 (American Broadcasting Companies, transcript produced by Journal Graphics, New York).

[6] National Public Radio's *Morning Edition,* 28 January 1992.

[7] Proverbs 29:18 NRSV.

[8] Martin Luther King Jr., *Where Do We Go from Here? Chaos or Community?* (Boston: Beacon Press, 1967), 186.

[9] Ellen Goodman, "Making War over What We Waste," *Washington Post,* 25 August 1990, A21.

[10] Wendell Berry, "What We Learned from the Gulf War," *Progressive* 55, no. 11 (November 1991): 26.

[11] May Sarton, introduction to *The Russia House,* by John LeCarré (New York: Alfred A. Knopf, 1989).

[12] Matthew 6:25–33 NRSV.

8. *Signs of Transformation*

[1] Amos 5:23–24; Isaiah 58:6–7 NRSV.

[2] See Leviticus 25:1–55 NRSV.

[3] Luke 1:51b–53 NRSV.

[4] Luke 4:18–19 NRSV.

[5] Luke 6:20b; Matthew 5:3a; James 2:1–7 NIV; Acts 4:34a NRSV.

[6] These words are from an Aboriginal woman, who gave her permission to use the quote but prefers that her name not be used.

[7] Jim Wallis, Introduction to Karl Gaspar's *How Long?: Prison Reflections from the Philippines,* ed. Helen Graham and Brenda Noonan (Maryknoll, NY: Orbis Books, 1986), 165.

[8] Joyce Hollyday, *Crucible of Fire: The Church Confronts Apartheid,* ed. Jim Wallis and Joyce Hollyday (Maryknoll, NY: Orbis Books, 1989), 124.

[9] This story also appears in Wallis and Hollyday, *Crucible of Fire,* 122–4.

[10] Allan Boesak, "An Interview with Allan Boesak," interview by Jim Wallis in *Crucible of Fire: The Church Confronts Apartheid,* ed. Jim Wallis and Joyce Hollyday (Maryknoll, NY: Orbis Books, 1989), 43.

[11] This story also appears in Wallis and Hollyday, *Crucible of Fire*, 43.

[12] Dorothy Day, *The Long Loneliness: An Autobiography* (San Francisco: Harper & Row, 1952), 285.

[13] Dorothy Day, *By Little and By Little: The Selected Writings of Dorothy Day,* ed. Robert Ellsberg (New York: Alfred A. Knopf, 1983), 330.

[14] Much research and writing has been done about the vast discrepancy between the CEOs' and employees' salaries. For a comprehensive study of this, see *In Search of Excess: The Overcompensation of American Executives* by Graef S. Crystal (New York: W. W. Norton, 1991).

[15] This comes from several sources within the alternative investment community, primarily the National Association of Community Development Loan Funds, 924 Cherry Street, Third Floor, Philadelphia, PA 19107–2405.

[16] According to Tim Smith from the Inter-Faith Center for Corporate Responsibility. For more than 25 years, ICCR has coordinated economic justice and corporate responsibility issues for the church community.

[17] Luke 12:34 NRSV.

[18] See *Toxic Waste and Race in the United States: A National Report on the Racial and Socio-economic Characteristics of Communities with Hazardous Waste Sites* by Charles Lee (United Church of Christ Commission for Racial Justice, 1987). The report is available from the UCC Commission for Racial Justice, 475 Riverside Drive, Ste. 1950, New York, NY 10115.

[19] Isaiah 11:9 NRSV.

[20] "A Nation in Transition: Census Reveals Striking Stratification of U.S. Society," *Washington Post,* 29 May 1992.

[21] William A. Henry III, "Beyond the Melting Pot," *Time* 135, no. 15 (9 April 1990): 28–31.

[22] Richard Lacayo, "Between Two Worlds," *Time* 133, no. 7 (13 March 1989): 58.

[23] Vincent Harding, conversation with author, Washington, D.C., summer 1987.

[24] Daniel Berrigan, in *Seeds of Peace: A Catalogue of Quotations,* comp. Jeanne Larson and Madge Micheels-Cyrus (Philadelphia: New Society Publishers, 1986), 219.

[25] Colonel David Hackworth, "Gulf War, One Year Later," discussion on *Weekend Edition,* National Public Radio, 18 Jan. 1992 (transcript copyright 1992, National Public Radio).

[26] Mohandas K. Gandhi, "On the Verge of It," *Young India,* 21 May 1925.

[27] Robert E. White, "Paying the Price: An Interview with Robert E. White," interview by editors, *Sojourners* 19, no. 10 (December 1990): 19–21.

[28] Matthew 7:3, 5a NRSV.

[29] Luke 6:27b–28 NRSV.

[30] Matthew 22:39b NRSV.

[31] Matthew 5:6 NRSV.

[32] Luke 6:46 NIV; James 2:17 NRSV.

[33] According to *Bright Futures or Broken Dreams: The Status of Children of the District of Columbia and an Investment Agenda for the 1990s* (Washington, D.C.: The Children's Defense Fund, 1991), 50, the infant mortality rate for Ward 1, where Sojourners Neighborhood Center is, from 1985 to 1989 was 20.6 per 1,000 live births. "An infant born in the District [of Columbia] was less likely to survive one year than a baby born in Jamaica, Costa Rica, or Cuba."

[34] Walter Brueggemann, "Powered By The Spirit," *Sojourners* 20, no. 4 (May 1991): 11.

[35] Exodus 3 & 4 NRSV.

[36] Bishop Leroy Matthiessen, "Bomb Builders Urged to Quit," *Sojourners* 10, no. 10 (October 1981): 8–9.

[37] Archbishop Raymond Hunthausen, "Archbishop Calls for Tax Refusal," *Sojourners* 10, no. 8 (August 1981): 6.

[38] Tim Unsworth, "In Chicago, Catholics React with Relief, Lingering Anger," *National Catholic Reporter* 30, no. 19, 11 March 1994, 5.

[39] "Bernardin Ordeal Ends with 'Deo Gratis'," *National Catholic Reporter* 30, no. 19, 11 March 1994.

[40] Jim Wallis, "Grace Under Pressure," *Sojourners* 23, no. 4 (May 1994): 4.

[41] Jim Wallis, "Faithful to the Truth," *Sojourners* 18, no. 11 (December 1989): 4.

[42] Jim Wallis, "Faithful to the Truth," *Sojourners* 18, no. 11 (December 1989): 5.

[43] Jim Wallis, "Faithful to the Truth," *Sojourners* 18, no. 11 (December 1989): 5.

[44] Jim Wallis, "Faithful to the Truth," *Sojourners* 18, no. 11 (December 1989): 5.

[45] Isaiah 58:6a, 7a NRSV.

[46] Jim Wallis, "A Different Kind of Leadership," *Sojourners* 22, no. 6 (July 1993): 50.

[47] Habakkuk 2:2–3 RSV.

[48] Matthew 16:3b RSV.

[49] Jonathan Schell, "Reflections: A Better Today," *The New Yorker* 61, no. 50 (3 February 1986): 47.

[50] Clarence Jordan, *The Substance of Faith and Other Cotton Patch Sermons,* ed. Dallas Lee (New York: Association Press, 1972), 42–43.

[51] Clarence Jordan, *The Cottonpatch Version of Hebrews 11* (Clinton, N.J.: New Wyn, 1963), 35.

[52] Nehemiah 1–2 NRSV.

[53] Principal authors: Jeffrey L. Brown, Union Baptist Church; Ray A. Hammond, Bethel African Methodist Episcopal Church; Eugene F. Rivers, Azusa Christian Community; Susie Thomas, Mt. Olive Temple of Christ; Gilbert A. Thompson, New Covenant Christian Center; Bruce H. Wall, Dorchester Temple Baptist Church; Samuel C. Wood, Lord's Family African Methodist Episcopal Zion Church, "Ten Point Plan to Mobilize the Churches: Taking Action in Boston," *Sojourners* 23, no. 2 (February–March 1994): 13.

[54] Hebrews 11:1 KJV.

[55] I Corinthians 3:19a NRSV.

[56] Pat Conroy, *The Prince of Tides* (New York: Bantam Books, 1991), 324.

[57] This story also appears in Wallis and Hollyday, *Crucible of Fire,* 1–3.

[58] Jim Wallis, "Drum Major in the Music of Freedom," *Sojourners* 19, no. 7 (August/September 1990): 50.

[59] Gardner Taylor, introduction of Nelson Mandela at Riverside Church, New York City, 21 June 1990.

[60] Nelson Mandela, sermon delivered at Riverside Church, New York City, 21 June 1990.

[61] Nelson Mandela quoted by Jim Wallis, "Drum Major in the Music of Freedom," *Sojourners* 19, no. 7 (August/September 1990): 50.

[62] Jim Wallis, "Drum Major," 50.

[63] C. S. Lewis, *Surprised by Joy* (New York: Harcourt, Brace & World, 1956).

Acknowledgments

There are many people to thank for this book. Several friends and co-workers read parts or the whole of the manuscript and offered their feedback. Others have been regular partners in dialogue around the ideas presented in the book. Many have contributed, sometimes in ways they are not even aware. The list includes Bill and Jeanie Wylie-Kellermann, Shelley Douglass, Richard J. Barnet, Jamie Edgerton, Joyce Hollyday, Rose Berger, Bill Moyers, Joe Nangle, Cornel West, Garry Wills, Sherrie Aeschliman, Richard Rohr, Marie Dennis, Jim Rice, Elizabeth Holler Hunter, Julie Polter, Jennifer Johnson, Jill Laferty, Mary Ann Richardson, Phoebe Smith, Joe Agne, Nane Alejandrez, Daniel Berrigan, Ed Browning, Joan Chittister, James Cone, Gordon Cosby, Yvonne Delk, Marian Wright Edelman, James Forbes, Sharon Gallagher, Wes Granberg-Michaelson, Tom Gumbleton, Vincent Harding, Mac Charles Jones, Sam Mann, Chuck Matthei, Ken Medema, Calvin Morris, Ched Myers, Reeves Nahwooks, Bill Pannell, John Perkins, Eugene Rivers, Joe Roos, Bob Sabath, Ken and Nancy Sehested, Ron Sider, Jean Sindab, Jim and Barb Tamialis, Gaylord Thomas, George Tinker, Beverly Vander Molen, David Wade, and Bill Weld-Wallis. Karen Lattea was also a principal reader and applied her considerable editing skills to the first draft. Priscilla Stuckey did a fine job of copyediting the final manuscript.

Additional members of Sojourners staff and community who have been part of the environment out of which this book has grown include Scot DeGraf, Aaron Gallegos, Dan Goering, David King, Doris Lavender, Barbara Ryan, Jeff Shriver, Ed Spivey Jr., Laura Zylstra-Garth and the many interns who have passed through.

Mary Ann Richardson and the staff of the El Caribe Motel in Daytona Beach, Florida, offered generous hospitality and support for the writing of this book. Excellent work was done by Susan Higman and Kari Verhulst in preparing the manuscript and researching footnotes, for which I am especially grateful. I'm also thankful to Tevera Ephriam, Jeremy Lloyd, and Wendy Smith-McCarroll, who have worked hard to help promote the book.

It was a pleasure to work with both my hardcover publishers, André Schiffrin of The New Press and Robert Gormley and Robert Ellsberg of Orbis Books. They are a rare breed these days—publishers with a conscience. They and their creative and hard-working co-workers (especially Bernadette Price, Patricia Gatzke, and Catherine Costello at Orbis and Paul Bennett and Matt Weiland of The New Press) put enthusiastic energy behind *The Soul of Politics*. And because the book is written to both a general and a religious audience, the unique alliance between The New Press, one of the country's liveliest and freshest new trade publishers, and Orbis Books, the religious house that brought the world liberation theology, has been an interesting and exciting experiment.

I am also very pleased that Harcourt Brace is publishing the paperback edition. It has been a great pleasure to work with Beverly Fisher, Hannah Robinson, and my fine editor, Diane Sterling, who together make a very creative and energetic team. Some revisions and updating add helpful improvements.

Most of all, I want to thank my friend/editor/agent Roy Carlisle, who really saw me through this project. He believed in this book long before it was conceived and pushed me to carve out the time to write it. Together we spent many hours over ideas and outlines until it all fell together. Roy convinced me, after many years of activism and writing on the run, to write books again. I have him to thank for the balance, reflection, and creativity that commitment is bringing to my life and work.

Finally I want to thank all the people whose stories fill this book. They are the ones who are transforming the face of politics in this country and around the world. These are the brothers and sisters who inspire my hope, and I am richly blessed to have them as companions on the journey toward justice.

Index

The Next Step . . .

In 1971, Jim Wallis and a group of other young seminary students had a dream. It was a dream of a place where concerned people who wanted to connect their commitments to social transformation and spiritual renewal could gather. It was a dream of a place where the voice of change could be heard, where steps of action could be taken, and where an alternative vision could take root and become reality.

Today that dream is called Sojourners. Through the publication of a bimonthly magazine, creative public action focusing on the major issues of our day, and a growing network of individuals, groups, churches, and organizations that want to work for change in their lives, the nation, and the world, Sojourners is working to change "the soul of politics."

If you have been stirred by this book and want to get involved in this transformation, we invite you to join us. The next step is to become a member of Sojourners. Simply write or call. As a member, you will receive the bimonthly magazine, featuring a regular column by Jim Wallis as well as news, features, and reviews all written from the perspective of social transformation and spiritual renewal. You will also support concrete activities such as *The Things That Make for Peace,* a church-based, Anti-Violence Network working with urban youth, and other peace and justice efforts around the world.

Sojourners
2401 15th St. NW
Washington, DC 20009
1 (800) 714-7474